Tara Forrest
The Politics of Imagination

Tara Forrest (PhD) lectures in Film and Cultural Studies at the University of Technology, Sydney.

TARA FORREST

The Politics of Imagination. Benjamin, Kracauer, Kluge

[transcript]

Bibliographic information published by Die Deutsche Bibliothek
Die Deutsche Bibliothek lists this publication in the Deutsche Nationalbibliografie; detailed bibliographic data are available in the Internet at http://dnb.d-nb.de

Layout by: Kordula Röckenhaus, Bielefeld
Cover: Deutschland im Herbst, @ Alexander Kluge
Typeset by: Justine Haida, Bielefeld
Printed by: Majuskel Medienproduktion GmbH, Wetzlar
ISBN 978-3-89942-681-6

Contents

Introduction
9

PART 1: WALTER BENJAMIN

Chapter 1:
Benjamin, Proust and the Rejuvenating Powers of Memory
21

1.1 Benjamin's Childhood Reminiscences
28

1.2 Children's Play and Proletarian Children's Theatre
36

1.3 Creative Writing and Play
39

Chapter 2:
The Politics of Aura and Imagination in Benjamin's Writings on Hashish
43

2.1 Auratic Experience and Involuntary Memory
52

2.2 Imagination and Mimesis
57

Chapter 3:
"Reproducibility – Distraction – Politicization"
65

3.1 The Aura, Contemplation, and Distraction
70

3.2 Changing Film's Technical Standards
75

3.3 Autonomy and Unity in Film
79
3.4 Film and Epic Theatre
81

Part 2: Siegfried Kracauer

Chapter 4:
"Film as the Discoverer of the Marvels of Everyday Life": Kracauer and the Promise of Realist Cinema
89
4.1 Photography, Proust, and the Task of a Realist Cinema
92
4.2 The Child's Capacity for Perception and Imagination
103

Chapter 5:
On the Task of a Realist Historiography in Kracauer's History: The Last Things Before the Last
107
5.1 Photography, History, and Memory
111
5.2 The Task of a Realist Historiography
115

Part 3: Alexander Kluge

Chapter 6:
From History's Rubble: Kluge on Film, History, and Politics
127
6.1 Autorenkino and Counter-histories
130
6.2 The Construction Site of History
140

**Chapter 7:
Raw Materials for the Imagination:
Kluge's Work for Television**
149
7.1 Information, Storytelling, and Experience
154
7.2 Raw Materials for the Imagination
159

Conclusion
169
Bibliography
175
Other Works Cited
191
Acknowledgements
193

Introduction

In "Convolute J" of *The Arcades Project*, Walter Benjamin quotes Joseph de Maistre's account, in *Les Soirées de Saint-Pétersbourg*, of the havoc wreaked by an earthquake on the organisation of exhibits displayed in a natural history museum:

> The door to the collection rooms is open and broken; there are no more windows. Whole drawers have fallen out, while others hang by their hinges, ready to drop. Some shells have rolled out into the hall of minerals, and a hummingbird's nest is resting on the head of a crocodile. What madman, though, could have any doubt of the original intention, or believe that the edifice was built to look this way? [...] The order is as visible as the disorder; and the eye that ranges over this mighty temple of nature reestablishes without difficulty all that a fatal agency has shattered, warped, soiled, and displaced.[1]

In Siegfried Kracauer's 1927 essay on photography, a similar image emerges in his analysis of the scrambling of "natural reality" performed by the intermingling of the undated, disorganised contents of a massive photographic archive. The images contained in this archive (which together constitute a "*general inventory* of [...] nature"[2]) have, Kracauer writes, "lost [their] relationship to the present".[3] That is to say, the historical "place" of each image is, from the viewer's perspective, not something that can be easily determined.

In a similar vein to the intermingling of the natural history exhibits described by de Maistre, Kracauer argues that the hodgepodge of images contained in the photographic archive produces a situation in which the

---

1. De Maistre quoted in: Walter Benjamin: [J86, 2], The Arcades Project, Cambridge, Mass. and London, England: Harvard University Press 1999, p. 377.

2. Siegfried Kracauer: "Photography", in: Kracauer: The Mass Ornament: Weimar Essays, ed. by Thomas Y. Levin, Cambridge, Mass. and London, England: Harvard University Press 1995, p. 61.

3. Ibid., p. 62.

viewer's "habitual" understanding of the "relationship among the elements of nature" is suspended.[4] In contrast, however, to de Maistre, Kracauer argues that it is neither straightforward, nor desirable, to reestablish the previously ordered relationship between these elements by seeking – as if they were parts of a jigsaw puzzle – to reinstate them to their so-called "natural" positions. On the contrary, Kracauer claims that the freeing up of the order of nature performed by the jumbling of the photographic images encourages the viewer to reconceive the possibilities of both the past and the future outside of the evolutionary conception of the relationship between the past and the present espoused by those who "subject [...] the historical process to the very kind of necessity which we are accustomed to attribute to the workings of nature".[5]

In both Benjamin's writings on history and in Kracauer's final book, *History: The Last Things Before the Last*, the relationship between the natural sciences and historicist accounts of history are discussed in some detail. For both Benjamin and Kracauer, what is problematic about the practice of "assimilating historiography to natural science"[6] is the degree to which it naturalises the idea that history is constituted out of a series of causally related events that are bound together (under the banner of abstract concepts such as "culture", "enlightenment", and "objective spirit"[7]) by a form of evolutionary progress.

"Historicism", Benjamin writes,

> contents itself with establishing a causal nexus among various moments in history. But no state of affairs having causal significance is for that very reason historical. It became historical posthumously, as it were, through events that may be separated from it by thousands of years.[8]

For Benjamin, what is problematic about the historicist conception of history as a form of evolutionary progress is the extent to which it naturalises the choices and decisions made by those who are in positions

---

4. Ibid.

5. Siegfried Kracauer: History: The Last Things Before the Last, Princeton: Markus Wiener Publishers 1995, p. 36. Hereafter referred to as History.

6. Walter Benjamin: "Paralipomena to 'On the Concept of History'", in: Benjamin: Selected Writings, Vol. 4, ed. by Howard Eiland/Michael W. Jennings, Cambridge, Mass. and London, England: Harvard University Press 2003, p. 401.

7. Ibid., p. 403.

8. Benjamin: "On the Concept of History", in: Benjamin: Selected Writings, Vol. 4, p. 397.

of power. "The rulers at any time", he writes, "are the heirs of all those who have been victorious throughout history".[9] Historicism, in this sense, can thus be seen as a form of "empathy with the victor".[10] Its delineation of political decisions and events as stepping stones in history's so-called march of progress toward the future creates a climate within which it is difficult to conceive of the possibilities of the past, the present and the future outside of the parameters established and maintained by the ruling status quo.

In his reading of Benjamin's "On the Concept of History", Kracauer argues that in order to critique this model of historical development, one must also critique the concept of chronology upon which it is based – a model within which the passing of time is heralded as "the matrix of a meaningful process".[11] In *History: The Last Things Before the Last*, Kracauer states that the historicists "unquestionably confide in the magic of chronology" in their delineation of the historical process. But how, he asks, would our conception of history change if "their confidence turn[ed] out to be unwarranted?" What if "calendric time is not the all-powerful medium they suppose it to be", but rather "an empty indifferent flow which takes along with it a conglomerate of unconnected events?"[12]

In an attempt to not only debunk the historicist conception of the significance of chronological time, but also to provide an alternative to the historicist perspective, Kracauer outlines the workings of memory in a manner reminiscent of Marcel Proust (the writings of whom had a significant impact on the development of both Kracauer and Benjamin's analyses of a form of historical knowledge that would challenge the historicist position). The irrelevance of chronological time, Kracauer notes, can be "confirmed by the mechanics of our memory".[13] Echoing Proust's distinction, in *In Search of Lost Time*[14], between voluntary and involuntary forms of recollection (the details, and significance, of which will be discussed in Chapter 1) Kracauer claims that the most vivid memories of the past are often those we are unable to date. "Perhaps", he speculates, this is because

9. "Paralipomena to 'On the Concept of History'", p. 406.

10. Ibid.

11. History, p. 150.

12. Ibid., p. 38.

13. Ibid., p. 149.

14. Marcel Proust: In Search of Lost Time, (6 Vols.), London: Vintage 1996. Only the volume and page numbers will be given hereafter.

the memory for qualities develops in inverse ratio to the chronological memory: the better equipped a person is to resuscitate the essential features of encounters that played a role in his life, the more easily will he misjudge their temporal distances from the present or play havoc with their chronological order. These errors must be laid to the difficulty for him to transfer his memories from their established places on his subjective time curve to their objective positions in chronological time – a time he never experienced.[15]

For Benjamin too, what is significant about Proust's conception of involuntary memory is the extent to which the experience of "*Jetztzeit*" ("now time") with which it is associated exists "outside the range of time and its measurements".[16] According to Proust, the experience of the past in the present evoked by involuntary memory is not the past as viewed from the perspective of the present, but rather "the past just as it was *at the moment when it was itself the present*".[17] Thus, in stark contrast to the image of the past presented by historicism (within which each period or event is viewed retrospectively as a transitional point in history's so-called journey of progress toward the present), the experience of the past evoked by involuntary memory is one in which the historical "place" of the past has not yet been determined.

In Benjamin's writings on history, it is clear that Proust's account of the experience of the past in the present evoked by involuntary memory had an important impact on the development of his analysis of a form of historical knowledge that would challenge the historicist position. "The concept of historical time", Benjamin writes, must form "an antithesis to the idea of a temporal continuum".[18] In contrast to historicism, the "founding concept" of a political engagement with the past "is not progress but actualization".[19] Echoing Proust, he claims that to treat the past politically means to create a situation in which "everything past (in its time) can acquire a higher grade of actuality than it had at the mo-

15. History, p. 149.

16. Proust: Vol. 4, p. 441.

17. Proust: Vol. 6, p. 429. My emphasis. In "Convolute N", Benjamin states of this experience: "It's not that what is past casts its light on what is present, or what is present its light on what is past; rather, image is that wherein what has been comes together in a flash with the now to form a constellation. In other words: Image is dialectics at a standstill". [N2a, 3], The Arcades Project, p. 462.

18. "Paralipomena to 'On the Concept of History'", p. 407.

19. [N2,2], The Arcades Project, p. 460.

ment of its existing", because it is the "actualization of former contexts [which] puts the truth of all present action to the test".[20]

Within this schema, the shake-up of the natural history exhibits performed by the earthquake described by de Maistre could be said to exemplify what Benjamin describes as the "blasting of historical continuity"[21] performed by a political historiographical practice that has liberated itself from the "vulgar historical naturalism"[22] characteristic of historicist accounts of history as a form of evolutionary progress. In a similar vein to Kracauer's analysis of the disordered state of the photographic archive, the jumbling of the natural history exhibits (so whimsically embodied in the image of the hummingbird's nest that has landed on the head of a crocodile) could be said to open up a space within which the historical "place" of the exhibits (and, by extension, the relationship between the past and the present) can be re-imagined and re-explored.

Indeed, the disorder among the exhibits described by de Maistre also resembles the rubble heap of historical materials out of which Alexander Kluge's 1979 film *The Patriot* (*Die Patriotin*) is constructed: a film which challenges the viewer to reconceive the possibilities of both the past and the future outside of the framework imposed by historicism, whose "identification of history with nature", Kracauer states, "not only unduly minimizes[s] the role of contingencies in history", but "preclude[s] man's freedom of choice, his ability to create new situations".[23] As I discuss in detail in Chapter 6, this desire to emphasise the "role of contingencies in history" is a driving force behind Kluge's highly experimental film, television and literary work. Why, Kluge asks, do "we carry in us such a fixed conception of the probable order of events, which is only the sum of what is impressed upon us by the objective history or the media? Why do we hang on to it so energetically, while the imagination circles elsewhere [...] and while] the sum of improbabilities is just as great as the sum of all probabilities"?[24]

In keeping with Kluge, the work of Benjamin and Kracauer discussed in this book is driven by a desire to emphasise the role of contingencies in history, to maximise one's freedom of choice, and to stimulate one's capacity for imagination into reconceiving the possibilities of

20. [0,5], The Arcades Project, p. 857.

21. [N10a,1], The Arcades Project, p. 475.

22. [N2,6], The Arcades Project, p. 461.

23. History, p. 37.

24. Claus Philipp: "Vertrauenswürdige Irrtümer: Ein Gespräch", Kolik, No. 13 (2000), p. 10.

the past and the present outside of the parameters of the status quo. The aim of the book is thus not to provide an overview of the work of each of these three figures. Rather, through a detailed analysis of Benjamin, Kracauer, and Kluge's engagements with a range of different subjects (including topics as diverse as literature, film, theatre, photography, historiography, and television), each of the chapters seeks to draw out the extent to which the concept of imagination plays a central role in their analyses of a mode of perception and experience that could serve as a catalyst for the creation and sustenance of a desire for "a better nature".[25]

The concept of imagination to which the title of the book refers is, however, not a strictly defined, stable concept. Rather, it is a term which is employed (in a fashion reminiscent of Benjamin's delineation of the mimetic faculty[26]) to refer to a capacity which facilitates both a process of mediation between the outside world and one's own experiences and memories, and an active, creative relationship to one's environment that is neither circumscribed, nor hindered by the conception of the possibilities and limitations of the present maintained by the ruling status quo.[27]

In Benjamin's writings on both mimesis and proletarian children's theatre, it is the capacity for imagination demonstrated in children's play which serves as a model for a mode of perception and cognition that is not inhibited by what the adult world deems to be appropriate and/or possible. Within this schema, the child's imagination functions in a manner comparable to the earthquake described by de Maistre. Indeed, what is significant about the capacity for imagination demonstrated in children's play (a topic which also emerges in my analysis of the work of Kracauer and Kluge) is the extent to which "it decomposes all creation;

25. [J76, 1], The Arcades Project, p. 362.

26. See "Doctrine of the Similar" and "On the Mimetic Faculty", in: Benjamin: Selected Writings, Vol. 2, ed. by Michael W. Jennings/Howard Eiland/Gary Smith, Cambridge, Mass. and London, England: Harvard University Press 1999, pp. 694-698, and 720-722 respectively. Benjamin's analysis of the significance of the mimetic faculty will be discussed in Chapter 2.

27. As Kluge and Oskar Negt have pointed out, within this schema, the imagination is "not a particular substance (as when one says 'so-and-so has a lot of imagination'), but the organizer of mediation". See Oskar Negt and Alexander Kluge: Public Sphere and Experience: Toward an Analysis of the Bourgeois and Proletarian Public Sphere, Minneapolis and London: University of Minnesota Press 1993, p. 37.

and with the raw materials accumulated [...], it creates a new world – it produces the sensation of newness".[28]

In Parts 1 and 2 of the book (which focus on the writings of Benjamin and Kracauer) the sense of possibility associated with the production of this "sensation of newness" is discussed across a range of different contexts. While Chapter 1 focuses on Benjamin's writings on Marcel Proust (and the impact that Proust's conception of involuntary memory had on the development of Benjamin's childhood reminiscences), Chapters 3 and 4 explore Benjamin and Kracauer's analyses of the role that an experimental film practice could play in stimulating the spectator's capacity for imagination into reconceiving the possibilities of the present.

As I discuss in detail in each of these chapters, absolutely central to Benjamin and Kracauer's analyses of the radical possibilities of film is the extent to which the camera's extension of the spectator's vision beyond the realm of subjective intention facilitates a mode of perception and experience which challenges our previously held conceptions about the material world -- a theme which is also taken up, in Chapter 2, via an analysis of Benjamin's delineation of the expansion of the capacity for perception and experience generated by his experiments with hashish.

Indeed, what is fascinating about Benjamin's analysis of the mode of perception facilitated by both hashish intoxication and the camera is the extent to which it is associated with the opening up of an "image space" within which the "natural" order of things is momentarily suspended. In a passage that resonates strongly with the effects of the earthquake described by de Maistre, Benjamin argues that the significance of film lies in its capacity (through devices such as framing, close-up, slow motion, and editing) to "explode [...] the prevailing world into rubble"[29] and, in

28. Charles Baudelaire quoted in: Benjamin: [J34a,1], The Arcades Project, p. 290. Benjamin's delineation of "the destructive character" also resonates with this image. "The destructive character", Benjamin writes, "sees nothing permanent. But for this very reason he sees ways everywhere. Where others encounter walls or mountains, there, too, he sees a way. [...] Because he sees ways everywhere, he always stands at a crossroads. No moment can know what the next will bring. What exists he reduces to rubble – not for the sake of the rubble, but for that of the way leading through it". Benjamin: "The Destructive Character", in: Benjamin: Selected Writings, Vol. 2, p. 542.

29. Gertrud Koch: "Cosmos in Film: On the Concept of Space in Walter Benjamin's 'Work of Art' essay", in: Walter Benjamin's Philosophy: Destruction and Experience, ed. by Andrew Benjamin/Peter Osborne, London and New York: Routledge 1994, p. 210.

doing so, to open up a space within which the possibilities and limitations of the current situation can be re-imagined and re-explored. In this regard, Benjamin writes, film

> manages to assure us of a vast and unsuspected field of action [*Spielraum*]. Our bars and city streets, our offices and furnished rooms, our railroad stations and our factories seemed to close relentlessly around us. Then came film and exploded this prison-world with the dynamite of the split second, so that now we can set off calmly on journeys of adventure among its far-flung debris [*weitverstreuten Trümmern*].[30]

The role that an experimental film and television practice could play in rejuvenating our capacity for perception and imagination is also taken up in Part 3 of the book via an analysis of the work of Alexander Kluge – a figure who is, in many regards, an heir to the ideas and concerns that preoccupied Benjamin and Kracauer. In a similar vein to both these figures, Kluge argues that the task of a political film practice is not to immerse the spectator in a fictional world, but to rejuvenate the audience's capacity for imagination into reconceiving the possibilities of the past and the present. Indeed, if Benjamin argues that film's radical potential lies in its capacity to explode the world around us into rubble, then Kluge's film and television work (which is itself constructed out of a diverse collection of "raw materials" – including photographs, diagrams, interviews, maps, clips from movies, and documentary footage) could be said to take this potential a step further.

In a similar vein to the undated, disorganised contents of the photographic archive described by Kracauer, what is significant about the "raw materials" out of which Kluge's film and television work is constructed is the extent to which they actively encourage the audience to draw on their own imagination and experience in aid of the creation of different cultural and historical imaginaries. Indeed, as I argue in Chapter 6 of the highly eclectic imaging practice characteristic of *The Patriot*, meaning is not to be found in any particular image (nor in the film as a whole), but in the thoughts, associations, and impressions sparked by the relationship between the materials – connections that encourage the

---

30. See Benjamin: "The Work of Art in the Age of its Technological Reproducibility" (Third Version), in: Benjamin: Selected Writings, Vol. 4, p. 265, and Benjamin: "Das Kunstwerk im Zeitalter seiner technischen Reproduzierbarkeit", in: Benjamin: Gesammelte Schriften (7 Vols.), ed. by Rolf Tiedemann/Hermann Schweppenhäuser, Frankfurt am Main: Suhrkamp 1991, Vol. I.2, pp. 499-500.

spectator to think about the "place" of both the past and the present in different terms.

For Kluge, Kracauer, and Benjamin, the task of a political film/literary/historiographical/television practice is not to provide the audience/reader with the image of a different kind of future, nor to channel the viewer's/reader's observations and associations into conceiving of the benefits of a particular political outlook. Rather, as I demonstrate in the book (through an analysis of a diverse range of topics that span a broad range of historical periods), the work of each of these figures is driven not only by a desire to denaturalise the current state of affairs, but to cleave open a space within history's so-called march of progress toward the future within which the possibilities of both the past and the present can be imagined and explored anew.

Finally, in the conclusion to the book, I seek (via an analysis of a short but, nonetheless, highly evocative passage in Kluge's 2003 *Die Lücke, die der Teufel läßt*) to draw out the relevance of some of the concerns addressed in the book for the contemporary political context, within which war and violence continue to be waged in the name of historical progress.

Part 1: Walter Benjamin

Chapter 1: Benjamin, Proust and the Rejuvenating Powers of Memory

The impact that Benjamin's fascination with the writings of Marcel Proust had on the development of his ideas in the 1920s and 30s cannot be underestimated. The significance of this fascination (which can be traced in Benjamin's correspondence to the early 1920s) first takes on concrete form in 1925 in his decision to undertake the "enormous task" of translating *Sodom and Gomorrah* (or what Benjamin, in a letter to Gershom Scholem, describes as the "main novel" of Proust's *In Search of Lost Time*).[1] While Benjamin's translation of *Sodom and Gomorrah* was never published, two other volumes of the book which he translated in collaboration with Franz Hessel were released as *Im Schatten der jungen Mädchen* and *Die Herzogin von Guermantes* in 1927 and 1930 respectively.[2] Throughout this period, the significance of Benjamin's close engagement with Proust's writings is revealed in his correspondence with friends and associates. In the above mentioned letter to Scholem, Benjamin's acknowledgment of the close affinity between Proust's "philosophical perspective" and his own prompts him to describe their relationship as one of "kindred souls". "I am eager to see", Benjamin writes, "whether this feeling will be maintained now that I will be intimately involved with his work".[3] In a letter to Rainer Maria Rilke written four months later, the continuation of these feelings is confirmed:

---

1. This letter to Scholem was written on July 21, 1925. See The Correspondence of Walter Benjamin: 1910-1940, ed. by Gershom Scholem/Theodor W. Adorno, Chicago and London: University of Chicago Press 1994, pp. 277-278. Hereafter referred to as Correspondence.

2. Momme Broderson: Walter Benjamin: A Biography, ed. by Martina Dervis, London and New York: Verso 1997, pp. 166-168.

3. Correspondence, p. 278.

The deeper I delve into the text [*Sodom and Gomorrah*], the more grateful I am for the circumstances that caused it to be entrusted to me! What I have gained from having been so deeply involved with this great masterpiece will in time become very tangible for me.[4]

However, despite Benjamin's own claims about the philosophical affinities between his own ideas and those of Proust, there has been much speculation about the extent to which Benjamin and Proust are in fact "kindred souls". This speculation has, in part, been fuelled by Theodor W. Adorno's account of a conversation he had with Benjamin about the Proust translations. In "On Proust" Adorno writes that Benjamin once told him "that he did not want to read one word more of Proust than he had to translate, because otherwise he would fall into an addictive dependency that would impede him in his own production".[5]

In "Hope in the Past: On Walter Benjamin", Peter Szondi claims that Benjamin's remark can be read not as a confirmation of his felt affinity to Proust, but rather as a sign of trepidation about his concentrated engagement with a work "only apparently similar to his own".[6] According to Szondi's argument, Proust and Benjamin's shared concern to capture "lost time" (as manifested in *In Search of Lost Time* and "Berlin Childhood around 1900" respectively[7]) obscures "the fact that the intentions of the two works are not only not related but are in fact totally opposed".[8] Szondi claims that Proust's search for, and experience of lost time (through the conjunction of the past and the present triggered by involuntary memory) is primarily motivated by a desire to "escape from the sway of time itself".[9] He argues that this desire (the goal of which is to evade the future, and with it death) stands in stark contrast to

4. Ibid., p. 285.

5. Adorno: "On Proust", in: Adorno: Notes to Literature: Volume 2, ed. by Rolf Tiedemann, New York: Columbia University Press 1992, p. 313.

6. Szondi: "Hope in the Past", Critical Inquiry, Vol. 4, No. 3 (Spring, 1978), p. 496.

7. Marcel Proust: In Search of Lost Time (6 Vols.), London: Vintage 1996. Only the volume and page numbers will be given hereafter. Benjamin: "Berlin Childhood around 1900", in: Benjamin: Selected Writings, Vol. 3, ed. by Howard Eiland/Michael W. Jennings, Cambridge, Mass. and London, England: Harvard University Press 2002, pp. 344-386. Hereafter referred to as "Berlin Childhood".

8. "Hope in the Past", p. 496.

9. Ibid., p. 497.

the promise of the future that Benjamin seeks in the past evoked by involuntary memory.

The evidence for such a claim can, in part, be found in the comments of Proust's narrator Marcel in the final volume of the book: *Time Regained*. In a discussion of the effects evoked by the taste of the madeleine (which was the catalyst for his first sojourn into the realm evoked by involuntary memory) Marcel states that the "joy" induced by these "impressions" hinges on their extra-temporality:

> A minute freed from the order of time has re-created in us [...] the man freed from the order of time. And one can understand that this man should have confidence in his joy, even if the simple taste of a madeleine does not seem logically to contain within it the reasons for this joy, one can understand that the word 'death' should have no meaning for him; situated outside time, why should he fear the future?[10]

As Szondi and others have pointed out, the desire to escape the future by submerging oneself in a timeless, idealised past does not sit comfortably with Benjamin's analysis of the significance of the experience of the past in the present evoked by involuntary memory.[11] While Benjamin is not openly critical of Proust in this regard, in his 1929 essay "The Image of Proust", he does point out that there are "rudiments of an enduring idealism" in Proust's writings, but adds that "it would be a mistake to make these the basis of an interpretation".[12] For while the concerns that underpin Benjamin's interest in involuntary memory do differ from those of Proust in certain regards, there are, nonetheless, a number of important similarities between each of their analyses of the "rejuvenating" effects precipitated by an experience of "convoluted time". While Marcel's trepidation about the future is quelled by his encounters with the past, to claim this as the primary motivation behind his search for lost time is to radically undermine the significantly more complex, nuanced conception of the powers of involuntary memory that emerges from the six volumes of *In Search of Lost Time*.

In order to get a fuller sense of the important influence that Proust's writings had on the development of Benjamin's conception of a radical

10. Proust: Vol. 6, p. 225.

11. See also John McCole: Walter Benjamin and the Antinomies of Tradition, Ithaca and London: Cornell University Press 1993, p. 261.

12. Walter Benjamin: "The Image of Proust", in: Benjamin: Illuminations, ed. by Hannah Arendt, London: Fontana Press 1992, p. 206.

historical consciousness, an analysis of Proust's distinction between voluntary and involuntary memory is required. In *In Search of Lost Time,* Marcel argues that the "desiccated" and "insubstantial" images evoked by voluntary memory (which is otherwise referred to as "the memory of the intellect") do not preserve anything of the "reality" of the past. He argues that the true past (which is located "beyond the reach of the intellect") "lies hidden" within "some material object" or "in the sensation which that material object will give us" – the location of which can only be discovered by chance.[13] This is because the reality of the past consists of impressions (of colours, scents, feelings and sounds) which have been separated by the intellect from the events or moments with which they were associated, because – as Marcel points out – it "could make nothing of them for its own rational purposes".[14] Although excluded from the realm in which they could be voluntarily recalled, Marcel claims that these impressions nonetheless remain "immured as within a thousand sealed vessels", each of which is filled with scents, colours, and temperatures which, when discovered, provide us with "the sensation of extraordinarily diverse atmospheres".[15] For Marcel, the "essential character" of these ephemeral encounters (which, like "a propitious breeze", blow in from the past[16]) is that they cannot be recalled at will, and this – he claims – is the "mark of their authenticity".[17]

As Benjamin argues in his 1939 essay "Some Motifs in Baudelaire", a comparison can be drawn between Proust's ideas and those elaborated by Sigmund Freud in his 1921 essay "Beyond the Pleasure Principle" (an essay which Benjamin describes in *The Arcades Project* as "probably the best commentary" that exists on Proust's writings[18]). In a similar vein to Marcel's analysis of the desiccating function of the intellect, Freud argues that consciousness plays an important role in parrying stimuli from the realm in which they could leave behind an imprint in memory. "The basic formula of this hypothesis", Benjamin writes:

---

13. Proust: Vol. 1, p. 51. See also Proust's analysis of the differences between voluntary and involuntary memory in his letter to Antoine Bibesco (written in 1912). Letters of Marcel Proust, ed. by Nina Curtiss, New York: Random House 1949, pp. 226-227.

14. Proust: Vol. 6, p. 221.

15. Ibid.

16. Proust: Vol. 1, p. 187.

17. Proust: Vol. 6, p. 232.

18. Walter Benjamin: [S2,3], The Arcades Project, Cambridge, Mass. and London, England: Harvard University Press 1999, p. 547.

is that 'becoming conscious and leaving behind a memory trace are processes incompatible with each other within one and the same system'. Rather, memory fragments are 'often most powerful and most enduring when the incident which left them behind was one that never entered consciousness'. Put in Proustian terms, this means that only what has not been experienced explicitly and consciously, what has not happened to the subject as an experience [*Erlebnis*], can become a component of the *mémoire involontaire*.[19]

For Benjamin, the "special achievement" of the intellect can be found in its "function of assigning to an incident a precise point in time in consciousness at the cost of the integrity of its contents".[20] This process not only turns the incident into "a moment that has been lived (*Erlebnis*)" but, in doing so, "sterilize[s it [...] for poetic experience" ("*dichterische Erfahrung*").[21] "Experiences", Benjamin writes, "are lived similarities". "What is decisive here is not the causal connections established over the course of time" (which characterise the kind of experience designated by the term *Erlebnis*)[22], but rather "the capacity for endless interpolations into what has been".[23] While "a *lived* event is finite – at any

19. Walter Benjamin: "Some Motifs in Baudelaire", in: Benjamin: Charles Baudelaire: A Lyric Poet in the Era of High Capitalism, London and New York: Verso 1997, p. 114.

20. Ibid., p. 117.

21. Ibid., pp. 116-117. See also Benjamin: "Über einige Motive bei Baudelaire", in: Benjamin: Gesammelte Schriften (7 Vols.), ed. by Rolf Tiedemann/Hermann Schweppenhäuser, Frankfurt am Main: Suhrkamp 1991, Vol. I.2, p. 614. "The *mémoire volontaire*", Benjamin writes in *The Arcades Project*, "is a registry providing the object [or incident] with a classificatory number behind which it disappears. 'So now we've been there.' ('I've had an experience')". See [H5, 1], p. 211. In a letter to Adorno (written in May, 1940) Benjamin "trace[s] the roots of [his] 'theory of experience' to a childhood memory". "My parents", Benjamin writes, "naturally took walks with us wherever we spent our summers. There were either two or three of us children. The one I have in mind is my brother. After we had visited one of the obligatory tourist attractions around Freudenstadt, Wengen, or Schreiberhau, my brother used to say, 'Now we can say that we've been there.' This statement made an unforgettable impression on me." Correspondence, p. 629.

22. "Experience", in: Benjamin: Selected Writings, Vol. 2, ed. by Michael W. Jennings/Howard Eiland/Gary Smith, Cambridge, Mass. and London, England: Harvard University Press 1999, p. 553, and "Zur Erfahrung", in: Benjamin: Gesammelte Schriften, Vol. VI, pp. 88-89.

23. Benjamin: "A Berlin Chronicle", in: Selected Writings, Vol. 2, p. 603.

rate, confined to one sphere of experience [*des Erlebens*]; a remembered event is infinite, because it is only a key to everything that happened before it or after it".[24]

Like Benjamin, Marcel argues that the images of the past which can be voluntarily recalled have been "made arid by the intellect" through and by which they have been filtered and systematised.[25] While the "snapshots taken by [his] memory" do not reveal anything of the substance of his trip to Venice, for example, an experience of a very different kind is communicated to him after the event via a chance encounter, in Paris, with an uneven path like the one he had encountered in the baptistery at St.Mark's.[26] For Marcel, what is important about this encounter is not so much the uncanny recurrence of the sensation of bumpy paving stones underfoot, but rather the extent to which this recurrence serves as a trigger for the mood and emotions associated with that time. Marcel's discovery of an old book, for example, not only reignites within him the memory of reading it as a child, but serves as a catalyst for an encounter with "the brilliant sunshine that prevailed while [he was] reading it", and the desires and dreams "that were then shaping themselves in his mind".[27]

This emphasis on the evocation of feeling and mood (rather than a purely imagistic encounter with the past) plays an important role in Benjamin's analysis of *In Search of Lost Time.* In his observations on Proust collected in the "Proust-Papiere", he writes:

> [w]hat Proust discovered was that once he had broken open the secret compartment of 'mood', what lay inside [...] could be appropriated: this disorderly pile of things [*dies Ungeordnete, Gehäufte*] which we ourselves having [...] faithfully crammed there, had forgotten, and which now overwhelms the person who stands before it, like the man at the sight of a drawer which is stuffed to the brim with useless, forgotten toys. It is this playfulness [*Verspieltheit*] of true life, of which only memory speaks to us, that one must seek in Proust, and make the central point of reflection.[28]

---

24. "The Image of Proust", p. 198. I have modified the English translation of "*ein erlebtes Ereignis*" as "an experienced event" to "a lived event" because the translation of "*erlebtes*" as "experienced" is confusing in this context. See "Zum Bilde Prousts", Gesammelte Schriften, Vol. II.I, p. 312.

25. Proust: Vol. 6, p. 224.

26. Ibid., pp. 217-218.

27. Ibid., pp. 241-242.

28. Gesammelte Schriften, Vol. II. 3, p. 1057. In his 1928 review of a book

This sense of "playfulness" (which is also central to Benjamin's analysis of the radicality of childhood perception and cognition) is, in his analysis of Proust, entwined with the relationship he draws between involuntary memory and "rejuvenation" (*Verjüngung*).[29] Anticipating Benjamin's fascination with both the child's capacity for imagination, and his/her refusal to accept the form of something as it exists[30], Marcel argues that the rejuvenating power of the impressions evoked by involuntary memory lies in their capacity to evoke a sense of "fresh emotion" and "spiritual renewal"[31] which could serve as a "starting-point" or "foundation-stone" for the construction of a different kind of existence[32]. This sentiment is also echoed in "The Image of Proust", when Benjamin claims that *In Search of Lost Time* is marked by a "constant attempt to charge an entire lifetime with the utmost awareness"[33] – a consciousness which springs from the "shock of rejuvenation" that occurs when "the past is reflected in the dewy fresh 'instant'".[34]

---

written by Karl Gröber, Benjamin claims that it is amongst the contents of a box of toys that one can find the most important images of one's life; images for which one "would be willing to give the whole world". See Benjamin: "Toys and Play", in: Selected Writings, Vol. 2, p. 120. The review is of Gröber's Kinderspielzeug aus alter Zeit: Eine Geschichte des Spielzeugs, Berlin: Deutscher Kunstverlag 1928.

29. In his "Notizen über Proust und Baudelaire", Benjamin makes a number of references to the rejuvenating powers of memory. See, for example, Gesammelte Schriften, Vol. II.3, p. 1063, and "The Image of Proust", pp. 206-207. It is important to note in this context that the German term for rejuvenation (*"Verjüngung"*) contains within it the word *"jung"* (young) – a term which connects the German word with the process of rendering someone younger than they were previously. In Benjamin's writings, this association takes on a greater significance when considered in the light of his analysis of the extent to which the experiences evoked by involuntary memory could be said to rejuvenate one's capacity for imagination (a capacity which, in Benjamin's writings, is predominantly associated with children).

30. See, for example, Benjamin: "Sammlung von Frankfurter Kinderreimen", Gesammelte Schriften, IV-2, p. 792.

31. See, for example, Proust: Vol. 1, p. 187, and Vol. 6, p. 237.

32. Proust: Vol. 5, p. 294.

33. "The Image of Proust", p. 207.

34. Ibid., p. 206.

1.1 Benjamin's Childhood Reminiscences

Benjamin's analysis of the significance of the relationship between this "shock of rejuvenation" and the experience of the past in the present evoked by involuntary memory is also manifest in his childhood reminiscences. In both "A Berlin Chronicle" and "Berlin Childhood around 1900", the past as recalled via involuntary memory emerges as a preserve of hope for a different kind of future. According to Scholem, Benjamin started work on "A Berlin Chronicle" in Berlin in January 1932, and in the following months continued to work on it while living in Ibiza.[35] As Benjamin explains in a letter written to Scholem in April of that year, his stay on the island was prompted "first and foremost" by his very poor financial situation, and the "strain of inconceivable proportions" engendered by the difficulties associated with making ends meet in Berlin.[36] Benjamin completed "A Berlin Chronicle" in Ibiza, and in July travelled to France, where he planned to take his own life in a Hotel in Nice. In a letter to Scholem (written on July 26) Benjamin describes the "profound fatigue"[37] that had overcome him as a result of the political events in Germany which were "preparing the way for Hitler's assumption of power"[38] – the impending consequences of which Benjamin was facing "with a grimness verging on hopelessness".[39] However, despite the mood of despair which pervades his letters of this period, Benjamin did not take his life, but travelled instead to Italy and Berlin, where he worked – until the end of the year – on "a series of sketches

35. Gershom Scholem: Walter Benjamin: The Story of a Friendship, Philadelphia: The Jewish Publicaton Society of America 1981, p. 181.

36. Correspondence, pp. 389-390.

37. Ibid., p. 395.

38. "Chronology", Selected Writings, Vol. 2, p. 844. The situation is described by the editors of Benjamin's Selected Writings as follows: "On July 20, 1932, Franz von Papen, who had been German chancellor for only a month, suspended the democratically elected Prussian government, naming himself 'Imperial Commissar for Prussia' and preparing the way for Hitler's assumption of power. Benjamin was all too aware of the immediate and possibly future results of Germany's political demise. By the end of July he had already, as a Jew, received a letter from the building-safety authorities ordering him to abandon his apartment because of alleged code violations; his radio work had also been brought to a halt by the dismissal of the left-leaning directors of the Berlin and Frankfurt stations." p. 844.

39. Correspondence, p. 396.

concerning memories of [his] early life" entitled "Berlin Childhood around 1900".[40]

The conditions under which Benjamin wrote "Berlin Childhood" are not insignificant. As Anna Stüssi has pointed out, the fragmentary images of his childhood out of which the book is constructed correspond with those memories ("which flash [...] up in a moment of danger") which Benjamin describes in "On the Concept of History".[41] For our concerns here, however, another more productive comparison can be drawn between the images collected in "Berlin Childhood" and the delineation of involuntary memory that emerges from Benjamin's short, but nonetheless significant, study "Aus einer kleinen Rede über Proust, an meinem vierzigsten Geburstag gehalten" ("From a small speech on Proust, delivered on my fortieth birthday") – a piece which was written around the time of Benjamin's planned suicide in 1932:

On the knowledge of the *mémoire involontaire*: not only do its images come when they are not summoned, but they appear rather as images that we have never seen before we remember them. This is most obvious in those images, in which – as in some dreams – we can see ourselves. We stand before ourselves, as we probably stood once somewhere in a primal past (*Urvergangenheit*) but as we have never stood before our gaze. And precisely the most important images – those which are

40. Letter to Adorno (written on September 3, 1932) in: Adorno and Benjamin: The Complete Correspondence, ed. by Henri Lonitz, Cambridge, Mass.: Harvard University Press 1999, pp. 16-17. In the same letter, Benjamin notes that included among the books contained in the "small library" that he has brought with him to Ibiza are "four volumes of Proust" which he "frequently peruse[s]". See p. 16. While Benjamin sent Scholem a "provisional" manuscript of "Berlin Childhood" in December 1932, as attested by his correspondence, he continued to work on the project for several years. See Benjamin's letter to Scholem of December 10, 1932, in: The Correspondence of Walter Benjamin and Gershom Scholem: 1932-1940, ed. by Gershom Scholem, New York: Schocken Books 1989, p. 24. During this time, Benjamin developed, refined, replaced and rearranged a number of sections, several of which were published in the Frankfurter Zeitung between 1933 and 1934. See Bernd Witte: Walter Benjamin: An Intellectual Biography, Detroit: Wayne State University Press, 1997, pp. 134-135.

41. Anna Stüssi: Erinnerung an die Zukunft: Walter Benjamins "Berliner Kindheit um Neunzehnhundert", Göttingen: Palaestra 1977, p. 83, and Benjamin: "On the Concept of History", in: Benjamin: Selected Writings, Vol. 4, ed. by Howard Eiland/Michael W. Jennings, Cambridge, Mass. and London, England: Harvard University Press 2003, p. 391.

developed in the darkroom of the lived moment – are the ones we get to see. One could say that our deepest moments [...] come with a little image, a photo of ourselves. And that 'entire life' that we often hear about, which passes before the dying, or those people who are hovering in danger of dying, is composed precisely out of these little images. They provide a quick procession like those booklets, the forerunners of the cinematograph, in which we, as children, could admire the skills of a boxer, swimmer, or tennis player.[42]

In both "A Berlin Chronicle" and "Berlin Childhood", it is these "little images" that Benjamin seeks to capture and represent, and which distinguish his reminiscences from the chronological, narrative based content of autobiographies which are developed primarily from the memory of the intellect. In "A Berlin Chronicle", he writes:

Reminiscences, even extensive ones, do not always amount to an autobiography. And these quite certainly do not, even for the Berlin years that I am exclusively concerned with here. For autobiography has to do with time, with sequence and what makes up the continuous flow of life. Here, I am talking of a space, of moments and discontinuities.[43]

In both "A Berlin Chronicle" and "Berlin Childhood" the temporal spaces opened up by involuntary memory are associated with rooms, objects, places, streets, sounds, and colours which surrounded Benjamin as a child, and later as a young man, growing up in Berlin. The images

42. Gesammelte Schriften, Vol. II.3, p. 1064. See also Benjamin's 1936 essay "The Storyteller: Reflections on the Works of Nikolai Leskov", in which he states something very similar. Illuminations, p. 93. "It is", he writes, "characteristic that not only a man's knowledge or wisdom, but above all his real life – and this is the stuff that stories are made of – first assumes transmissible form at the moment of his death. Just as a sequence of images is set in motion inside a man as his life comes to an end – unfolding the views of himself under which he has encountered himself without being aware of it – suddenly in his expressions and looks the unforgettable emerges and imparts to everything that concerned him that authority which even he poorest wretch in dying possesses for the living around him".

43. "A Berlin Chronicle", p. 612. In a letter to Scholem written in September 1932, Benjamin writes of "Berlin Childhood": "[Y]ou will have guessed that they are not narratives in the form of a chronicle, but rather portray individual expeditions into the depths of memory". The Correspondence of Walter Benjamin and Gershom Scholem: 1932-1940, p. 19.

in "Berlin Childhood" (which Hermann Hesse describes as having been "sketched out with the most careful hand and lightly hued as if with watercolours"[44]) bear titles such as "Winter Morning", "The Sewing Box", "Hiding Places", "Butterfly Hunt", "The Moon", "The Carousel", "Market Hall", and "Colors", while the memories captured in "A Berlin Chronicle" revolve around places such as the *Tiergarten*, New Lake, the Viktoria Café, and other meeting places of the Youth Movement with which Benjamin was associated. As Benjamin writes in the preface to "Berlin Childhood", this emphasis on Berlin was due partly to his realisation while abroad in 1932 that in the near future he could be forced "to bid a long, perhaps lasting farewell" to the city in which he was born, and partly because – for someone living in exile – the images that "are most apt to awaken homesickness" are those of childhood.[45]

In "The Image of Proust", Benjamin argues that Proust's writings, too, are infused with an almost debilitating sense of homesickness. For Benjamin, however, Proust's homesickness is not the catalyst for a desire to escape into the realm of childhood and away from time itself, but is the product of his longing for a "world distorted in the state of resemblance".[46] Benjamin argues that the world that involuntary memory opens up to Proust is not a world of "boundless time" but rather a "universe of convolution"[47], and it is through this experience of "convoluted time" (which is achieved through the interweaving of memory with the present) that Benjamin locates the possibility for rejuvenation, and with it a sense of promise for a different kind of future. As John McCole has argued, this "entwinement" of memory stands in stark contrast to "the perpetual present of immediate, living experience (*Erlebnis)*". It consists

44. Hermann Hesse: "Welche Bücher begleiten Sie", Die Weltwoche, 20 (July, 1951). Quoted in: Brodersen: Walter Benjamin: A Biography, p. 212.

45. "Berlin Childhood", p. 344.

46. "The Image of Proust", p. 200.

47. Ibid., p. 206. Benjamin's analysis is supported by Proust's comments in a letter written to Princess Marthe Bibesco in 1912: "A sensation", Proust writes, "however disinterested it may be, a perfume, a ray of light [...] are still too much in my power to make me happy. It is when they bring back to my mind some other sensation, when I savor them between the present and the past (and not in the past – impossible to explain this here), that they make me happy". Letters of Marcel Proust, p. 213. See also the narrator's description of the impressions evoked by involuntary memory in Vol. 6, pp. 222-223: "A moment of the past, did I say? Was it not perhaps very much more: something that, common both to the past and the present, is much more essential than either of them?"

"neither in recalling discrete moments whose entire significance was given in the instant of their occurance nor in freeing them from time", but rather in "the ability to interpolate endlessly in what has been".[48]

Although it is clear that the emphasis Benjamin places on certain aspects of Proust's search for lost time is driven by his own conception of the powers of involuntary memory, he is not uncritical of Proust. On the contrary, one of the key criticisms that he levels at Proust's writing revolves around the two fundamentally different forms taken by the desire for happiness fuelling Proust's homesickness. One of these forms, Benjamin argues, is associated with an experience of memory which revolves around "the unheard-of, the unprecedented, the height of bliss", while the other is characterised by "eternal repetition, the eternal restoration of the original, the first happiness".[49] While the latter – in its evocation of a self-enclosed, timeless space – is a recognition of the emphasis Proust places on the past as a refuge from the future, the former – in its reference to that which is "unprecedented" – evokes an experience of time much closer to that privileged by Benjamin in his reading of Proust's "impassioned cult of similarity".[50]

For both Benjamin and Proust, the experiences provoked by these encounters are associated not with those incidents or events that one would ordinarily deem "memorable", but rather with the fleeting experience of mood that Benjamin associates with "the night, a lost twittering of birds, or a breath drawn at the sill of an open window".[51] It is the moody, atmospheric quality of these encounters (which are themselves prompted by everyday impressions such as the flavour of a certain blend of coffee or the sight of a book) that draws Benjamin, despite his reservations, to the writings of Proust. "The sight", Marcel notes,

> of the binding of a book once read may weave into the characters of its title the moonlight of a distant summer night. The taste of our breakfast coffee brings with it that vague hope of fine weather which so often long ago – as with the day still intact and full before us, we were drinking it out of a bowl of white porcelain, creamy and fluted and itself looking almost like vitrified milk – suddenly smiled upon us in the pale uncertainty of the dawn.[52]

---

48. McCole: Walter Benjamin and the Antinomies of Tradition, p. 262.

49. "The Image of Proust", p. 200.

50. Ibid.

51. Ibid., p. 199.

52. Proust: Vol. 6, p. 245. I have slightly modified the punctuation in this passage in an attempt to render it more clear.

For "[a]n hour", he continues, "is not merely an hour, it is a vase full of scents and sounds and projects and climates", and real experience is borne of a "connexion between these immediate sensations and the memories which envelop us simultaneously with them".[53]

It is also out of such moments that both "A Berlin Chronicle" and "Berlin Childhood" are constituted. In one of the most beautiful images contained in his childhood reminiscences, Benjamin recounts the memory of ice-skating on New Lake via an evocation of the sensation of weight (and, later, weightlessness) which accompanied the wearing (and removal) of his childhood skates. Nothing, Benjamin writes,

> would bring back New Lake and a few hours of my childhood so vividly as to hear once more the bars of music to which my feet, heavy with their skates after a lone excursion across the bustling ice, touched the familiar planks and stumbled past the chocolate-dispensing machines [...] to the bench where you now savored for a while the weight of the metal blades strapped to your feet, which did not yet reach the ground, before resolving to unbuckle them. If you then slowly rested one calf on the other knee and unfastened the skate, it was as if in its place you had suddenly grown wings, and you went out with steps that nodded to the frozen ground.[54]

The promise of the "scents and sounds and projects and climates" evoked by Benjamin's images of the loggias, the Zoo, and ice-skating on New Lake do not lie, however, in the objects and spaces, occasions and conversations with which they are associated, nor in their capacity to provide a model for a different kind of future. Rather, in a similar vein to Marcel's impression of the flavour of an early morning coffee when the day was "still intact and full before [him]", their significance lies in their evocation of a time when the future was still open, and the past not yet completed.[55] For Benjamin, this experience of time contains within it its own revolutionary possibility, because it opens up a space in the so-

53. Ibid., pp. 245-246.

54. "A Berlin Chronicle", pp. 610-611. See also "Berlin Childhood", p. 384.

55. See Szondi: "Hope in the Past", p. 499. See also the section entitled "Winter Morning" in: "Berlin Childhood" in which Benjamin describes the extent to which the scent of the apple which his nursemaid baked for him daily on the coal stove evoked "the aromas of all the things the day held in store for [him]". p. 357.

called forward march of history within which the remembering subject is able to imagine the possibility of a different kind of future.[56]

In *In Search of Lost Time,* Proust also draws a connection between the experience of "breathing the atmosphere" of childhood and the rejuvenation of one's capacity for imagination. In *Time Regained,* for example, Marcel refers to the "celestial nourishment" which involuntary memory provides him, commenting later that his encounters with impressions such as the sight of the sea, and the smell of a room provoked by the texture of a starched napkin play an important role in "caress[ing his] imagination".[57]As I will discuss in detail in the following chapter, this relationship between childhood and imagintion plays an important role in Benjamin's analysis of childhood perception and cognition in both "On the Mimetic Faculty" and "Doctrine of the Similar"[58]. In the context of this chapter, however, the heightened capacity for imagination that Benjamin attributes to children helps to shed light on the nature of the promise for the future that he locates in the spaces opened up by his childhood reminiscences. For, as Benjamin suggests in the preface to the book, the images that constitute "Berlin Childhood" are not specific to his own particular childhood.[59] Rather, as attested to by his delight upon hearing that Scholem had recognised his own childhood in the book, what is important for Benjamin is the degree to which "Berlin Childhood" captures not only something of the urban childhood of the middle classes, but something of the experience of childhood more generally.[60]

56. In "Some Motifs in Baudelaire", Benjamin notes that the time of involuntary memory is "outside history". p. 143.

57. See Proust: Vol. 6, pp. 224 and 229 respectively.

58. As Benjamin notes in a letter to Scholem (written in February, 1933) his ideas on mimesis were "formulated while [he] was doing research for the first piece of the Berliner Kindheit". Correspondence, pp. 402-403. See also Scholem's comments on the significance of Benjamin's fascination with childhood perception and cognition: "It is one of Benjamin's most important characteristics that throughout his life he was attracted with almost magical force by the child's world and ways", including "the as yet undistorted world of the child and its creative imagination, which the metaphysician describes with reverent wonder and at the same time seeks conceptually to penetrate". "Walter Benjamin", in: Scholem, Jews and Judaism in Crisis, New York: Schocken Books 1976, p. 175.

59. Benjamin notes in the preface that "certain biographical features, which stand out more readily in the continuity of experience than its depths, altogether recede in the present undertaking". p. 344.

In his writings on Proust, Benjamin is critical of what he describes as the private, self-absorbed focus of Proust's conception of the powers of involuntary memory. In "Some Motifs in Baudelaire", for example, he argues that Proust "nonchalantly and constantly strives to tell the reader: Redemption is my private show".[61] Benjamin, however, claims in his later writings that "where there is experience in the strict sense of the word", aspects of one's "individual past" are entwined with those of the "collective".[62] In his notes on Proust written after the publication of "The Image of Proust" in 1929, this collective emphasis features heavily. In his notes for *The Arcades Project*, for example, Benjamin argues that in order for a desire for change to become manifest, the experiences provoked by Proust's childhood recollections would have to be experienced at the level of the collective. Indeed, for Benjamin, the promise of the impressions evoked by involuntary memory lies not only in the particular content of the memories which are recollected, but in the extent to which the capacity for imagination that he associates with children's play is reignited along with those memories.

60. See "Berlin Childhood", p. 344. In a letter to Scholem (written in January, 1933) Benjamin writes: "[Y]ou could hardly have said anything more encouraging than that in fact now and again certain passages seemed to bear on your own childhood." See Correspondence, p. 400. In a letter to Benjamin (written in April, 1934) Adorno comments that Erich Reiss also "felt he could recognize his own childhood" in the images of Benjamin's childhood captured in the book. See Walter Benjamin and Theodor Adorno: The Complete Correspondence, p. 37.

61. "Some Motifs in Baudelaire", note 80, p. 145. See also Benjamin's comments in "The Image of Proust" in which he writes: "Since the spiritual exercises of Loyola there has hardly been a more radical attempt at self-absorbtion". p. 207.

62. "Some Motifs in Baudelaire", p. 113.

1.2 Children's Play and Proletarian Children's Theatre

This fascination with children's play stands as the heart of Benjamin's 1929 "Program for a Proletarian Children's Theatre".[63] Although the concerns addressed in this essay are intermeshed with those which are central to Benjamin's writings from this period (including, in particular, his writings on mimesis, Proust, hashish, and Surrealism), the impetus for the project sprang from his meeting with the Latvian performer and theatre director Asja Lacis – a "Russian revolutionary from Riga" with whom Benjamin first came into contact in 1924 during a six month stay on the island of Capri.[64]

In the account of their first meeting outlined in *Revolutionär im Beruf*, Lacis describes the "extraordinary interest" demonstrated by Benjamin in the children's theatre she had established in 1918 in Orel.[65] Benjamin, Lacis recounts, was so "inflamed"[66] with enthusiasm for her work that he was inspired to write a "program" for the theatre which would provide her practical work with a theoretical grounding.[67] The central concern of this program is the development of a child-centred model for education based on experimentation and play that seeks to avoid the emphasis on morality and discipline characteristic of the bourgeois education system.[68] Instead of a teacher, proletarian children's

---

63. Benjamin: "Program for a Proletarian Children's Theatre", in: Selected Writings, Vol. 2, pp. 201-206.

64. This description of Lacis appears in a letter to Scholem written in July, 1924. See Correspondence, p. 245. For a more detailed account of Benjamin's relationship with Lacis, see Susan Ingram: "The Writing of Asja Lacis", New German Critique, No. 86 (Spring/Summer, 2002), pp. 159-177, and Walter Benjamin, 1892–1940: Marbacher Magazin, No. 55, ed. by Rolf Tiedemann/Christoph Gödde/Henri Lonitz, Marbach am Necker: Deutsche Schillergesellschaft, 1990, pp. 161-70.

65. See Asja Lacis: "Orel 1918/1919: Proletarisches Kindertheater – Programm einer ästhetisch-politischen Erziehung (Benjamin)", in: Lacis: Revolutionär im Beruf: Berichte über proletarisches Theater, über Meyerhold, Brecht, Benjamin und Piscator, ed. by Hildegard Brenner, München: Rogner & Bernhard, 1971, pp. 25-26. Hereafter referred to as Revolutionär im Beruf. See also Lacis' discussion of their meeting in "Capri 1924, Benjamin – 'Neapel'", in: Revolutionär im Beruf, pp. 41-42.

66. Ibid., p. 42.

67. Ibid., pp. 25-26.

68. "Program for a Proletarian Children's Theatre", p. 205. Benjamin argues

theatre is organised by a "leader" who seeks neither to dictate, nor influence the children's behaviour, but rather to guide their activities indirectly through his or her choice of subject material.[69] What is specific to the development of the learning process at the heart of the proletarian children's theatre is that the emphasis is placed on the children, not the leader, on observation rather than instruction or direction. "No pedagogic love", Benjamin writes,

> is worth anything unless in nine-tenths of all instances of knowing better and wanting better it is deprived of its courage and pleasure by the mere observation of children's lives. [...] For the true observer, however – and this is the starting point of education – every childhood action and gesture becomes a signal. Not so much a signal of the unconscious, of latent processes, repressions, or censorship (as the psychologists like to think), but a signal from another world, in which the child lives and commands.[70]

What fascinates Benjamin about the world inhabited by children is the extent to which the capacity for imagination demonstrated in children's play infuses both their world, and their audience, with a sense of possibility. "[W]e the educators", Lacis writes, "learnt and saw many new things. How easily children can adapt themselves to situations, how inventive they are, [... how] they make the wild imagination of their inventions visible".[71] Elaborating on this idea, Benjamin argues that the children's performance "represents in the realm of children what the carnival was in the old cults. Everything was turned upside down; and just as in Rome the master served the slaves during the Saturnalia, in the same way in a performance children stand on stage and instruct and teach the attentive educators".[72]

For Benjamin, one of the most important lessons to be learnt from the active, creative behaviour of children is their refusal to accept the form of something as it is. As he demonstrates in both "One Way Street" and "Berlin Childhood", children are particularly adept at transforming

---

that just as "the discipline which the bourgeoisie demands from *children* is the mark of shame", the "proletariat must not pass on its own class interest to the next generation with the tainted methods of an ideology that is destined to subjugate the child's suggestible mind". p. 205.

69. Ibid., p. 203.

70. Ibid., pp. 203-204.

71. Revolutionär im Beruf, p. 25.

72. "Program for a Proletarian Children's Theatre", p. 205.

both themselves, and the world around them, into something radically different. In "One-Way Street", for example, Benjamin describes the child's transformation of his "dresser drawers" into an "arsenal and zoo, crime museum and crypt". "To tidy up", he writes, "would be to demolish an edifice full of prickly chestnuts that are spiky clubs, tinfoil that is hoarded silver, bricks that are coffins, cacti that are totem poles, and copper pennies that are shields".[73] While in "Berlin Childhood", Benjamin recounts his own experience of playing hide-and-seek, and his attempts to blend himself – chameleon like – into his surroundings in order to evade discovery by his pursuer.[74]

In his "Program for a Proletarian Children's Theatre", Benjamin argues that it is the responsibility of the leader to "release" the creative energies generated in children's play from the "world of sheer fantasy" by encouraging the children to apply themselves to materials – an activity which takes place in the various workshops in which children take part in activities such as "the making of stage props, painting, recitation, music, dance, [and] improvisation".[75] Anticipating his writings on mimesis, Benjamin argues that what is revealed in the workshops is the direct connection between "receptive innervation" and creativity characteristic of the gestures and activities of children – the traces of which can be found in the activities of the painter who, like the child, is particularly adept at transferring "the receptive innervation of the eye muscles into the creative innervation of the hand".[76]

It is this process of transferral (between perception and creative action) demonstrated in children's play, which – as we will see in the following chapters – provides Benjamin with a model for his analysis of the innervating mode of perception cultivated by hashish and film. Indeed, in a similar vein to his delineation of the rejuvenating effects evoked by involuntary memory, the significance of this playful, innervating mode of perception lies in the extent to which the experience of the past in the present with which it is associated can serve as a catalyst for the creation and sustenance of a desire for a different kind of future.

73. "One-Way Street", p. 465. See also Benjamin's analysis, in "The Image of Proust", of the child's playful, imaginative transformation of a "stocking" into a range of different objects and shapes. p. 200.

74. "Berlin Childhood", p. 375.

75. "Program for a Proletarian Children's Theatre", p. 204.

76. Ibid.

1.3 Creative Writing and Play

In his analysis of Benjamin's "Program for a Proletarian Children's Theatre", Gerhard Fischer draws a highly productive comparison between Benjamin's analysis of the significance of the child's imagination and Freud's discussion of children's play in his 1907 lecture "Creative Writers and Daydreams".[77] In this short piece, Freud argues that the child's "intense occupation" with play (an activity which he or she takes very seriously) can be likened to the practices of the creative writer insofar as both seek to "create [...] a world of [their] own, or, rather, rearrange [...] the things of [their] world in a new way which pleases [them]".[78] He argues that the creative practices of both the child and the writer are fuelled by a desire for the fulfillment of "unsatisfied wishes".[79] "[A] happy person", Freud writes, "never phantasies, only an unsatisfied one [...] and every single phantasy is the fulfilment of a wish, a correction of [an] unsatisfying reality".[80]

What is particularly interesting about Freud's analysis for our concerns here, is not only the relationship he draws between childhood play and an active desire to transform one's reality into something different, but his analysis of the extent to which this desire is reflected in the practices of the creative writer, which he argues are "a continuation of, and a substitute for, what was once the play of childhood".[81]

This conception of creative writing (as a practice which is driven by a dissatisfaction with the prevailing conditions) certainly provides us with an insight into the writings of Proust, which are – as Adorno has pointed out – infused by a "fidelity to childhood" borne of an implacable desire for happiness.[82] "Proust", Adorno writes,

77. Gerhard Fischer: "Benjamin's Utopia of Education as Theatrum Mundi et Vitae: On the Programme of a Proletarian Children's Theatre", in: With the Sharpened Axe of Reason: Approaches to Walter Benjamin, ed. by Gerhard Fischer, Oxford and Herndon: Berg 1996, p. 214, and Sigmund Freud: "Creative Writers and Day-dreaming", in: Art and Literature – Vol. 14: The Penguin Freud Library, ed. by Albert Dickson, London: Penguin 1990, pp. 131-141.

78. Freud: "Creative Writers and Daydreaming", p. 132.

79. Ibid., p. 134.

80. Ibid., p. 133.

81. Ibid., p. 139.

82. Adorno: "On Proust", p. 316.

looks at even adult life with such alien and wondering eyes that under his immersed gaze the present is virtually transformed into prehistory, into childhood. This has an aspect that is not at all esoteric but rather democratic. For every somewhat sheltered child whose responsiveness has not been driven out of him in his earliest years has at his disposal infinite possibilities of experience.[83]

Contrary, however, to Benjamin's claims about the private, self-absorbed focus of Proust's analysis of the experiences evoked by involuntary memory, it is clear from both Proust's letters and the narrator's comments in *Time Regained* that Proust conceived of the task of the novel somewhat differently. In a letter to Camille Vetard (written in 1922), Proust claims that the task of the book is "to reveal to the conscious mind unconscious phenomena which, wholly forgotten, sometimes lie very far back in the past"[84] – the significance of which is framed, in *Time Regained,* in terms of a collective, rather than an individual recollection of the past. In a passage towards the end of the novel, Marcel claims that "it would be inaccurate [...] to say that I thought of those who would read [the book] as 'my' readers. For it seemed to me that they would not be 'my' readers but the readers of their own selves, [...] it would be my book, but with its help I would furnish them with the means of reading what lay inside themselves".[85] "The writer's work", he states, "is merely a kind of optical instrument which he offers to the reader to enable him to discern what, without this book, he would perhaps never have perceived in himself".[86]

In his article "On Proust", Adorno expresses a similar sentiment. In a passage which reveals an important affinity between the childhood reminiscences of Benjamin and Proust that was not explicitly recognised by Benjamin himself, Adorno argues that the reader of Proust "feels addressed by [his descriptions] as if by an inherited memory".[87] It is from "under the mask of autobiography" that he is able to give away "the secrets of every person while at the same time reporting on something extremely specialized".[88] In the recollections of his childhood collected in "A Berlin Chronicle" and "Berlin Childhood" Benjamin has sought to achieve something very similar.[89] Confronted with a future eclipsed by

83. Ibid., p. 315.

84. Letters of Marcel Proust, p. 405.

85. Proust: Vol. 6, pp. 431–432.

86. Ibid., p. 273.

87. Adorno: "On Proust", p. 315.

88. Ibid., p. 313.

the horrors of Fascism, the value of his childhood reminiscences lies not in the extent to which they open up a space within which Benjamin can escape into the past, and away from the terror of the present. On the contrary, what is significant for Benjamin about the impressions evoked by involuntary memory is not only the degree to which they can reignite the capacity for imagination hidden within the crevices of one's childhood but – more significantly – the extent to which the child's capacity for imagination can be harnessed in the service of the creation of a different kind of future.

89. It would also be interesting to read Adorno's own childhood reminiscences in this context. Unfortunately, however, such a reading lies beyond the scope of this chapter. See Theodor W. Adorno: Kindheit in Amorbach: Bilder und Erinnerungen, ed. by Reinhard Pabst, Frankfurt am Main and Leipzig: Insel 2003.

Chapter 2: The Politics of Aura and Imagination in Benjamin's Writings on Hashish

The immediate reality of the surrealist revolution is not so much to change anything in the physical and apparent order of things as to create a movement in men's minds.

Surrealists' Declaration of January 27, 1925[1]

In a letter to Gershom Scholem written in July 1932, Benjamin recounts with disappointment a list of projects that – due to the prolonged precariousness of his financial situation – remain untouched or uncompleted. He writes that amongst the books which "mark off the real site of ruin or catastrophe" is "a truly exceptional book about hashish". "Nobody", he cautions Scholem, "knows about this [project], and for the time being it should remain between us"[2]. However, while Benjamin's plans for a book on hashish appear concretely for the first time in this letter, as early as 1919 he had expressed an interest in exploring the psychological effects produced by hashish and opium. Inspired by Charles Baudelaire's writings on the topic in *Artificial Paradise* (which was written in

1. Quoted in Maurice Nadeau: The History of Surrealism, Middlesex: Penguin Books 1978, p. 114. Nadeau claims that this declaration, which was published as a tract in 1925, has not – to his knowledge – been reprinted. p. 112.

2. The Correspondence of Walter Benjamin: 1910-1940, ed. by Gershom Scholem/Theodor W. Adorno, Chicago and London, University of Chicago Press 1994, p. 396. Hereafter referred to as Correspondence.

the 1850s[3]) Benjamin's interest lay in examining what the effects of these drugs could "teach us philosophically"[4].

It wasn't, however, until some eight years later (in December 1927) that Benjamin began the first of a series of experiments with hashish that continued sporadically over the next seven years. His first experiment (and several which followed) was undertaken under the supervision of Doctors Fritz Fränkel and Ernst Joël (both of whom Benjamin had known from his days in the Berlin Youth Movement[5]). In 1926, Fränkel and Joël (who jointly ran a clinic for drug addicts in Berlin) published an article on the psychopathological effects induced by hashish intoxication in *Klinische Wochenschrift*. The range of effects outlined in this article (which include a heightened perceptual acuity, the experience of an expansion of space, the "derangement of one's sense of time (*Zeitsinn*)", a return to the infantile, and the frequent activation of memory[6] were to feature significantly, not only in Benjamin's own writings about the effects induced by the drug, but also in his delineation of auratic experience. As I will endeavour to show in this chapter, the contours of Benjamin's conception of auratic experience – and the important role it occupies in relation to his analysis of the significance of both mimetic perception and the impressions evoked by involuntary memory – grew out of his experiences while under the influence of hashish[7], even though his analysis of the political significance of auratic experience wasn't developed in his writings until some years later.

While Benjamin did not transform or incorporate his writings on

---

3. Charles Baudelaire: Artificial Paradise: On Hashish and Wine as Means of Expanding Individuality, New York: Herder and Herder 1971. Hereafter referrred to as Artificial Paradise.

4. See Benjamin's letter to Ernst Schoen of September 19, 1919, Correspondence, p. 148.

5. For Benjamin's comments on his reacquaintance with Fränkel and Joël, see his letter to Scholem of January 30, 1928, Correspondence, p. 323.

6. Fränkel, Fritz and Ernst Joël: "Der Haschisch-Rausch: Beiträge zu einer experimentellen Psychopathologie", Klinische Wochenschrift, 5, Nr.37 (1926), pp. 1707-1709. A long quote from this article appears at the beginning of Benjamin's "Hashish in Marseilles". See Benjamin: Selected Writings, Vol. 2, ed. by Michael W. Jennings/Howard Eiland/Gary Smith, Cambridge, Mass. and London, England: Harvard University Press 1999, pp. 673-679.

7. This observation is confirmed by the editors of Benjamin's Selected Writings. See the "Chronology", in: Selected Writings, Vol. 2, p. 827.

hashish into a book length study, the protocols he wrote while under the influence of the drug, as well as a number of more formally constructed pieces, were published posthumously in 1972 under the title *Über Haschisch*.[8] As Benjamin claims in a letter written to Scholem in January 1928: These writings "may well turn out to be a very worthwhile supplement to my philosophical observations, with which they are most intimately related, as are to a certain degree even my experiences while under the influence of the drug".[9] While the ideas explored in Benjamin's writings on hashish (which were written between 1927 and 1934) are intermeshed with those developed in his childhood reminiscences, and in his essays on Marcel Proust and photography (which were also written during this period)[10], the most significant influences shaping his conception of the radical experiential effects induced by hashish intoxication were *Artificial Paradise* and the writings of the Surrealists.

Benjamin's "burning interest"[11] in Surrealism during this period was, as Peter Osborne has pointed out, fuelled by its "contribution to the expansion of the idea of political experience"[12] at a time when Benjamin was arguing that the capacity for experience had been significantly diminished. The extent of Benjamin's interest in the writings of the

---

8. Benjamin: Über Haschisch: Novellistisches, Berichte, Materialien, ed. by Tillman Rexroth, Frankfurt am Main: Suhrkamp 1972. A selection of Benjamin's writings on hashish has been published in English translation in Vol. 2 of Benjamin's Selected Writings. See "Main Features of my Second Impression of Hashish", pp. 85-90, "Hashish, Beginning of March 1930", pp. 327-330, "Myslovice-Braunschweig- Marseilles", pp. 386-393, and "Hashish in Marseilles", pp. 673-679. Not included in this volume are the "Crocknotizen" and most of the material from the "Protokolle". See Über Haschisch, pp. 57-61 and 65-143 respectively.

9. Correspondence, p. 323.

10. See "A Berlin Chronicle", in: Selected Writings, Vol. 2, pp. 595-637, "Berlin Childhood around 1900" (Final Version), in: Selected Writings, Vol. 3, ed. by Howard Eiland/Michael W. Jennings, Cambridge, Mass. and London, England: Harvard University Press 2002, pp. 345-386, "The Image of Proust", in: Benjamin: Illuminations, ed. by Hannah Arendt, London: Fontana Press 1992, pp. 197-210, and "Little History of Photography", in: Selected Writings, Vol. 2, pp. 507-530.

11. Gershom Scholem: Walter Benjamin: The Story of a Friendship, Philadelphia: The Jewish Publication Society of America 1981, p. 134.

12. Peter Osborne: "Small-scale Victories, Large-scale Defeats: Walter Benjamin's Politics of Time", in: Walter Benjamin's Philosophy: Destruction and Experience, ed. by Andrew Benjamin/Peter Osborne, London and New York: Routledge, 1994, p. 63.

group can be gauged from his 1935 letter to Theodor W. Adorno, in which he reflects upon the impact that Louis Aragon's 1926 Surrealist narrative *Paris Peasant* had had upon him when he first came upon the book in the late 1920's.[13] "Evenings", Benjamin writes, "lying in bed, I could never read more than 2 or 3 pages by him because my heart started to pound so hard that I had to put the book down".[14]

Although Aragon's magical descriptions of the *Passage de l'Opera* in *Paris Peasant* are not explored by Benjamin in any detail in his 1929 essay "Surrealism: The Last Snapshot of the European Intelligentsia"[15], it is nonetheless clear that Aragon's book had a significant impact, not only on the development of the radical conception of intoxication which emerges from this essay, but also on Benjamin's analysis of the political significance of the perceptual and experiential effects induced by hashish intoxication. "To win the energies of intoxication [*die Kräfte des Rausches*] for the revolution", Benjamin writes, "is the project on which Surrealism focuses in all its books and enterprises. This it may call its most particular task"[16] – the significance of which can be traced to the manner in which the perceptual effects induced by hashish intoxication provide access to the "image space" that both Benjamin and the Surrealists associate with the activation of involuntary memory.

In the opening pages of *Paris Peasant*, the "image spaces" opened up by the intoxicated gaze of its narrator are revealed as he strolls through the wondrous "aquarium" into which the *Passage de l'Opera* has been transformed. Attracted by a sound emanating from a shop that sells walking canes, the narrator's attention is drawn to the "greenish, almost submarine light" radiating from the window display, the contents of

13. The first mention of Aragon in Benjamin's correspondence appears in a letter to Hugo von Hofmannsthal written in June, 1927. See Correspondence, p. 315.

14. Ibid., p. 488. As Bernd Witte has pointed out, Benjamin also translated sections of Paris Peasant for publication in the Literarische Welt in 1928. See Bernd Witte: Walter Benjamin: An Intellectual Biography, Detroit: Wayne State University Press 1997, p. 91.

15. Benjamin: "Surrealism: The Last Snapshot of the European Intelligentsia", in: Selected Writings, Vol. 2, pp. 207-221. Hereafter referred to as "Surrealism".

16. Ibid., p. 215, and "Der Sürrealismus: Die Letzte Momentaufnahme der europäischen Intelligenz", in: Benjamin: Gesammelte Schriften (7 Vols.), ed. by Rolf Tiedemann/Hermann Schweppenhäuser, Frankfurt am Main: Suhrkamp 1991, Vol. II.1, p. 307.

which – under the gaze of the narrator – are transformed into images from his childhood. "It was", he recounts, "the same kind of phosphorescence that, I remember, emanated from the fish I watched, as a child, from the jetty of Port Bail on the Cotentin peninsula".[17] The canes – which "possess[ed] the illuminating properties of creatures of the deep" – "floated gently like seaweed".[18] While some time later – as he gazes through the window of a beauty salon – the sight of a woman's "remodelled coiffure" is promptly transformed into "a great maroon insect".[19] These experiences of contiguity – or similarity – across time are, however, not isolated incidents, but the mark of the renewal of the capacity for perception and imagination that, for both Aragon and Benjamin, are hallmarks of Surrealist experience.

In an important fragment in "One-Way Street" (in which the relationship between perceptual renewal and this rejuvenation in the capacity for imagination is rendered more clear) Benjamin argues that the significance of the latter rests upon the extent to which it "subserves the *past*"[20]. The "faculty of imagination", he writes, is

> the gift of interpolating into the infinitely small, of inventing, for every intensity, an extensiveness to contain its new, compressed fullness – in short, of receiving each image as if it were that of the folded fan, which only in spreading draws breath and flourishes, in its new expanse, the beloved features within it.[21]

The experiences provoked by the impressions that emerge from the folded fan that is the image (which Aragon's narrator finds manifested in objects and materials as diverse as telephone switchboards, drinking straws, lamps, and the wickerwork of armchairs[22]) activates an experience of the past in the present that Benjamin describes as a "*profane illumination*", that is, "a materialistic, anthropological inspiration, to which hashish, opium, or whatever else can give an introductory lesson".[23]

---

17. Louis Aragon: Paris Peasant, London: Pan Books 1987, pp. 36-37.

18. Ibid., p. 36.

19. Ibid., p. 54.

20. Benjamin: "My Second Impression of Hashish", p. 89.

21. "One-Way Street", in: Benjamin: Selected Writings, Vol. 1, ed. by Marcus Bullock/Michael W. Jennings, Cambridge, Mass. and London, England: Harvard University Press 1996, p. 466.

22. Aragon: Paris Peasant, p. 94.

23. "Surrealism", p. 209.

The political significance of this "inspiration" (which the Surrealists associated with dreams and practices such as automatic writing, hypnosis, and drug taking) is rendered more clear in André Breton's analysis of the highly circumscribed character of modern existence in his 1924 "Manifesto of Surrealism". Experience today, Breton writes,

> paces back and forth in a cage from which it is more and more difficult to make it emerge. It too leans for support on what is most immediately expedient, and it is protected by the sentinels of common sense. Under the pretense of civilization and progress, we have managed to banish from the mind everything that may rightly or wrongly be termed superstition or fancy; forbidden is any kind of search for truth which is not in conformance with accepted practices.[24]

For Breton, the most significant side-effect of the diminution in the quality of experience is the breakdown of the capacity for imagination and, with it, the waning of the ability to envision a different kind of existence. He argues that the capacity for imagination (which "knows no bounds" in the realm of children) is only exercised "in strict accordance with the laws of an arbitrary utility". Because "it is incapable of assuming this inferior role" for a prolonged period, he claims that it "generally prefers to abandon man to his lusterless fate" in "the vicinity of [his] twentieth year".[25] For Breton, this abandonment has dire consequences for those whose lives are characterised by emptiness and atrophy, because he argues that it is the "[i]magination alone" which "offers [...] some intimation of what *can be*".[26]

The role of Surrealism, in this context, is to rid the mind of the "cancer" which "consists of thinking all too sadly that certain things 'are,' while others, which well might be, 'are not'"[27], through the rejuvenation of the imagination, and with it, the activation of an encounter with the unconscious. "For this", Breton writes, "we must give thanks to the discoveries of Sigmund Freud", on the basis of which the imagination is able to reassert itself.[28] Like Proust, Breton argues that it is only

---

24. Andre Breton: "Manifesto of Surrealism", in: Breton: Manifestoes of Surrealism, Ann Arbor: University of Michigan Press 1972, p. 10.

25. Ibid., p. 4.

26. Ibid., p. 5.

27. André Breton: "Second Manifesto of Surrealism", in: Manifestoes of Surrealism, p. 187.

28. Breton: "First Manifesto", p. 10.

through the mobilisation of an individual's past and present[29] (through the "connection established under certain conditions between two things whose conjunction would not be permitted by common sense"[30]) that the limitations of the conscious mind can be obliterated, opening up a space in which one's capacity for imagination can once again assert itself. As Benjamin stresses in both the preparatory notes for his essay on Surrealism, and the essay itself, the Surrealists are concerned "with experiences, not with theories" and "the showplace of [their] revelation is memory".[31]

In a similar vein to his analysis of Proust's delineation of the powers of involuntary memory, Benjamin claims that it is only in a heightened state of moodiness or intoxication that these experiences can become manifest. "Breton and Nadja", he writes in "Surrealism", "convert everything that we have experienced on mournful railway journeys [...], on Godforsaken Sunday afternoons[...], in the first glance through the rain-blurred window of a new apartment, into revolutionary experience [*Erfahrung*], if not action. They bring the immense forces of 'atmosphere' concealed in these things to the point of explosion".[32] Similarly, Breton argues that just as the intensity and duration of a spark are enhanced in "rarefied gases", the "atmosphere" created by Surrealist practices is particularly conducive to the activation of involuntary memory.[33] "The mind", he writes, "which plunges into Surrealism relives with glowing excitement the best part of its childhood. [...] From childhood memories, and from a few others, there emanates a sentiment of being unintegrated, and then later of *having gone astray*, which I hold to be the most fertile that exists".[34] Quoting Baudelaire, Breton claims that these explo-

---

29. André Breton: Communicating Vessels, Lincoln and London: University of Nebraska Press 1990, p. 122.

30. Breton quoted in Ruth Brandon: Surreal Lives: The Surrealists, 1917-1945, London: Papermac 2000, p. 449.

31. See "Surrealism", p. 208, and "Zum großen Aufsatz über Sürrealismus", Gesammelte Schriften, Vol. II.3, p. 1021.

32. "Surrealism", p. 210. See also Gesammelte Schriften, Vol. II.1, p. 300.

33. "Manifesto of Surrealism", p. 37.

34. Ibid., pp. 39-40. This passage, when read in full, bears a number of similarities to Benjamin's delineation of involuntary memory in "Aus einer kleinen Rede über Proust, an meinem vierzigsten Geburstag gehalten", in: Gesammelte Schriften, Vol. II.3, p. 1064. See also Theodor W. Adorno's account of the significance of the Surrealists' attempts to "uncover" childhood memories in "Looking

sions of memory cannot be willed, but rather "come to [man] spontaneously, despotically. He cannot chase them away; for the will is powerless now and no longer controls the faculties".[35]

Both the dissolution of the will – and its precipitation by a range of different factors – are the central features of Baudelaire's analysis of the experiential effects induced by hashish intoxication in *Artificial Paradise*.[36] As in Joël and Fränkel's study of the effects induced by the drug, Baudelaire argues that central among these factors is the derangement of perception ushered in by hashish, in which one's experience of the dimensions of time and space is expanded to "monstrous" proportions[37]. He argues that it is through this process of expansion that a heightened sensitivity becomes apparent in each of the senses: "One's ear perceives near-imperceptible sounds in the very midst of the loudest tumult" and under the "magnifying mirror" of hashish, objects and spaces take on "strange appearances".[38] In a passage which foreshadows Benjamin's analysis of the "magical correspondences"[39] evoked by language in his essays on mimesis, Baudelaire claims that "[e]ven grammar – sterile grammar" is transformed by hashish into a form of "evocative witchcraft": "[W]ords come to life, wrapped in flesh and bone – the noun, in all its substantive majesty; the adjective, transparent garb that dresses and colors it like glaze; and the verb, angel of motion, that sets the sentence moving."[40]

Back on Surrealism", in: Adorno: Notes to Literature, Vol. 1, ed. by Rolf Tiedemann, New York, Columbia University Press 1991, p. 88.

35. Breton: "Manifesto of Surrealism", p. 36.

36. The roots of Baudelaire's fascination with the drug can be traced back to his involvement in the 1840's with the "Club des Hachichins", a group of artists and writers (including Gérard de Nerval, Honoré de Balzac, Eugène Delacroix, and Dr. Jacques-Joseph Moreau) who would meet in Paris to take, and discuss the effects of the drug. See Claude Pichois and Jean Ziegler: Baudelaire, London: Vintage 2002, pp. 128-129, and Sadie Plant: Writing on Drugs, London: Faber and Faber 2001, pp. 41-42. As Edouard Roditi argues in his introduction to Baudelaire's Artificial Paradise, it is also likely that Baudelaire experimented with the drug as a young man. Artificial Paradise, p. xv.

37. Artificial Paradise, p. 70.

38. Ibid., pp. 43 and 54.

39. See Benjamin: "Doctrine of the Similar", in: Selected Writings, Vol. 2, p. 695.

40. Artificial Paradise, p. 69. See also Aragon's discussion of the manner in which words can function as "mirrors" in Paris Peasant, p. 103.

Although Baudelaire refers to this intoxicated state as "hallucinatory", he is careful to distinguish his use of the term from the manner in which it is employed by physicians. Hallucination in its strict sense, Baudelaire argues, is characterised by a sense of self-sufficiency, insofar as the experience it designates is sealed off from, and is therefore not influenced by, external conditions. Put simply, the person who hallucinates will see things and hear sounds which in reality do not exist, while the "hallucinations" induced by hashish intoxication are fuelled by the surroundings in which one finds oneself.[41] In a passage which evokes Benjamin's review of a book of plant photographs taken by Karl Blossfeldt[42], Baudelaire claims that the hashish eater "endu[es] all the external world with an intensity of interest": The "hue of a blade of grass", the "shape of a trefoil", the "gleaming of a dew-drop" and "the quivering of a leaf"[43] each take on the most striking appearance when viewed under the "magic glaze" of hashish.[44]

As per the Surrealists, Baudelaire argues that concomitant with this increase in sensitivity comes the enhancement of one's capacity to perceive similarities between things which would ordinarily be conceived of as disparate: "Sounds are clad in color, and colors contain a certain music", "[m]usical notes become numbers", and analogies (which "attack, pervade, and overcome the mind") "assume an unaccustomed vivid-

41. In "Der Haschisch-Rausch: Beiträge zu einer experimentellen Psychopathologie", Joël and Fränkel also make a distinction between the images induced by hashish and hallucinations proper. See p. 1708.

42. See Benjamin: "News about Flowers", in: Selected Writings, Vol. 2, pp. 155-157. This short piece is a review of Karl Blossfeldt's Urformen der Kunst: Photographische Pflanzenbilder, Berlin: Ernst Wasmuth 1928. It is interesting to note that this review was written in 1928 in the midst of Benjamin's experiments with hashish.

43. Artificial Paradise, p. 65. Baudelaire is quoting Edgar Allan Poe here, although he does not cite the source.

44. Ibid., p. 68. Blossfeldt's photographs, Benjamin writes, "reveal an entire, unsuspected horde of analogies and forms in the existence of plants". For example: "The oldest forms of columns pop up in horsetails; totem poles appear in chestnut and maple shoots enlarged ten times; and the shoots of a monk's-hood unfold like the body of a gifted dancer. Leaping toward us from every calyx and every leaf are inner image-imperatives [*Bildnotwendigkeiten*], which have the last word in all phases and stages of things conceived of as metamorphoses". "News about Flowers", p. 156.

ness".[45] It would however, as Benjamin states in "Convolute J" of *The Arcades Project*, be a mistake to conceive of these experiences as "a simple counterpart to certain experiments with synaesthesia".[46] In keeping with his analysis of Proust's delineation of the significance of the impressions evoked by involuntary memory, what is significant, for Benjamin, about these correspondences is not the sensory connections themselves, but the medium of memory through which these sense impressions become intermingled. In "Convolute J", Benjamin argues that memory in Baudelaire's writings is

> possessed of unusual density. The corresponding sensory data correspond in it; they are teeming with memories, which run so thick that they seem to have arisen not from this life at all but from some more spacious *vie antérieure*.[47]

It is the shards of this *vie antérieure* which the hashish eater glimpses in the images, thoughts, and experiences which – under his or her intoxicated gaze – "surge up and are projected with the ambitious energy and sudden flare of fireworks" which, "like the explosive powders and coloring chemicals of a pyrotechnic display, [...] blaze up and vanish in the darkness".[48]

2.1 Auratic Experience and Involuntary Memory

The political significance of Benjamin's fascination with the "intermittent" "visitation[s]"[49] of memory evoked by hashish intoxication (and the practices of the Surrealists more generally) is rendered more clear when read alongside his analysis of the atrophy of modern experience in his 1939 essay "Some Motifs in Baudelaire". Central to Benjamin's analysis of the decline of the capacity for experience is his delineation of the destruction of the aura – the significance of which can be traced to the important role that Benjamin's conception of auratic experience occupies in his analysis of the conditions that would lay the

45. Artificial Paradise, pp. 54-55.
46. Benjamin: [J79, 6], The Arcades Project, p. 367.
47. Ibid.
48. Artificial Paradise, p. 72.
49. Ibid., p. 34.

ground for the creation and sustenance of an "imaginative conception of a better nature [*der Phantasievorstellung von einer bessern Natur*]".[50]

In both "The Work of Art in the Age of its Technological Reproducibility" and "Some Motifs in Baudelaire", the concept of the aura emerges as the mark of an experience born of a non-reified relationship between man and nature. "We define the aura", Benjamin writes in the former,

> as the unique apparition of a distance, however near it may be. To follow with the eyes – while resting on a summer afternoon – a mountain range on the horizon or a branch which casts its shadow on the beholder is to breathe the aura of those mountains, of that branch. In the light of this description, we can readily grasp the social basis of the aura's present decay.[51]

In "Some Motifs in Baudelaire", Benjamin argues that this experience of distance (which is of a temporal order) designates "the associations which, at home in the *mémoire involontaire*, tend to cluster around the object of perception".[52] The act of looking at someone or something, he writes, "carries the implicit expectation that our look will be returned". "Where this expectation is met [...], there is an experience of the aura to the fullest extent".[53] Thus, to experience the aura of something

> we look at means to invest it with the ability to look at us in return. This experience corresponds to the data of the *mémoire involontaire*. (These data, incidentally, are unique; they are lost to the memory that seeks to retain them. Thus they lend support to a concept of the aura that comprises the 'unique manifestation of a distance'.[54]

---

50. In [J76,1] Benjamin claims that "[t]he decline of the aura and the waning of the imaginative conception of a better nature – this latter conditioned on its defensive position in the class struggle – are one and the same". The Arcades Project, p. 362. Translation modified. See Gesammelte Schriften, Vol. V.1, p. 457.

51. Benjamin: "The Work of Art in the Age of its Technological Reproducibility" (Third Version), in: Benjamin, Selected Writings, Vol. 4, ed. by Howard Eiland/ Michael W. Jennings, Cambridge, Mass. and London, England: Harvard University Press 2003, p. 255. Hereafter referred to as "Work of Art".

52. "Some Motifs in Baudelaire", in: Benjamin, Charles Baudelaire: A Lyric Poet in the Era of High Capitalism, London and New York: Verso 1997, p. 145.

53. Ibid., p. 147.

54. Ibid., p. 148. In the final sentence, Benjamin is quoting himself from "The Work of Art" essay. See p. 255.

If the image of someone gazing at a mountain range on the horizon "makes it easy to comprehend the social bases of the contemporary decay of the aura", as Benjamin argues in his analysis of Baudelaire, it is because "the expectation roused by the look of the human eye" in this image in not fulfilled under the conditions of modernity.[55] In contrast to the mood of tranquillity which permeates this image, Benjamin argues that life in the modern city – from the structure of newspapers and crowds, to the organisation of production-line labour – is everywhere permeated by a sense of shock and collision. Influenced by Georg Simmel's analysis of the psychological effects of urban living in "The Metropolis and Mental Life" (the details of which will be discussed in the following chapter)[56], Benjamin argues that the proliferation of shock in the modern city produces a subject who "is increasingly unable to assimilate the data of the world around him by way of experience [*Erfahrung*]".[57]

In "Some Motifs in Baudelaire", Benjamin argues that this decrease in the capacity for experience is bound with the role that consciousness plays as a "protective shield" which defends the organism from "excessive energies at work in the external world".[58] Drawing on Freud's analysis of the psychological effects produced by shock in "Beyond the Pleasure Principle", Benjamin argues that "[t]he greater the share of the shock factor in particular impressions, the more constantly consciousness has to be alert as a screen against stimuli; the more efficiently it is so, the less do these impressions enter experience (*Erfahrung*), tending to remain in the sphere of a certain hour of one's life (*Erlebnis*)".[59]

In "Some Motifs in Baudelaire", both the inability to assimilate data by way of one's experience, and the decline in one's capacity to *draw* on one's experience, is exemplified in Benjamin's description of the factory worker, whose relationship to both the product of his/her labour – and time more generally – allegorises the "perpetual present"[60] which de-

55. "Some Motifs in Baudelaire", p. 149.

56. Georg Simmel: "The Metropolis and Mental Life", in: Simmel on Culture – Selected Writings, ed. by David Frisby/Mike Featherstone, London, Thousand Oaks, New Delhi: Sage Publications 1997, pp. 174-185.

57. "Some Motifs in Baudelaire", p. 112. Benjamin's analysis of the role that newspapers play in contributing to this inability will be discussed in detail in Chapter 7.

58. Benjamin quoting Freud, "Some Motifs in Baudelaire", p. 115.

59. Ibid., p. 117.

60. I have borrowed this description from John McCole's analysis of "Erleb-

fines Benjamin's conception of "*Erlebnis*". In contrast to the emphasis on "practice" which is central to the art of craftsmanship (in which the capacity to draw on one's experience is essential to the development of one's practice), Benjamin – drawing on Karl Marx's analysis of alienated labour practices in *Capital* - argues that the "drilling of the workers" in production-line labour makes "a speciality of the absence of all development".[61] "The unskilled worker", he writes, "is the one most deeply degraded by the drill of the machines. His work has been sealed off from experience; practice counts for nothing there".[62]

Expanding on this idea, Benjamin argues that the experiences of the factory worker can be compared to those of the gambler (a familiar figure in both *The Arcades Project* and Baudelaire's poetry[63]). While production-line labour "lacks [the] touch of adventure" which is central to the appeal of gambling, Benjamin argues that gambling is nonetheless marked by the same sense of "emptiness" borne of an "inability to complete something which is inherent in the activity of a wage slave in a factory"[64]. "The manipulation of the worker at the machine", he writes,

> has no connection with the preceding operation for the very reason that it is its exact repetition. Since each operation at the machine is just as screened off from the preceding operation as a *coup* in a game of chance is from the one that preceded it, the drudgery of the labourer is, in its own way, a counterpart to the drudgery of the gambler. The work of both is equally devoid of substance.[65]

This passage is significant for an understanding of Benjamin's delineation of the atrophy of modern experience because it allegorises the temporal structure of his conception of *Erlebnis*. In contrast to the experience of contiguity across time which is central to Benjamin's delineation of auratic experience (*Erfahrung*), *Erlebnis* designates the experience of a series of self-contained, finite moments; each of which is "screened off"

nis" in Walter Benjamin and the Antinomies of Tradition, Ithaca and London: Cornell University Press 1993, p. 262.

61. "Some Motifs in Baudelaire", p. 133.

62. Ibid.

63. See, for example, Baudelaire's poem "The Clock", in: Baudelaire: The Flowers of Evil, Oxford and New York: Oxford University Press 1998, pp. 160-163.

64. "Some Motifs in Baudelaire", p. 134.

65. Ibid., pp. 134-135.

from those which precede it by the process of "starting all over again" upon which the temporal structure of *Erlebnis* is based.[66]

If Benjamin is drawn to Baudelaire's poetry, then it is not only because of the manner in which he gives voice to this degeneration of the capacity for auratic experience[67], but because of the extent to which he invests these self-contained, finite moments with "the weight of an experience (*Erfahrung*)"[68] through his evocation – in the form of the "*correspondances*" – of an experience of time which exists outside of the "homogenous, empty time"[69] characteristic of *Erlebnis*. These "*correspondances*" (which emerge when the perception of something in the present evokes an impression of the past with which it is unconsciously associated) are, Benjamin writes, the "data of remembrance"[70]. They are moments of "completing time" which are "not marked by any experience [*Erlebnis*]".[71]

In Baudelaire's poetry, these *correspondances* are associated with the evocation of the glimmer and density of certain colours, images of trees, masts, oarsmen, crashing waves, the flavour of fruit, dazzling sunlight, and the chant of boatmen. For Benjamin, however, their significance lies not in the particular content of the recollected memories (many of which would appear to derive from Baudelaire's voyage across the Indian ocean at the age of 20[72]). Rather, what is significant for Benjamin about these *correspondances* is the extent to which the opening up of time provoked by involuntary memory generates a space within which the remembering subject is able to envision the possibility of a different kind of relationship to his or her environment, and with it, the possibility of a different kind of existence. "In reality", Benjamin writes in his notes for "On the Concept of History", "there is not a moment that

---

66. Ibid., p. 137.

67. See, for example, Baudelaire's delineation of the experience of time characteristic of modernity in "The Clock", and in his prose poem "The Double Room", in: Baudelaire in English, ed. by Carol Clarke/Robert Sykes, London: Penguin 1997, pp. 237-239.

68. "Some Motifs in Baudelaire", p. 154.

69. "On the Concept of History", in: Benjamin: Selected Writings, Vol. 4, p. 395.

70. "Some Motifs in Baudelaire", p. 141.

71. Ibid., p. 139, and Gesammelte Schriften, Vol. I.2, p. 637.

72. See, for example, "Exotic Perfume", "Head of Hair", and "The Dancing Serpent", in: The Flowers of Evil, pp. 48-49, 50-53, and 56-59 respectively. For a detailed account of Baudelaire's voyage, see Chapter 9 of Baudelaire, pp. 74-81.

would not carry with it *its* revolutionary chance [...] the chance for a completely new resolution of a completely new problem [*Aufgabe*]".[73] It is precisely in these moments in which the "empty passage"[74] of time as *Erlebnis* is torn asunder by the experience of the past in the present that the political significance of Benjamin's delineation of auratic experience manifests itself.

2.2 Imagination and Mimesis

If, as Benjamin suggests, the experience of the past in the present evoked by the *correspondances* is associated with a heightened sensitivity, then the emphasis that Benjamin and Baudelaire place on the increase in sensitivity to their surroundings induced by hashish intoxication takes on a greater significance. In "Hashish in Marseilles", for example, Benjamin describes the extraordinary tenderness to his environment induced by the drug:

> It was not far from the first café of the evening, in which, suddenly, the amorous joy dispensed by the contemplation of some fringes blown by the wind had convinced me that the hashish had begun its work".[75] Baudelaire, too, expresses a similar sentiment: "[A] new sharpness – a greater keenness – becomes apparent in all the senses. The senses of smell, sight, hearing and touch alike participate in this development[76].

What is significant about this increase in sensitivity described by both Benjamin and Baudelaire is the extent to which it is attributed to the freeing up of one's experience of time induced by hashish intoxication. For the hashish eater, Baudelaire writes in *Artificial Paradise*, "the *dimension* of time" is "abolished".[77] Similarly, in his "Protokoll des Haschischversuchs vom 11. Mai 1928", Benjamin claims that a "complete disorientation of the sense of time [*Zeitsinn*]" characterises his experience – the significance of which he corroborates by quoting the observations of

73. "Paralipomena to 'On the Concept of History'", in: Selected Writings, Vol. 4, p. 402.

74. See [J69,5], The Arcades Project, p. 351.

75. "Hashish in Marseilles", p. 678.

76. Artificial Paradise, p. 54.

77. Ibid., p. 61. See also p. 21, 22, 24, and 70.

Ernst Joël (with whom he undertook the experiment): "I have miscalculated the time. [...] My watch is going backwards".[78]

In a similar vein to his delineation of the significance of Baudelaire's poetry, it is in the loosening up of one's experience of time provoked by hashish intoxication that Benjamin locates the possibility for the rejuvenation of auratic experience. The connections between the perceptual and experiential capacities of the hashish eater and auratic experience are drawn most suggestively in Benjamin's description – in "Hashish in Marseilles" – of the hashish eater as a "physiognomist".[79]

Although he is referring specifically, in this essay, to the hashish eater's capacity for recognising – in a crowd of unfamiliar faces – facial characteristics reminiscent of friends and acquaintances, as revealed in his notes on the effects of the drug in *The Arcades Project*, this capacity is not limited to the observation of human faces, but extends to the manner in which the intoxicated gaze of the hashish eater animates face-like qualities inherent within objects and spaces. In "Convolute M", Benjamin argues that, for the hashish eater, everything develops a face: "[E]ach thing", he claims, "has the degree of bodily presence that allows it to be searched – as one searches a face – for such traits as appear. Under these conditions even a sentence (to say nothing of the single word) puts on a face".[80]

What is significant about these comments in the light of Benjamin's analysis of the decline in the capacity for experience is the extent to which this perceptual capacity is rendered synonymous with the definition of a non-reified, auratic form of experience outlined in "Some Motifs in Baudelaire". "Experience of the aura", Benjamin writes, "rests on the transposition of a response common in human relationships to the

78. "Walter Benjamin: Protokoll des Haschischversuchs vom 11. Mai 1928", in: Über Haschisch, p. 84. The feeling that "the chronological order" has been freed up also features in Benjamin's account of Ernst Bloch's experiment with hashish in "Bloch's Protokoll zum Versuch vom 14. Januar 1928". See Über Haschisch, p. 78. See also Benjamin's analysis of "the hashish eater's demands on time and space" in "Hashish in Marseilles", p. 674.

79. "Hashish in Marseilles", p. 675.

80. [M1a,1], The Arcades Project, p. 418. In "Hashish in Marseilles", Benjamin (quoting Karl Kraus) writes: "'The more closely you look at a word, the more distantly it looks back' – appears to extend to the optical". p. 678. See also Benjamin's comments about the manner in which his surroundings "wink" at him in "Main Features of My Second Impression of Hashish", p. 88, and "First Sketches" in: The Arcades Project, p. 841.

relationship between the inanimate or natural object and man. The person we look at, or who feels he is being looked at, looks at us in return". Thus, to recapitulate a point made earlier: "To perceive the aura of an object we look at means to invest it with the ability to look at us in return. This experience corresponds to the data of the *mémoire involontaire*"[81].

In a similar vein to Benjamin's analysis of the "image-spaces" opened up by the writings and practices of the Surrealists, the conception of involuntary memory that emerges from Benjamin's writings on hashish revolves around the involuntary production and recollection of images:

> As this very evening proved, there can be an absolutely blizzard-like production of images, independently of whether our attention is directed toward anyone or anything else. Whereas in our normal state free-floating images to which we pay no heed simply remain in the unconscious, under the influence of hashish images present themselves to us seemingly without requiring our attention. Of course, this process may result in the production of images that are so extraordinary, so fleeting, and so rapidly generated that we can do nothing but gaze at them simply because of their beauty and singularity.[82]

In "Convolute M", this increase in the activation of involuntary memory is associated with the enhancement of the hashish eater's capacity for recognising similarities – the significance of which is traced in the analysis of mimetic perception outlined in Benjamin's 1933 essays "Doctrine of the Similar" and "On the Mimetic Faculty"[83].

In "Doctrine of the Similar", Benjamin argues that "[i]nsight into the realms of the 'similar' is of fundamental significance for the illumination of major sectors of occult knowledge" – the importance of which is demonstrated, not in the content of the similarities themselves, but in the replication of the processes through which such similarities are manifested.[84] Benjamin claims that the capacity for recognising similarities (which is a "a weak rudiment of the once powerful compulsion to become similar and also to behave mimetically") has been significantly attenuated in modern times – resulting in a "perceptual world" which

81. "Some Motifs in Baudelaire", p. 148.

82. "Hashish, Beginning of March 1930", pp. 328-329.

83. Both essays are contained in: Selected Writings, Vol. 2. See pp. 694-698, and pp. 720-722 respectively.

84. "Doctrine of the Similar", p. 694.

"contains only minimal residues of the magical correspondences and analogies that were familiar to ancient peoples".[85] These correspondences – which the ancients traced in the constellations of stars with which the "spirits and forces of life were shaped in accordance"[86] – extended significantly beyond the limited confines within which modern man is able to recognise similarity: "The similarities perceived consciously – for instance, in faces – are", Benjamin writes, "compared to the countless similarities perceived unconsciously or not at all, like the enormous underwater mass of an iceberg in comparison to the small tip one sees rising above the water".[87]

In "The Lamp" (which served as a preliminary draft for the ideas discussed in "Doctrine of the Similar"[88]) Benjamin argues that one of the few realms within which what was "the natural heritage of mankind in its early stages" can be found today, is in the play of children.[89] "Children's play", he writes in "Doctrine of the Similar", "is everywhere permeated by mimetic modes of behaviour, and its realm is by no means limited to what one person can imitate in another". Particularly adept at both recognising and producing similarities, "[t]he child plays at being not only a shopkeeper or teacher but also a windmill and a train"[90] in a realm which is free from what Breton describes as the "imperative [of] practical necessity".[91] For Benjamin, it is by remaining loyal to that "animistic" relationship to the world of nature and things (which is both a mark of the life of the ancients and the hallmark of auratic experience) that the "liberating" dimension of childhood play manifests itself.[92]

In "Convolute M", Benjamin argues that the "category of similarity, which for the waking consciousness has only minimal relevance" also "attains unlimited relevance" for the person intoxicated by hashish.[93] In "Myslovice-Braunschweig-Marseilles", for example, he recounts the story of a man, who – in a late night search for chocolate prompted by

85. See Ibid., p. 698, and "On the Mimetic Faculty", p. 721.

86. See "The Lamp", p. 691, and "On Astrology", in: Selected Writings, Vol. 2, pp. 684-685.

87. "Doctrine of the Similar", p. 695.

88. See the translator's notes to the "The Lamp", p. 693.

89. "The Lamp", p. 691.

90. See "Doctrine of the Similar", p. 694, and "On the Mimetic Faculty", p. 720.

91. "Manifesto of Surrealism", p. 4.

92. See Benjamin: "Toys and Play", in: Selected Writings, Vol. 2, p. 100.

93. [M1a,1], The Arcades Project, p. 418.

the "pangs of hunger" occasioned by the drug – is beckoned by the contents of a barber shop which (under his intoxicated gaze) have been transformed into confectionary products: "Only now", he writes, "did I realize that the hashish had begun to work, and if I had not been alerted by the way in which boxes of powder had changed into candy jars, nickel trays into chocolate bars, and wigs into cakes, my own loud laughter would have been warning enough".[94] While in his experiment of May 11, Benjamin describes the "curious [...] mimetic anticipations" which dominate both his and Ernst Joël's experience of the drug. Joël, for his part, transforms the corner of a writing table into a "naval base, coal station, something between Wittenberg and Jüterbog" – the significance of which, he notes, can be traced to a memory of his childhood.[95] While under Benjamin's intoxicated gaze, an oven metamorphoses into a cat, a writing table into a fruit stall [*Fruchtbude*], and "the creases in [his] white beach trousers" into "the creases of a burnous"[96]. When Joël takes a biscuit, Benjamin offers him a light, and while his cousin Egon Wissing is talking, Benjamin's "apprehension of his words [is] instantly translated into the perception of colored, metallic sequins that coalesce [...] into patterns" (like "the beautiful colored knitting patterns" in the *Herzblättchens Zeitvertreib* Benjamin had loved as a child).[97]

Although the "image spaces" opened up by hashish intoxication are, in Benjamin's writings, often associated with memories of the hashish eater's childhood, what is significant is not so much the particular content of the memories themselves, but rather the extent to which the experience of childhood in the present evoked by involuntary memory rejuvenates the capacity for perception and imagination that Benjamin, Baudelaire, and Breton each associate with childhood. Citing his own re-encounter as an adult with sounds such as the "dull pop with which the flame [lit] up the gas mantle" in his childhood home, and "the jangling of [his] mother's keys in her basket" as examples, Benjamin

94. "Myslovice-Braunschweig-Marseilles", p. 390.

95. "Protokoll des Haschischversuchs vom 11. Mai 1928", pp. 83 and 86 respectively, and Ernst Joël: "Protokoll zu demselben Versuch", in: Über Haschisch, p. 90.

96. See "Hauptzüge der ersten Haschisch-Impression", in: Über Haschisch, p. 67, and "Myslovice-Braunschweig-Marseilles", p. 392.

97. See "Protokoll des Haschischversuchs vom 11. Mai 1928", p. 83, and "Hashish, Beginning of March 1930", p. 328.

argues that it is through the recollection of childhood memories that one's capacity for mimetic perception can be reignited.[98]

Central not only to Benjamin's, but also to Baudelaire's and Breton's analyses of the radicality of childhood perception and cognition is not only the child's heightened mimetic capacity for recognising and producing similarities, but the extent to which the child's capacity for imagination is not limited by what the adult world deems appropriate and/or possible. "Imagination", Baudelaire writes, "is not fantasy", but "a virtually divine faculty that apprehends immediately, by means lying outside philosophical methods, the intimate and secret relation of things, the correspondences and analogies."[99] To reiterate a point made earlier, Baudelaire argues that the significance of imagination lies in the extent to which it "decomposes all creation and with the raw materials accumulated [...] it creates a new world, it produces the sensation of newness".[100]

In *Artificial Paradise*, Baudelaire argues that, "if we were wise", we would harness this "bubbling-over of imagination" occasioned by the effects of hashish in order to derive, not only "the certainty of a better life", but also "the hope of attaining it through daily exercise of our will".[101] His concern, however, lies with the danger that the "image spaces" opened up by the drug could be experienced not as catalysts for action, but rather as spectacles conceived of as ends or "paradises" in themselves. For Baudelaire, it is the dissolution of the will occasioned by the drug which is responsible for this development. For while this dissolution opens up a space within which the imagination can flourish, he argues that it also guards against "the ability [of the hashish eater] to

98. "Modern man", Benjamin writes in "The Lamp", "is transported into this very force field [of mimesis] by memories of his childhood". p. 692.

99. Baudelaire: "Further Notes on Edgar Poe", in: Baudelaire: Selected Writings on Art and Literature, ed. by P.E. Charvet, London: Penguin Books 1992, p. 199. Benjamin also quotes this passage in "Convolute J" of The Arcades Project. See [J31a,5], p. 285.

100. Baudelaire: "The Salon of 1859 – Letters to the Editor of the Revue Française", in: Baudelaire: Art in Paris: 1845-1862, Salons and other Exhibitions, ed. by Jonathan Mayne, Oxford: Phaidon 1981, p. 156. Benjamin also includes this passage in The Arcades Project. See [J34a,1], p. 290. See also Baudelaire's delineation of the radicality of childhood perception and cognition in "The Painter of Modern Life", in: Baudelaire: Selected Writings on Art and Literature, p. 398, and Benjamin's analysis of the "renewal of existence" accomplished by children in "Unpacking my Library", in: Illuminations, p. 63.

101. Artificial Paradise, pp. 34 and 57.

profit by it"[102]. According to Baudelaire, "[i]f a man can instantly procure all wealth in heaven and earth by taking a teaspoon of jelly, then he will never seek to acquire the slightest fraction of it by working. And our most urgent need is to live and work! [...] Indeed, what point is there in working, toiling, writing, creating anything at all, when it is possible to obtain Paradise in a single swallow?"[103]

For Benjamin, a similar shadow is cast upon the writings and practices of the Surrealists by what he describes as their "inadequate, undialectical conception of the nature of intoxication".[104] He argues that the "histrionic or fanatical stress on the mysterious side of the mysterious"[105] (which reveals itself, at times, in the writings of the Surrealists) is not politically productive in itself. Rather, what *is* productive is the "fruitful, living experience that allowed these people to step outside the charmed space of intoxication"[106] by bringing the experience of the past in the present occasioned by Surrealist practices to bear on the exigencies of the present situation.[107] "The task", Benjamin writes in "Surrealism", is "to discover in the space of political action the one hundred percent image space".[108] This space will not "be measured out by contemplation"[109], but is borne out of a rejuvenation of the capacity for auratic experience – the significance of which lies in the extent to which both the experience of the past in the present that it designates (and the renewal of the capacity for imagination with which it is associated) can serve as a catalyst for the creation and sustenance of a desire for a different kind of existence.

---

102. Ibid., p. 81.

103. Ibid., p. 26.

104. "Surrealism", p. 216.

105. Ibid.

106. Ibid., p. 208.

107. "The point", as John McCole has argued, "was not to revel in the ecstasy of a complementary world but to return with a sharpened sense for the realities of the world that lie [...] *this* side of the charmed circle". McCole: Walter Benjamin and the Antinomies of Tradition, p. 226.

108. "Surrealism", p. 217.

109. Ibid.

Chapter 3: "Reproducibility – Distraction – Politicization"[1]

In "The Work of Art in the Age of its Technological Reproducibility"[2], the various avenues pursued in what is an extremely complex analysis of the radical possibilities of film culminate at the end of the essay in Benjamin's call for communism to politicise art.[3] Although Benjamin's conjoining of politics and art in this passage may appear, at first glance, to be a straightforward comment on the role that art could play in the political struggle against fascism, a more detailed analysis reveals the extent to which Benjamin's understanding of what it means to "politicize art" is intimately bound with the desire for a rejuvenation of the capacity for perception and imagination elaborated in his previous writings.

As Susan Buck-Morss has pointed out, it is in the "Epilogue" to the "Work of Art" essay that the stakes of Benjamin's analysis of the complex relationship between politics and aesthetics is played out in his cri-

---

1. This phrase is taken from Benjamin's notes on film in "Theory of Distraction", in: Benjamin: Selected Writings, Vol. 3, ed. by Howard Eiland/Michael W. Jennings, Cambridge, Mass. and London, England: Harvard University Press: 2002, p. 142.

2. Although the first draft of the essay was written in 1936, Benjamin continued to work on it up until 1939. Throughout the course of this chapter I will refer predominantly to the third and final version of the essay (which was completed in 1939). See Walter Benjamin: "The Work of Art in the Age of Its Technological Reproducibility", in: Benjamin: Selected Writings, Vol. 4, ed. by Howard Eiland/Michael W. Jennings, Cambridge, Mass. and London, England: Harvard University Press: 2003, pp. 251-283. Hereafter referred to as "Work of Art".

3. Ibid., p. 270.

tique of the "*aestheticizing of political life*" undertaken by the Nazi government.[4] Although Benjamin is referring specifically in this passage to the fascists' "glorification of war", his aim is not to provide a detailed account of fascist propaganda, but to show – in more general terms – the extent to which the aestheticisation of violence and war has (in his own time and, indeed, our own) "reached the point where [humankind] can experience its own annihilation as a supreme aesthetic pleasure"[5] – a point which is illustrated via a quote from Tomaso Marinetti's 1909 "Futurist Manifesto":

> For twenty-seven years we Futurists have rebelled against the idea that war is anti-aesthetic. [...] We therefore state: [...] War is beautiful because – thanks to its gas masks, its terrifying megaphones, its flame throwers, and light tanks – it establishes man's dominion over the subjugated machine. War is beautiful because it inaugurates the dreamed-of metallization of the human body. War is beautiful because it enriches a flowering meadow with the fiery orchids of machine-guns. War is beautiful because it combines gunfire, barrages, cease-fires, scents, and the fragrance of putrefacation into a symphony. War is beautiful because it creates new architectures, like those of armored tanks, geometric squadrons of aircraft, spirals of smoke from burning villages, and much more. [...] Poets and artists of Futurism, [...] remember these principles of an aesthetic of war, that they may illuminate [...] your struggles for a new poetry and a new sculpture![6]

Fascism, Benjamin argues, has sought to achieve something very similar: "'Fiat ars – pereat mundus' [Let art flourish – and the world pass away], says fascism, expecting from war, as Marinetti admits, the artistic gratification of a sense perception altered by technology". "*Such*", Benjamin writes, "*is the aestheticizing of politics, as practiced by fascism. Communism replies by politicizing art*".[7]

If, as Buck-Morss argues, the kind of "sensory alienation" that enables one to experience human destruction as an "aesthetic pleasure" can be seen as a symptom of the "aestheticizing of politics" (that is, an alienated mode of perception cultivated by the enlisting of art in aid of a

---

4. Ibid., p. 269, and Susan Buck-Morss: "Aesthetics and Anaesthetics: Walter Benjamin's Artwork Essay Reconsidered", New Formations, No. 20 (Summer, 1993), pp. 123-4. Hereafter referred to as "Aesthetics and Anaesthetics".

5. "Work of Art", p. 270.

6. Marinetti quoted in: Ibid., pp. 269-270.

7. "Work of Art", p. 270. See also Walter Benjamin: "The Signatures of the Age", in: Selected Writings, Vol. 3, p. 139.

particular political outcome) then Benjamin's call at the end of the essay for communism to politicise art must, she argues, extend beyond a desire for communism to employ art in the aid of its own political struggle.[8] Rather, working closely within the parameters sketched out in the final pages of the essay, Buck-Morss claims that Benjamin is in fact "demanding of art a task far more difficult – that is, to *undo* the alienation of the corporeal sensorium, to *restore the instinctual power of the human bodily senses for the sake of humanity's self-preservation,* and to do this, not by avoiding the new technologies, but by *passing through* them".[9]

Although what it might mean to "pass through" new technologies such as film is not rendered clear in this passage, Buck-Morss' reading of Benjamin's call for the politicisation of art as a statement on the role that art *could* play in undoing "the alienation of the corporeal sensorium" resonates with the emphasis on the desire for a rejuvenation of the capacity for perception and experience elaborated in Benjamin's writings on Proust, Baudelaire, Surrealism, and hashish. In more specific terms, Benjamin's analysis, in the "Work of Art" essay, of the role that film could play in sensually reconnecting the audience with their everyday environment could, as Miriam Hansen has argued[10], be seen to mitigate against the decline in the capacity for auratic experience (and the concomitant "waning of the imaginative conception of a better nature"[11]) that Benjamin describes as a key symptom of urban alienation in "Some Motifs in Baudelaire".[12]

What is striking about Buck-Morss' reading of the "Work of Art" essay is the extent to which she situates Benjamin's call for the politicisation of art within the broader context of both the decline in the capacity

8. "Aesthetics and Anaesthetics", p. 124. "Otherwise", Buck-Morss argues, "the two conditions, crisis and response, would turn out to be the same. Once art is drawn into politics (Communist politics no less than Fascist politics), how could it help but put itself into its service, thus to render up to politics its own artistic powers, ie., 'aestheticize politics'". See note 9, pp. 123-124.

9. Ibid., p. 124.

10. Miriam Hansen: "Benjamin, Cinema and Experience: 'The Blue Flower in the Land of Technology'", New German Critique, No. 40 (Winter, 1987).

11. Walter Benjamin: [J76,1] in The Arcades Project, Cambridge, Mass. and London, England: Harvard University Press 1999, p. 362. Translation modified. See Gesammelte Schriften, Vol. VI, p. 457.

12. Walter Benjamin: "Some Motifs in Baudelaire", in: Benjamin: Charles Baudelaire: A Lyric Poet in the Era of High Capitalism, London and New York: Verso 1997.

for auratic experience and the modern transformation that has taken place in our understanding of the term "aesthetics". Drawing on Terry Eagleton's critical history of the term, Buck-Morss traces its etymological roots to "*Aisthitikos*" – "the ancient Greek word for that which is 'perceptive by feeling'".[13] The original field of aesthetics, Eagleton writes,

> is nothing less than the whole of our sensate life together – the business of affections and aversions, of how the world strikes the body on its sensory surfaces, of that which takes root in the gaze and the guts and all that arises from our most banal, biological insertion into the world.[14]

For Buck-Morss, how and why our understanding of "aesthetics" has been transformed via "the course of the modern era" from connoting a close, "sensate" relationship to the world, to invoking the realm of art with which it is – and was in Benjamin's time – predominantly associated, is "not self-evident".[15] While she refrains from charting a causal or parallel history between this shift and Benjamin's analysis of the diminution in the capacity for perception and experience under conditions of modernity, she draws them into a constellation so that the transformation in our understanding of "aesthetics" can illuminate – and be illuminated by – what she describes as the "synaesthetic system's" modern reorganisation as an "anaesthetic" which numbs us to such a degree that we are able to "experience [our] own annihilation" as an "aesthetic pleasure".[16]

As discussed in previous chapters, Benjamin argues (via Freud and Simmel) that the decline in the capacity to integrate perception with memory and bodily sensation is a by-product of the role that consciousness plays as a stimulus shield which protects the urban dweller from excess energies characteristic of everyday life in the city. According to Simmel's 1903 analysis of the experiential effects of urbanisation in "The Metropolis and Mental Life"[17], the "sharp discontinuity" and "un-

---

13. "Aesthetics and Anaesthetics", p. 125.

14. Terry Eagleton: The Ideology of the Aesthetic, Oxford: Blackwell 1990, p. 13.

15. "Aesthetics and Anaesthetics", p. 125.

16. Ibid., p. 131. As Buck-Morss points out, her employment of the term "synaesthetic" in this context "identifies the mimetic synchrony between outer stimulus (perception) and inner stimulus (bodily sensations, including sense-memories) as the crucial element of aesthetic cognition". See note 53, p. 132.

17. Georg Simmel: "The Metropolis and Mental Life", in: Simmel on Culture

expectedness of onrushing impressions" characteristic of big city environments create "psychological conditions" which differ significantly from those cultivated by small town and rural environments.[18] In a similar vein to Freud's analysis, in "Beyond the Pleasure Principle", of the protective function performed by consciousness, Simmel argues that it is the responsibility of the "intellect" ("that organ which is least sensitive and quite remote from the depth of the personality") to "preserve subjective life against the overwhelming power of metropolitan life".[19] Faced, however, with a constant bombardment with stimuli, Simmel argues that the intellect quickly loses its capacity to respond with the amount of energy required – resulting in the "blasé", anaesthetised manner in which the "metropolitan type" relates to his or her environment.[20] As Buck-Morss argues, within this schema, the urban dweller's mimetic capacities serve not – as in Benjamin's writings on mimesis – as a means of "incorporating the outside world as a form of empowerment, or 'innervation'", but rather as a means of "deflection"[21] – a process which seals the urban dweller off from the possibility of auratic experience, and stunts the capacity for imagination with which, for Benjamin, auratic experience is closely associated.

It is this crisis in the capacity for perception and imagination outlined by Buck-Morss, Simmel and Benjamin that provides the crucial background for an understanding of Benjamin's delineation of the radical possibilities of film. Although (as I will argue in the following sec-

– Selected Writings, ed. by David Frisby/Mike Featherstone, London, Thousand Oaks, and New Delhi: Sage Publications 1997, pp. 174-185.

18. Ibid., p. 175.

19. Ibid., p. 176. In "Some Motifs in Baudelaire", Benjamin states something very similar: "Moving through the traffic involves the individual in a series of shocks and collisions. At dangerous crossings, nervous impulses flow through him in rapid succession, like the energy from a battery. Baudelaire speaks of a man who plunges into the crowd as into a reservoir of electric energy. Circumscribing the experience of the shock, he calls this man "a *kaleidoscope* equipped with consciousness"". p. 132.

20. "The Metropolis and Mental Life", p. 178.

21. "Aesthetics and Anaesthetics", p. 131. For a detailed account of Benjamin's use of the term "innervation" as it pertains to his analysis of the radical possibilities of film, see Miriam Hansen: "Benjamin and Cinema: Not a One-Way Street", in: Benjamin's Ghosts: Interventions in Contemporary Literary and Cultural Theory, ed. by Gerhard Richter, Stanford, California: Stanford University Press 2002, pp. 41-73.

tion) Benjamin's analysis of the political significance of the medium does rest, in part, on the degree to which it undermines the "cult value" generated by the "aura" of traditional works of art, following the leads established by Buck-Morss and Hansen, this chapter will explore Benjamin's analysis of the extent to which film could be seen to rejuvenate our capacity for auratic experience, and with it, our ability to reconceive the possibilities of both the past and the present outside of the parameters of the status quo.

3.1 The Aura, Contemplation, and Distraction

Central to Benjamin's analysis, in the "Work of Art" essay, of the perceptual changes which have taken place under conditions of modernity is the withering of contemplative (auratic) experience and the rise of a distracted mode of perception. Although (as discussed in the previous chapter) the contours of Benjamin's conception of auratic experience can be traced in his delineation of the close, animistic relationship to one's environment generated by hashish intoxication, in the "Work of Art" essay, the "aura" of traditional artworks is associated with a markedly different kind of experience.

As outlined in Buck-Morss' analysis of the modern split between art and the sensory emphasis characteristic of the original realm of aesthetics, Benjamin argues that the contemplative mode of perception cultivated by traditional works of art "begins at a distance of two metres from the body"[22] – a gap which, he claims, is partly sustained by the "aura" of the artwork in question. In the "Work of Art" essay, Benjamin argues that the aura of traditional artworks (and the "cult value" with which it is associated) is bound with its "unique existence in a particular place" and the concomitant sense of authority and authenticity with which this uniqueness is associated.[23] He claims that the "cult value" of a sculpture or a painting is intimately bound with its "unapproachability", and that it is the aura generated by the uniqueness of the artwork which ensures that it retains a distance from the viewer "however near it may be"[24] – a quality which is exacerbated when a painting, for example, is rarely

22. Benjamin: "Dream Kitsch: Gloss on Surrealism", in: Benjamin: Selected Writings, Vol. 2, ed. by Michael Jennings/Howard Eiland/Gary Smith, Cambridge, Mass. and London, England: Harvard University Press 1999, p. 4.

23. "Work of Art", p. 253.

24. Ibid., note 11, p. 272.

placed on public display, or when a sculpture is only exhibited at certain times of the year.[25]

Within this context, what is significant about the technological reproducibility of both film and photography is the extent to which it undermines the sense of uniqueness, authority, and authenticity upon which the aura of the traditional artwork is based. "[F]or the first time in world history", Benjamin writes, "technological reproducibility emancipates the work of art from its parasitic subservience to ritual. To an ever-increasing degree, the work reproduced becomes the reproduction of a work designed for reproducibility".[26] While copies or reproductions of traditional artworks often function to enhance the aura and authority of the original, Benjamin claims that "to ask for the 'authentic' print" of a photograph "makes no sense". Thus, he argues, "*as soon as the criterion of authenticity ceases to be applied to artistic production, the whole social function of art is revolutionized. Instead of being founded on ritual, it is based on a different practice: politics*".[27]

While Benjamin's analysis of the political significance of film does rest, in part, on the degree to which it both enables – and virtually necessitates – mass exhibition and distribution (and, in doing so, opens up the realm of art to circles beyond those occupied by the socially privileged)[28], his understanding of the political promise of the medium is intimately bound with his analysis of the distracted mode of perception cultivated by film – the significance of which lies not only in the extent to which it undermines the contemplative mode of perception cultivated by traditional works of art, but the degree to which it is imbricated in his

25. Ibid., p. 257. Benjamin claims that »[c]ult as such tends today, it would seem, to keep the artwork out of sight: certain statues of gods are accessible only to the priest in the cella; certain images of the Madonna remain covered nearly all year round; certain sculptures on medieval cathedrals are not visible to the viewer at ground level«. p. 257.

26. Ibid., p. 256.

27. Ibid., pp. 256-257.

28. *"The technological reproducibility of films"*, Benjamin writes, *"not only makes possible the mass dissemination of films in the most direct way, but actually enforces it.* It does so because the process of producing a film is so costly that an individual who could afford to buy a painting, for example, could not afford to buy a [master print of a] film. It was calculated in 1927 that, in order to make a profit, a major film needed to reach an audience of nine million". See ibid., note 14, p. 273.

analysis of the role that film could play in counteracting the atrophy of experience associated with modernity.

In "This Space for Rent" (a short fragment in "One-Way Street" which anticipates a number of the concerns elaborated some ten years later in the "Work of Art" essay) Benjamin draws a distinction between the distant, contemplative gaze characteristic of the art critic, and the visceral, distracted mode of perception cultivated by advertising and film.[29] In a damning critique of the contemplative gaze that sustains the art critic's mode of analysis or interpretation, Benjamin states that only

> [f]ools lament the decay of criticism. For its day is long past. Criticism is a matter of correct distancing. It was home in a world where perspectives and prospects counted and where it was still possible to adopt a standpoint. Now things press too urgently on human society. The 'unclouded', 'innocent' eye has become a lie, perhaps the whole naïve mode of expression sheer incompetence.[30]

For Benjamin, the attentive, concentrated gaze of the art critic stands in stark contrast to the distracted mode of perception cultivated by film. In contrast to the contemplative manner in which one gazes at a sculpture or a painting, the shock-like organisation and sensation of film is said to create a spectatorial relationship more akin to the mode of perception cultivated by life in the city – the "distracting element" of which is "primarily tactile, being based on successive changes of scene and focus which have a percussive effect on the spectator".[31]

For Benjamin, what is significant about the manner in which film "hurls"[32] itself at the spectator is the extent to which it shatters the distance that sustains the sovereign, contemplative gaze (with all its preformed ideas, values, and prejudices) – opening up a space within which the film could animate thoughts and associations in the viewer which might challenge "the optical illusions" generated by one's own "isolated

29. In his notes on film in "Theory of Distraction", Benjamin states that "[d]istraction, like catharsis, should be conceived as a physiological phenomenon". p. 141.

30. "One Way Street", in: Benjamin: Selected Writings, Vol. 1, ed. by Marcus Bullock/Michael W. Jennings, Cambridge, Mass. and London, England: Harvard University Press 1996, p. 476.

31. "Work of Art", p. 267.

32. "One-Way Street", p. 476.

standpoint".[33] Moreover, although the shock-like organisation of film does, to a certain extent, cultivate a mode of perception analogous to the distracted mode of perception associated with urbanisation, Benjamin argues that the camera's capacity to extend the spectator's vision beyond the realm of subjective intention means that film is ideally placed to counter the diminution in the capacity for perception and experience that both Benjamin and Simmel associate with modernity.

In Benjamin's response to an article by Oscar A.H. Schmitz published in *Die literarische Welt* in 1927, film's capacity to open up "a *new realm of consciousness*" is described in no uncertain terms:

> To put it in a nutshell, film is the prism in which the spaces of the immediate environment – the spaces in which people live, pursue their avocations, and enjoy their leisure – are laid open before their eyes in a comprehensible, meaningful, and passionate way. In themselves these offices, furnished rooms, saloons, big-city streets, stations, and factories are ugly, incomprehensible, and hopelessly sad. Or rather, they were and seemed to be, until the advent of film. The cinema then exploded this entire prison-world with the dynamite of its fractions of a second, so that we can take extended journeys of adventure between their widely scattered ruins.[34]

Film, in this context, thus performs a similar function to Benjamin's delineation of the effects produced by hashish. By placing a "prism" between the spectator and his or her environment, the spectator is able to gaze anew at that which "had previously floated unnoticed on the broad stream of perception".[35] "Clearly", Benjamin writes, "it is another nature which speaks to the camera as compared to the eye. 'Other' above all in the sense that a space informed by human consciousness gives way to a space informed by the unconscious".[36] Employing examples reminiscent of those sketched out in observations he wrote while under the influence of hashish, Benjamin notes that although we are

33. Ibid., p. 453. In support of this claim, Benjamin quotes Georges Duhamel, who states of the mode of perception cultivated by film: "I can no longer think what I want to think. My thoughts have been replaced by moving images". "Work of Art", p. 267.

34. "Reply to Oscar A.H. Schmitz", in: Selected Writings, Vol. 2, p. 17. As quoted in the Introduction, this passage also appears, albeit in an altered format, in the "Work of Art" essay. See p. 265.

35. "Work of Art", p. 265.

36. Ibid., p. 266.

familiar with the movement of picking up a cigarette lighter or a spoon, [we] know almost nothing of what really goes on between hand and metal, and still less how this varies with different moods. This is where the camera comes into play, with all its resources for swooping and rising, disrupting and isolating, stretching or compressing a sequence, enlarging or reducing an object. It is through the camera that we first discover the optical unconscious, just as we discover the instinctual unconscious through psychoanalysis.[37]

This opening up of the "optical unconscious" enabled by the camera's extension of the spectator's vision beyond the realm of subjective intention results in what Benjamin describes as a "progressive" mode of spectatorship which is "characterized by an immediate, intimate fusion of pleasure – pleasure in seeing and experiencing – with an attitude of expert appraisal".[38] Drawing on Bertolt Brecht's delineation of the active, critical spectator generated by epic theatre (the details of which will be discussed later in this chapter), Benjamin argues that the audience's familiarity with the techniques via which the film re-presents a person, scene, or object counteracts the sense of distance via which the traditional work of art is constituted as auratic – an analysis which, as we will see, is significantly complicated by Benjamin's delineation of the role that film could play in counteracting the atrophy of experience associated with modernity.

37. Ibid. In an essay written some three years earlier, Benjamin argues that "[i]t is through photography that we first discover the existence of this optical unconscious, just as we discover the instinctual unconscious through psychoanalysis. Details of structure, cellular tissue, with which technology and medicine are normally concerned – all this is, in its origins, more native to the camera than the atmospheric landscape or the soulful portrait". See "Little History of Photography", in: Selected Writings, Vol. 2, pp. 510-12. See also the second version of the "Work of Art" essay, in which Benjamin draws a link between the camera's capacity in this regard, and the kind of perceptual effects generated by hallucinations. "[I]n most cases", Benjamin states, "the diverse aspects of reality captured by the film camera lie outside only the *normal* spectrum of sense impressions. Many of the deformations and stereotypes, transformations and catastrophes which can assail the optical world in films afflict the actual world in psychoses, hallucinations, and dreams. Thanks to the camera, therefore, the individual perceptions of the psychotic or the dreamer can be appropriated by collective perception". Selected Writings, Vol. 3, pp. 117-8.

38. "Work of Art", p. 264.

3.2 Changing Film's Technical Standards

"The history of every art form", Benjamin writes in the "Work of Art" essay, "has critical periods in which the particular form strains after effects which can be easily achieved only with a changed technical standard – that is to say, in a new art form".[39] In both the "Work of Art" essay, and critical accounts of Benjamin's argument, this "changed technical standard" is predominantly traced at the level of the distinction he draws between traditional works of art and new imaging technologies such as film and photography. However, if we situate this passage within the period in which Benjamin was writing, it is possible to view this reference to "a changed technical standard" not as an affirmative statement about changes to art that have already taken place with the advent of new imaging technologies, but as a comment on the degree to which the "technical standards" of film would have to change in order to cultivate the kind of spectatorial effects outlined in the "Work of Art" essay. As Marcus Bullock has pointed out:

> The essay is commonly read as an optimistic pronouncement on the intrinsically revolutionary and critical moment of the film medium. The conclusion which follows, that he is simply *too* optimistic, must surely be quite naive, however. This was not written in 1920 or 1925, but in 1935. The German film industry was in the increasingly adept hands of Josef Goebbels' ministry of propaganda, France had produced a masterpiece of reactionary mythopoeic aesthetics in Abel Gance's *Napolean*, and Hollywood was developing an analgesic consumer-product to draw a veil of dreams around the reality of the Depression.[40]

---

39. Ibid., p. 266.

40. Marcus Bullock: "The Rose of Babylon: Walter Benjamin, Film Theory, and the Technology of Memory", MLN, 103, 5 (1988), p. 1100. Hereafter referred to as "The Rose of Babylon". Miriam Hansen also makes a similar point, stating that, when Benjamin was writing the "Work of Art" essay, "instead of advancing a revolutionary culture, the media of 'technical reproduction' were lending themselves to oppressive social and political forces – first and foremost in the fascist restoration of myth through mass spectacles and newsreels, but also in the liberal-capitalist marketplace and in Stalinist cultural politics". This fact, she claims, "only enhances the utopian modality of [Benjamin's] statements, shifting the emphasis from a definition of what film *is* to its failed opportunities and unrealized promises". See "Benjamin, Cinema, and Experience: 'The Blue Flower in the Land of Technology'", pp. 181-182.

It is certainly true that Leni Riefenstahl's highly phantasmagoric representation of the Nazis' Nuremburg Party Convention – in her 1935 film *Der Triumph des Willens* (*The Triumph of the Will*) – is a prime example of the "aestheticization of political life" undertaken by the fascists. "The violation of the masses", Benjamin writes, "whom fascism, with its *Führer* cult, forces to their knees, has its counterpart in the violation of an apparatus which is pressed into serving the production of ritual values"[41] – a statement which is echoed in his analysis of the "putrid magic" of the "cult of the movie star" cultivated by the "money of the film industry".[42]

In more general terms, it is also true to say that the kind of "analgesic consumer product" described by Bullock in the above passage bears little trace of either the shock-like organisation and sensation, nor the emphasis on the "exploration of commonplace milieux" characteristic of the film practice for which Benjamin argues in the "Work of Art" essay.[43] Indeed, if we consider the "technical standards" around which classical narrative film is predominantly organised (an emphasis on character-driven narratives, continuity in time and space, and the creation of a sense of stylistic unity and narrative closure) we can begin to get a sense of the kind of changes to the "technical standards" of film which would be required in order to produce the kind of spectatorial effects outlined in the "Work of Art" essay.[44]

Foremost among these changes is the breakdown between art and reality that Benjamin describes as one of the most significant achievements of the Dadaists. "Dadaism", he writes, "attempted to produce with the means of painting (or literature) the effects which the public today

41. "Work of Art", p. 269.

42. Ibid., p. 261. Elaborating on this point, Benjamin states that "[s]o long as moviemakers' capital sets the fashion, as a rule the only revolutionary merit that can be ascribed to today's cinema is the promotion of a revolutionary criticism of traditional concepts of art". p. 261.

43. Ibid., p. 265.

44. Concerning the role played by characters in the film practice for which he argues, Benjamin quotes Bertolt Brecht's 1931 "The Threepenny Lawsuit": "Film [...] provides – or could provide – useful insight into the details of human actions. [...] Character is never used as a source of motivation; the inner life of the persons represented never supplies the principal cause of the plot and seldom is its main result". See "Work of Art", note 24, p. 276, and Bertolt Brecht: "The Film, the Novel and Epic Theatre (from 'The Threepenny Lawsuit')", in: Brecht on Theatre: The Development of an Aesthetic, ed. by John Willett, New York: Hill and Wang 1998, p. 48. This book will hereafter be referred to as Brecht on Theatre.

seeks in film". The significance of artists such as Hans Arp and John Heartfield lies in the extent to which they "attached much less importance to the commercial usefulness of their artworks than to the uselessness of those works as objects of contemplative immersion".[45] While the Dadaists, as Bullock points out, start out "within the enclosed territory of art", their construction of still lifes out of cigarette butts, train tickets, buttons, and spools of cotton "break down the dividing barrier separating [art] from the material existence of reality".[46]

In the "Work of Art" essay, Benjamin's analysis of the perceptual and experiential effects generated by autonomous works of art emerges most clearly in his criticism of painting which, to borrow Bullock's phrase, "does not look out with a straight gaze on the disorder of true conditions, but only through the restrictive filter of what may be admitted into the consistent, harmonious order of artistic construction".[47] Complicating his analysis of the distant, detached gaze characteristic of the art critic, Benjamin states that the "person who concentrates before a work of art is absorbed by it"[48] – a point which he elaborates via reference to a Chinese legend that is narrated in some detail in his childhood reminiscences. "The story", Benjamin writes,

> tells of an old painter who invited friends to see his newest picture. This picture showed a park and a narrow footpath that ran along a stream and through a grove of trees, culminating at the door of a little cottage in the background. When the painter's friends, however, looked around for the painter, they saw that he had

---

45. "Work of Art", p. 266. He states that "[b]efore a painting by Arp or a poem by August Stramm, it is impossible to take time for concentration and evaluation, as one can before a painting by Derain or a poem by Rilke". p. 267.

46. "The Rose of Babylon", p. 1108. See also "Work of Art", pp. 266-267, and "The Author as Producer", in: Benjamin: Understanding Brecht, London and New York: Verso 1998, p. 94. This breakdown between art and reality is also manifested in Benjamin's 1929 literary portrait of Marseilles – the structure and subject matter of which resonate strongly with the kind of film practice outlined in the "Work of Art" essay. See Benjamin: "Marseille", in: Selected Writings, Vol. 2, pp. 232-236.

47. "The Rose of Babylon", p. 1108. Bullock is referring, more specifically, here to "[t]he inner coherence which we prize most highly in our established aesthetics". According to Benjamin, the image of the world presented in paintings is a "total" one, in contrast to the images obtained by the cinematographer, which are "piecemeal". "Work of Art", p. 263-4.

48. "Work of Art", p. 268.

left them – that he was in the picture. There, he followed the little path that led to the door, paused before it quite still, turned, smiled, and disappeared through the narrow opening.[49]

In stark contrast to this image of the painter (who escapes into the harmonious, idyllic world which he himself has created), Benjamin argues that "the distracted masses *absorb the work of art into themselves*"[50] – a point which he elaborates via a comparison between the analogous mode of perception cultivated by film and architecture (the latter of which, he claims, is the "prototype" of a work of art which is received both "in a state of distraction and through the collective").[51]

In contrast to the "concentrated" manner in which a traveller gazes at an architectural work of art,[52] Benjamin argues that buildings are, on an everyday basis, received both "optically" (via visual perception) and "tactilely" (via use) – the latter of which, he claims, is accomplished "not so much by way of attention as by way of habit".[53] In a passage in the second version of the essay which explicitly links this "tactile" mode of

---

49. "Berlin Childhood around 1900" (1934 Version), in: Selected Writings, Vol. 3, p. 393.

50. "Work of Art", p. 268. My emphasis. In "Theory of Distraction", Benjamin states that the "relation of distraction to absorption [*Einverleibung*] must be examined". Selected Writings, Vol. 3, p. 141, and "Theorie der Zerstreuung", in: Gesammelte Schriften, Vol. VII-2, p. 678. As the editors of Benjamin's Selected Writings have pointed out, this idea of "absorption" is also discussed in Benjamin's 1929 radio talk "Children's Literature", in which he claims that the child engages with a book by means of "absorption" rather than by "empathy". See "Theory of Distraction", note 3, p. 142, and "Children's Literature", in: Selected Writings, Vol. 2, p. 256.

51. "Work of Art", p. 268.

52. Ibid. In "Paris – the Capital of the Nineteenth Century", Benjamin provides an extreme example of this tendency in the contemplation of Hausmann's Parisian boulevards: "Hausmann's urbanistic ideal was one of views in perspective down long street-vistas. It corresponded to the tendency which was noticeable again and again during the nineteenth century, to ennoble technical exigencies with artistic aims. The institutions of the worldly and spiritual rule of the bourgeoisie, set in the frame of the boulevards, were to find their apotheosis. Before their completion, boulevards were covered over with tarpaulins, and unveiled like monuments". See Charles Baudelaire: A Lyric Poet in the Era of High Capitalism, pp. 173-174.

53. "Work of Art", p. 268.

reception with his analysis of the role that film could play in rejuvenating our senses, Benjamin claims that film – "by virtue of its shock effects" – is not only "predisposed to this form of reception", but that it "proves to be the most important subject matter, at present, for the theory of perception which the Greeks call aesthetics"[54] – the tactile, bodily dimension of which is further emphasised in Benjamin's analysis of the extent to which the spectator "absorbs" the image on screen by way of his or her own experience. Circumscribing this mode of reception, Benjamin states in a highly evocative passage which clearly distinguishes this close, tactile spectatorial relationship from contemplative immersion, that the "waves" of the audience "lap around" the film which "[t]hey encompass [...] with their tide".[55]

3.3 Autonomy and Unity in Film

What is, however, to a certain extent elided by the sharp distinction Benjamin draws between the very different modes of engagement cultivated by the autonomous, "total" image presented by painting, and the shock-like, "piece-meal" organisation of film, is a detailed discussion of the perceptual effects generated by a film practice that is organised around the creation of a sense of autonomy and unity – effects which complicate the distinction between contemplation and distraction outlined in the "Work of Art" essay.

In Siegfried Kracauer's 1926 essay "Cult of Distraction: On Berlin's Picture Palaces" (an essay which had a significant impact on the development of Benjamin's conception of distraction) the spectatorial effects of such a film practice are discussed in some detail.[56] In an analysis of the distracted mode of perception cultivated by the Berlin picture palaces (in which films were screened in the 1920s and 30s as part of a broader program of visual and acoustic "attractions") Kracauer argues that the "stimulations of the senses" (provoked by the shock-like organisation of spotlights, music, images, glass fittings, and other forms of decoration) "succeed one another with such rapidity that there is no room left be-

54. "Work of Art" (Second Version), p.120.

55. Ibid., p. 119.

56. Siegfried Kracauer: "Cult of Distraction: On Berlin's Picture Palaces", in: Kracauer, The Mass Ornament: Weimar Essays, ed. by Thomas Y. Levin, Cambridge, Mass. and London, England: Harvard University Press 1995, pp. 323-8. Hereafter referred to as "Cult of Distraction".

tween them for even the slightest contemplation".[57] Such programs, Kracauer argues, fulfil an important function for the urban masses whose working hours are saturated with a "formal tension" which leaves them feeling profoundly unfulfilled. "Such a lack", he claims, "demands to be compensated, but this need can be articulated only in terms of the same surface sphere that imposed the lack in the first place"[58], and which finds expression in the interior design of the picture palaces, the "surface glamor of the stars", the display of "externality" characteristic of the revue programs, and the proliferation of images in newspapers and magazines.[59] "Here", Kracauer writes,

> in pure externality, the audience encounters itself; its own reality is revealed in the fragmented sequence of splendid sense impressions. Were this reality to remain hidden from the viewers, they could neither attack nor change it; its disclosure in distraction is therefore of *moral* significance.[60]

Kracauer argues, however, that – far from disclosing the current state of affairs – the programs of the picture palaces actually "rob distraction of its meaning" by artistically combining the diverse attractions characteristic of such programs into the kind of "organic whole" characteristic of certain kinds of literature and theatre. "Distraction", he writes,

> which is meaningful only as improvisation, as a reflection of the uncontrolled anarchy of the world – is festooned with drapery and forced back into a unity that no longer exists. Rather than acknowledging the actual state of disintegration that such shows ought to represent, the movie theaters glue the pieces back together after the fact and present them as organic creations.[61]

The closest that Benjamin comes, in the "Work of Art" essay, to discussing the spectatorial ramifications of a film practice that is organised around the creation of a sense of autonomy and unity is in the relationship he draws between the captions which accompany images in illustrated magazines, and the manner in which filmic images (or shots) are pieced together in the editing process. "The directives", he writes, "given by captions to those looking at images in illustrated magazines soon be-

57. Ibid., p. 326.
58. Ibid., p. 325.
59. Ibid., p. 326.
60. Ibid.
61. Ibid., p. 327-8.

come even more precise and commanding in films, where the way each single image is understood appears prescribed by the sequence of all the preceding images"[62]. Elaborating on this idea in an evocative comparison between the image of continuity striven for by certain filmmakers and historians, Benjamin states that, in film, the "continuous musical accompaniment" undermines the "downright jerky rhythm of the image sequence" – the latter of which "satisfies the deep-seated need of this generation to see the 'flow' of 'development' disavowed".[63]

What is significant about these comments is not only the degree to which they furnish a link between Benjamin's writings on film and history, but the extent to which they establish his concern with the degree to which the shock-like organisation and sensation of film can, as Kracauer points out, be undermined when the autonomy of each fragment is subordinated to a piece of a larger picture, or a cog driving a larger narrative – a process which could be said to culminate with classical narrative film, for example, in which filmic images are shot and cut together to draw the spectator in, and lead him or her through, the world of the narrative. Indeed, within this context, it is much more likely that the audience's familiarity with the techniques via which such films represent their subject would result not in an active, "testing" audience, but rather an audience whose familiarity with classical techniques would actually facilitate their *absorbtion* into the world of the narrative.

3.4 Film and Epic Theatre

The roots of Benjamin's aversion to such a film practice can, in part, be traced to his friendship with, and writings on, Bertolt Brecht – whom Benjamin first met, via Asja Lacis, in 1929, and whose delineation of the mode of spectatorship cultivated by epic theatre provided Benjamin with a model for the active, "testing" spectator outlined in the "Work of Art" essay.[64] In the second version of "What is Epic Theatre?" (in which he

62. "Work of Art", p. 258.

63. [H,16], The Arcades Project, p. 845. "To root out any trace of 'development' from the image of history", Benjamin writes in this passage, "is no less the tendency of this project".

64. For a detailed account of Benjamin's relationship to Brecht, see Bernd Witte: Walter Benjamin: An Intellectual Biography, Detroit: Wayne State University Press 1997, pp. 122-126, and Walter Benjamin, 1892-1940: Marbacher Magazin,

expands on ideas elaborated in an essay of the same title written some eight years earlier in 1931) Benjamin evokes an image of epic theatre that is in keeping with his analysis of the fragmentary, shock-like organisation of film:

> Epic theatre proceeds by fits and starts, in a manner comparable to the images on a film strip. Its basic form is that of the forceful impact on one another of separate, sharply distinct situations in the play. The songs, the captions, the gestural conventions differentiate the scenes. As a result, intervals occur which tend to destroy illusion. These intervals paralyse the audience's readiness for empathy.[65]

Anticipating both Benjamin and Kracauer's criticism of autonomous works of art, Brecht argues that the "fusing" together of the artwork's various elements produces a "*Gesamtkunstwerk*" ("total work of art") within which each of the elements serves as "a mere 'feed' to the rest" – a process which does not exclude the spectator, who is drawn into the work of art as a "passive" participant.[66]

In stark contrast to this passive mode of spectatorship, Brecht argues that the "radical *separation of the elements*"[67] characteristic of epic theatre cultivates a spectator who is actively encouraged to participate in the meaning-making process which is generated, but not circumscribed directly by, the various situations which are presented by the play. Within this schema, the audience retains a critical distance between themselves and the action on stage. The spectator is not drawn unconsciously (via character identification) into a fictional world, but is situated outside as an observer who brings his or her critical faculties to bear on the scenarios presented by the play. "The essential point", Brecht claims, is that epic theatre "appeals less to the feelings than to the spectator's reason. Instead of sharing an experience the spectator must come to grips with things".[68]

In Benjamin's writings on Brecht, this coming "to grips with things"

No. 55, ed. by Rolf Tiedemann/Christoph Gödde/Henri Lonitz, Marbach am Necker: Deutsche Schillergesellschaft 1990, pp. 190-198.

65. "What is Epic Theatre?" (Second Version), in: Benjamin, Understanding Brecht, p. 21.

66. Bertolt Brecht: "The Modern Theatre is the Epic Theatre", in: Brecht on Theatre, pp. 37-38.

67. Ibid., p. 37.

68. Brecht: "The Epic Theatre and its Difficulties", in: Brecht on Theatre, p. 23.

is framed very much within the terms employed in Benjamin's writings on history – terms which, transposed to a discussion of film, provide us with a clearer sense of the stakes of his analysis of the radical possibilities of the medium. In language remarkably reminiscent of that employed in both "Convolute N" and "On the Concept of History", Benjamin claims that the significance of epic theatre lies in its capacity to "expose the present".[69] "Epic theatre", he states, "makes life spurt up high from the bed of time and, for an instant, hover iridescent in empty space".[70] The situation it reveals (as if "by lightening") is "the dialectic at a standstill"[71]; a phrase which Benjamin employs in his writings on history to refer to those moments of "*Jetztzeit*" ("now time") which – in their disruption of the false image of historical continuity propagated by historicism – open up a space within which one is able to reconceive the possibilities of both the past and the present.[72]

In Benjamin's writings on Brecht, it is the "interruption of the action" characteristic of epic theatre which encourages the audience to "treat elements of reality as if they were an experimental set-up"[73] – an idea which he explores via an analysis of the image of history presented by epic theatre. The epic dramatist, Benjamin writes,

> will tend to emphasize not the great decisions which lie along the main line of history but the incommensurable and the singular. 'It can happen this way, but it can also happen quite a different way' – that is the fundamental attitude of one who writes for epic theatre. His relation to his story is like that of a ballet teacher to his pupil. His first aim is to loosen her joints to the very limits of the possible.[74]

Transposing these ideas to film, one could say that it is the loose, fragmentary structure of a film practice that is not organised around the creation of a sense of autonomy and unity which (in a similar vein to Benjamin's delineation of the mode of spectatorship cultivated by epic theatre) prompts the viewer to draw upon his or her own experience and imagination in an attempt to engage with the materials on screen.[75] In

---

69. Benjamin: "The Author as Producer", p. 100.

70. Benjamin: "What is Epic Theatre?" (First Version), in: Understanding Brecht, p. 13.

71. Ibid., pp. 12-13.

72. See, for example, [N2a,3], The Arcades Project, p. 462.

73. "The Author as Producer", p. 99.

74. "What is Epic Theatre?" (First Version), pp. 7-8.

75. In "What is Epic Theatre?" (Second Version), Benjamin notes that "the

contrast, however, to the image of the distant, reasoning spectator outlined by Brecht (the contours of which resemble Benjamin's negative delineation of the art critic), the mode of spectatorship cultivated by the film practice for which Benjamin argues is more akin to the animistic, innervating mode of perception which – in Benjamin's writings on Baudelaire, hashish, and mimesis – is associated with the rejuvenation of auratic experience. Indeed, in a similar vein to his analysis of the extent to which the intoxicated gaze of the hashish eater animates face-like qualities inherent within objects and spaces, Benjamin argues that the image spaces opened up by the camera reveal to the spectator "*physiognomic* aspects, image worlds, which dwell in the smallest things"[76] – the presence of which "assure us of a vast and unsuspected field of action [*Spielraum*]".[77]

As Hansen has argued, it is this emphasis on film's capacity to open up a "vast and unsuspected *Spielraum*" (or "space of play") which ties Benjamin's analysis of the possibilities of the medium to "the radical unleashing of play" cultivated by proletarian children's theatre and, more specifically, to his analysis of the connection between "receptive innervation" and creativity exhibited in the activities of children.[78] Indeed, expanding on this idea, one could say (within the terms of the framework set out by Benjamin in the "Work of Art" essay) that, in a similar vein to his analysis of the role of the children's leader, the task of the filmmaker is not to dictate, nor circumscribe the spectator's behaviour, but rather to encourage him or her to engage creatively with the images on screen.

As Kracauer states in an important passage in his 1927 essay on photography which anticipates Benjamin's analysis of the significance of the fragmented, "piecemeal" organisation of film, the basis for such a mode of spectatorship can only be realised "whenever film combines parts and segments to create strange constructs". In a passage reminiscent of the shake-up to the "natural order" of things precipitated by the damage sustained by the natural history museum, Kracauer argues that "the game film plays with the pieces of disjointed nature is reminiscent of *dreams* in which the fragments of daily life become jumbled". "This

---

events shown on stage [...] must be of such a kind that they may, at certain decisive points, be checked by the audience against its own experience". pp. 15-16.

76. "Little History of Photography", p. 512. My emphasis.

77. "Work of Art", p. 265.

78. Miriam Hansen: "Room-for-Play: Benjamin's Gamble with Cinema", October, No. 35 (Summer, 2004), p. 7.

game", Kracauer states, "shows that the valid organization of things remains unknown".[79]

For Benjamin (and, indeed, for Kracauer), the task of a political film practice is not to provide the audience with an image of a better world. As Benjamin states in his analysis of proletarian children's theatre, "what is truly revolutionary is not the propaganda of ideas, which leads here and there to impracticable actions and which vanishes in a puff of smoke upon the first sober reflection at the theatre exit".[80] Rather, what *is* revolutionary is the extent to which the "unsevered connection between perception and [creative] action"[81] exhibited in children's play can be rejuvenated by a film practice which actively encourages the audience to draw on their own imagination and experience in an atttempt to reconceive the possibilities of the present.

In keeping with Benjamin's analysis of the significance of the breakdown between art and reality enacted by the work of the Dadaists, the role of a political film practice is to put the spectator back *in touch* with his/her everyday environment and, in doing so, to contribute to the overcoming of the diminution in the capacity for auratic experience that Benjamin associates with modernity.

---

79. Siegfried Kracauer: "Photography", in: The Mass Ornament: Weimar Essays, pp. 62-63.

80. Benjamin: "Program for a Proletarian Children's Theatre", in: Selected Writings, Vol. 2, p. 206.

81. Susan Buck-Morss: The Dialectics of Seeing: Walter Benjamin and the Arcades Project, Cambridge, Mass. and London, England: The MIT Press 1995, p. 263.

Part 2: Siegfried Kracauer

Chapter 4: "Film as the Discoverer of the Marvels of Everyday Life": Kracauer and the Promise of Realist Cinema

In the years following the publication of Siegfried Kracauer's *Theory of Film: The Redemption of Physical Reality* in 1960[1], the book came under fire by a number of critics, whose reactions to Kracauer's delineation of the promise of the medium were both patronising and acrimonious. As Miriam Hansen has argued in her introduction to *Theory of Film*, foremost among those analyses of the book which "assumed an unusually condescending tone"[2] were Pauline Kael's hostile account of Kracauer's "German pedantry" and Dudley Andrew's dismissive references to the "utterly transparent" nature of the concerns addressed in Kracauer's "huge homogeneous block of realist theory"[3]. Indeed, as revealed by Richard Corliss's highly critical account of the book, it appears that Kracauer's "irredeemable sin" lies in the perceived extent to which,

---

1. Siegfried Kracauer: Theory of Film: The Redemption of Physical Reality, Princeton, New Jersey: Princeton University Press 1997. Hereafter referred to as Theory of Film.

2. Miriam Bratu Hansen: "Introduction", Theory of Film, p. ix

3. See ibid., pp. ix-x, Pauline Kael: "Is There a Cure for Film Criticism? Or: Some Unhappy Thoughts on Siegfried Kracauer's Nature of Film: The Redemption of Physical Reality", Sight and Sound, 31.2 (Spring, 1962), p. 57, and J. Dudley Andrew: The Major Film Theories: An Introduction, London, Oxford, New York: Oxford University Press 1976, p. 106. Kracauer's theory, Andrew argues, "comes down solidly, unmistakably, even fanatically on the realist side". p. 129.

in focusing upon the significance of cinematic realism, he "manages to debase the potentialities of film".[4]

What is interesting to note is the extent to which Kracauer himself actually anticipated the vehemence of such criticism, despite his own belief in the significance of the project. In a letter written to Rudolf Arnheim in the early stages of the book's production, Kracauer admits that despite his feeling that he has "found something essential", "[t]he worst is that [his] whole outlook antagonises most people".[5] While in a letter to his good friend Leo Löwenthal written upon completion of the project, Kracauer states that the book "will arouse violent controversies", and that "the art-minded will, all of them, be against it".[6]

One of the main sources of the antipathy expressed by the so-called "art-minded" critics anticipated in Kracauer's letter can be traced to the very specific criteria he employs in his analysis of the properties and possibilities of the medium. What appears to have particularly inflamed the ire of his critics is the extent to which his delineation of these possibilities is based not upon a comprehensive analysis of cinema as it exists[7], but on his own conception of what he describes as the task of the medium to "assist [...] us in discovering the material world with its psychophysical correspondences".[8] In a manner reminiscent of Benjamin's analysis of the camera's capacity to extend our vision beyond the realm of subjective intention, Kracauer argues that film "renders visible what we did not, or perhaps even could not, see before its advent"[9]. It

4. Richard Corliss: "The Limitations of Kracauer's Reality", Cinema Journal, 10.1 (Fall, 1970), p. 22. Kael makes a similar point at the end of "Is There a Cure for Film Criticism". See p. 64.

5. Letter to Arnheim, September 14, 1951, Kracauer Nachlaß, Deutsches Literaturarchiv, Marbach am Necker. The source of all references to materials contained in this archive will hereafter be referred to as the Kracauer Nachlaß.

6. Letter to Löwenthal, November 29, 1959, quoted in: Siegfried Kracauer, 1889-1966: Marbacher Magazin, No. 47, ed. by Ingrid Belke/Irina Renz, Marbach am Necker: Deutsche Schillergesellschaft 1989, p. 117.

7. In a letter to Löwenthal dated April 6, 1957, Kracauer describes that "which is considered film here and now" as "very remote" from his own concerns. Kracauer Nachlaß. This letter has also been published in In Steter Freundschaft, Leo Löwenthal – Siegfried Kracauer: Briefwechsel 1921-1966 ed. by Peter-Erwin Jansen/Christian Schmidt, Springe: zu Klampen 2003, pp. 194-195.

8. Theory of Film, p. 300.

9. Ibid.

enables us to "redeem this world from its dormant state" by allowing us to "experience it through the camera".[10]

In contrast, however, to the claims of "naïve realism"[11] that have been directed against the book, Kracauer's analysis of the significance of the redemptive task of the medium is bound, as Hansen has argued, not with the camera's capacity to "reflect its object as real but rather with [its] ability to render it strange"[12]. Indeed, in stark contrast to Andrew's claim that, for Kracauer, there is "little essential difference between perception in the cinema and in the world at large"[13], what I will demonstrate in this chapter is the degree to which Kracauer's conception of the promise of realist cinema is intimately bound with the extent to which it facilitates a mode of perception that is not inflected by the "ideas", "value judgements", and "desires" which actively shape and delimit our perception and experience of the world.[14] In this regard, Kracauer argues in a letter to Lucienne Astruc (dated September 10, 1959), *Theory of Film* is a "philosophical venture which goes far beyond film".[15] Similarly, in a letter to Theodor W. Adorno, Kracauer claims that his analysis of cinema in the book functions only as a "pretext" (*Vorwand*) which enables a much broader exploration of certain aesthetic

10. Ibid.

11. Dudley Andrew: Concepts in Film Theory, Oxford, New York: Oxford University Press 1984, p. 19

12. Miriam Hansen: "'With Skin and Hair': Kracauer's Theory of Film, Marseille 1940", Critical Inquiry 19 (Spring, 1993), p. 453. Hansen is referring, more specifically, here to Kracauer's analysis of the significance of photography. However, as I will discuss in detail in this chapter, Kracauer's analysis of the significance of photography is intimately bound with his analysis of the promise of cinema. In recent years, Kracauer's Theory of Film has been re-evaluated by critics who have sought to defend the book from the, at times, misguided claims made by the aforementioned critics. In addition to Hansen's "Introduction" to the book, see Heide Schlüpmann: "The Subject of Survival: On Kracauer's Theory of Film", New German Critique, No. 54 (Fall, 1991), and Chapter 6: "Space, Time, and Apparatus: The Optical Medium 'Theory of Film'", in: Gertrud Koch: Siegfried Kracauer – An Introduction, Princeton, New Jersey: Princeton University Press 2000, pp. 95-113.

13. See Concepts in Film Theory, p. 19.

14. See Kracauer's "Tentative Outline of a Book on Film Aesthetics" which he wrote in 1949, in Siegfried Kracauer – Erwin Panofsky, Briefwechsel: 1941-1966 ed. by Volker Breidecker, Berlin: Akademie 1996, p. 83.

15. Letter to Astruc, September 10, 1959, Kracauer Nachlaß.

and philosophical questions.[16] As I will explore in this chapter, these questions revolve around the extent to which film – in circumventing "the prejudices and preoccupations which normally interfere with our vision"[17] – can, in rejuvenating our capacity for perception and imagination, play a part in reanimating our capacity to conceive of the possibilities of the future in different terms.

4.1 Photography, Proust, and the Task of a Realist Cinema

In the "Preface" to *Theory of Film*, Kracauer argues that his analysis of the possibilities of the medium is based on "the assumption that film is essentially an extension of photography".[18] Kracauer's conception of the "nature" and "task" of photography is, however, a very specific one, which is bound with his analysis of the camera's unique capacity to "record and reveal physical reality".[19] The history of photography, he claims, can be divided into two opposing groups – one of which is characterised by "realist" traits, the other by "formative" tendencies. In contrast to the "artist photographers" of the "formative" camp (who are defined by their attempts to produce "artistic creations" which reflect

---

16. Letter to Adorno, February 12, 1949, Kracauer Nachlaß. This letter is also quoted in Belke and Renz: Siegfried Kracauer, 1889-1966, p. 107. See also Kracauer's letter to Rudolf Arnheim requesting that he review Theory of Film in the Journal of Aesthetics or the Art Bulletin: "You are one of the very few people", Kracauer writes, "who really understand what I want to convey and therefore may lend words to my inmost conviction – that this book reaches far beyond film; that actually it concerns general aesthetics and our whole attitude toward life. And so on. You know what I mean". Letter to Arnheim, October 16, 1960, Kracauer Nachlaß. Arnheim's review of the book was published as "Melancholy Unshaped", in The Journal of Aesthetics and Art Criticism (Spring, 1963). See also Kracauer's letter to Wolfgang Weyrauch in which he describes his interest in film as "only a hobby" and a "means for making certain sociological and philosophical statements". In this letter, Kracauer also asks Weyrauch not to introduce him as a "film man", but as a "cultural philosopher", a "sociologist", and a "poet". Letter to Weyrauch, June 4, 1962, Kracauer Nachlaß.

17. See Kracauer's undated "Entwurf über das Verhältnis direktor visueller Erfahrung und der durch Photographie vermittelten", Kracauer Nachlaß.

18. Theory of Film, p. xIix.

19. Ibid., pp. 27 and 28.

"painterly styles and preferences"[20]) Kracauer argues that the "realist" photographers remain true to the medium insofar as they are driven by a desire to capture "nature in the raw".[21]

The conception of "nature" which emerges from *Theory of Film* is, however, not bound with the natural world. As Kracauer himself points out, throughout the book the term "nature" is used interchangeably with "physical reality", "material reality", "physical existence", "actuality", and "camera reality"[22] in order to designate photographic scenes which – "alienated from ego-involved frames of reference"[23] – transform our conception and experience of the world. The camera, Kracauer states, has an affinity for that which is "fortuitous" and "indeterminate", and so if photographs are to be "true to the medium", then "it would seem natural to imagine the photographer as a 'camera-eye'", an "indiscriminating mirror" who is "devoid of formative impulses".[24]

The figure who had the greatest influence on Kracauer's conception of the significance of the camera's capacity to "transcend human vision"[25] was Marcel Proust, whose examination of the alienating effects of photography in *In Search of Lost Time* had an important impact on Kracauer's understanding of the promise of the photographic media.[26] The passage in *In Search of Lost Time* to which Kracauer refers most frequently appears in Volume 3 of the book, and revolves around Marcel's chance encounter with his grandmother, who – "absorbed in thoughts" in the drawing-room – is unaware that her grandson has arrived home.[27] Upon entering the room, Marcel – not having anticipated his grandmother's presence – is suddenly transformed into a "spectator of [his] own

---

20. Ibid., pp. 12 and 6 respectively. See, for example, Kracauer's analysis of the work of the "artist-photographer" Adam-Salomon, who employed "Rembrandt lighting" and "velvet drapery" in the production of his photographic portraits. p. 6.

21. Ibid., p. 18. For a more detailed account of the differences which separate the "formative" and "realist" camps, see Chapter 1 in Theory of Film, pp. 3-23.

22. See ibid., p. 28.

23. "Tentative Outline of a Book on Film Aesthetics", p. 84.

24. Theory of Film, pp. 19-20, and 14-15.

25. "Entwurf uber das Verhältnis direktor visueller Erfahrung und der durch Photographie vermittelten".

26. See Kracauer's letter to Lucienne Astruc (dated September 10, 1959) in which he describes the prominent role that Proust's ideas occupy in Theory of Film. Kracauer Nachlaß.

27. Marcel Proust: In Search of Lost Time, London: Vintage 1996, Vol. 3, p. 155. Only the volume and page numbers will be given hereafter.

absence", whose alienated view of the scene, he claims, is comparable to that of a "stranger", a "witness", or a "photographer".[28] "The process", Marcel argues,

> that automatically occurred in my eyes when I saw my grandmother was indeed a photograph. We never see the people who are dear to us save in the animated system, the perpetual motion of our incessant love for them, which, before allowing the images that their faces present to reach us, seizes them in its vortex and flings them back upon the idea that we have always had of them, makes them adhere to it, coincide with it. [...] I, for whom my grandmother was still myself, I who had never seen her save in my own soul, always in the same place in the past through the transparency of contiguous and overlapping memories, suddenly [...] saw, sitting on the sofa beneath the lamp, red-faced, heavy and vulgar, sick, day-dreaming, letting her slightly crazed eyes wander over a book, an overburdened old woman whom I did not know.[29]

Proust's analysis of the rejuvenation of the capacity for perception which emerges from this state of "self-effacement"[30] is not limited, however, to this passage in the book, but is a concern which winds its way like a thread through the six volumes of Proust's novel.[31] Like Kracauer, Proust's more general concern lies with the extent to which the memories, value judgements, desires, and expectations that colour and shape our perception of the world prohibit our capacity to conceive of both the promise of the past – and the possibilities of the future – in different terms. In a passage that anticipates Kracauer's criticism of the form and structure of "theatrical" cinema (the details of which will be elaborated in the following pages) Marcel argues that "our eyes, charged with thought, neglect, as would a classical tragedy, every image that does not

28. Proust, Vol. 3, pp. 155-156.

29. Ibid., pp. 156-157. Kracauer quotes this passage in more detail in Theory of Film, p. 14.

30. Kracauer: History: The Last Things Before the Last, Princeton, Markus Wiener Publishers 1995, p. 84. Hereafter referred to as History.

31. See, for example, Proust's description of the painter Elistir, and the "effort" which he made to "strip himself [...] of every intellectual notion" when painting his subjects. Vol. 2, p. 485. Another figure to whom Proust points in his delineation of an alienated perceptual state is the person who wakes up in an unfamiliar environment feeling somewhat disoriented and who is, for a moment, "newly born, ready for anything, the brain emptied of that past which was life until then". See Vol. 4, p. 440.

contribute to the action of the play and retain only those that may help to make its purpose intelligible".[32]

For Proust, this mode of perception stands in stark contrast to the alienated perceptual state he aligns with the photographer, whose estranged gaze – aided by the neutrality of the photographic plate – is comparable to the alienated state borne out of an unexpected encounter with something or someone to which one has become habituated. Referring back to the unexpected encounter with his grandmother as his example, Marcel claims that it is "chance" which prompts our eyes to "set to work mechanically, like films", and which reveals to us, "in place of the beloved person who has long ago ceased to exist but whose death our tenderness has always hitherto kept concealed from us, the new person whom a hundred times daily it has clothed with a loving and mendacious likeness".[33]

As per his analysis of the history of photography, Kracauer argues that the history of film is also marked by a split between "realist" and "formative" tendencies. This split, he claims, can be traced back to the beginnings of the cinema and, more specifically, to what he describes as the divergent conceptions of the possibilities of the medium embodied in the films of Georges Méliès and Louis Lumière. In keeping with his analysis of the significance of the realist photographers, Kracauer argues that the "bulk of [Lumière's] films" (he cites *Arrival of a Train, Lunch Hour at the Lumière Factory*, and *Baby's Breakfast* as examples) "recorded the world about us for no other purpose than to present it".[34] Lumière's films, he claims, are "[d]etached records"[35] of "nature caught in the act".[36] Their significance lies in the extent to which they reveal to us the state of the world as captured by the objective eye of the camera.

---

32. Proust: Vol. 3, p. 156. See also the passage in Vol. 6, p. 224 which anticipates Kracauer's analysis, in History, of the formativist impulse of "historicism". In this passage, Marcel argues that our conception of the possibilities of the present "languishes" in "the anticipation of a future which the will constructs with fragments of the present and the past, fragments whose reality it still further reduces by preserving of them only what is suitable for the utilitarian, narrowly human purpose for which it intends them". Kracauer's analysis of the formativist impulse of historicism will be discussed in detail in the following chapter.

33. Proust: Vol. 3, p. 156.

34. Theory of Film, p. 31.

35. Ibid.

36. Kracauer is quoting Henri de Parville's description of the films of Lumière. Ibid.

Kracauer argues that, in stark contrast to Lumière's "photographic realism", Méliès' films are organised around the creation of illusion and fantasy. Echoing his criticism of the artist-photographers, Kracauer claims that – in contrast to the presentation of everyday scenes and phenomena for which Lumière had become famous – Méliès' films are based upon "imagined events" which have been staged "according to the requirements of his charming fairy-tale plots."[37]

The distinction which Kracauer draws – between filmmakers who seek to "exhibit and penetrate physical reality for its own sake"[38], and those who employ the camera in aid of the creation of a fictional story or universe – is not limited to his discussion of Méliès and Lumière, but is a distinction which forms the basis of his analysis of the realist/cinematic, and formative/theatrical camps into which he divides the history of the medium.[39] In contrast to the "open-ended" quality of realist films (which focus upon such "cinematic" subjects as "trees", "waves", "buildings", "passers-by", and "inanimate objects"[40]) Kracauer argues that the emphasis which the formative/theatrical film places upon storytelling runs counter to the promise and capacities of the medium.

Building on his criticism of the "total work of art" elaborated in "Cult of Distraction", Kracauer claims that what is troubling about the theatrical film is the extent to which its tightly woven narrative structure is organised around the creation of "a whole with a purpose"[41]. According to Kracauer, the theatrical film's "purpose" is intimately bound with

37. Ibid., p. 32. In a prospectus in which he distinguishes his own work from that of Lumière, Méliès claims that his films "specialize mainly in fantastic or artistic scenes" and "reproductions of theatrical scenes" which differ "entirely from the customary views supplied by the cinematograph – street scenes or scenes of everyday life". Méliès quoted in Theory of Film, p. 32. Although Kracauer does acknowledge the enormous impact that Méliès' films (he cites A Trip to the Moon, The Haunted House, and An Impossible Voyage as examples) had on the subsequent development of cinematic technique, his criticism lies in the extent to which Méliès – in "interfering with the photographic reality" to which both the camera and the realists aspire – fails to transcend the limitations of the theatre in which he had previously worked as a director. See Theory of Film, pp. 32, 33, and 104.

38. Ibid., p. 69.

39. Kracauer argues that "[i]n strict analogy to the term 'photographic approach' […] the cinematic approach materializes in all films which follow the realistic tendency". Ibid., p. 38.

40. See, for example, ibid., pp. 27 and 170.

41. Ibid., p. 221

the creation and implementation of a story. Every element of the theatrical film, he writes, "has the sole function of serving that purpose"[42], and images of the environment, of faces, gestures, and inanimate objects are shown only insofar as they aid, or feed directly into the unfolding of the narrative.[43]

As Hansen argues in her introduction to the book, it would, however, be wrong "to label Kracauer's stance as *anti*-narrative". A better title, she suggests, is "*anti*-classical" – a designation which is more apt in its distancing of Kracauer's conception of realist film from classical narrative cinema (with its emphasis on tightly woven, character driven narratives, the creation of a unified sense of time and space, stylistic continuity, and narrative closure).[44] Indeed, in contrast to the classical/theatrical film (which, he claims, is organised around the creation of "a whole with an ideological centre") the film practice favoured by Kracauer must be "permeable" to environmental phenomena that is not subservient to the telling of a story[45]. While cinematic films will not "exhaust themselves in depicting these phenomena", Kracauer maintains that it is essential that the material world be allowed to speak to the viewer on its own terms.[46] Any films, he writes, "in which the inanimate [world] merely serves as a background to self-contained dialogue and the closed circuit of human relationships are essentially uncinematic".[47]

Echoing Sergei Eisenstein and Alberto Calvalcanti's concerns (as elaborated in the 1920s and 30s) about the impact that the coming of sound would have on the development of filmmaking, Kracauer argues that the emphasis that the theatrical film places upon dialogue undermines the properties and possibilities of the medium.[48] "At the beginning of sound", he writes, "the screen went 'speech-mad', with many film makers starting from the 'absurd assumption that in order to make a sound film it is only necessary to photograph a play'".[49] For Kracauer,

42. Ibid.

43. Ibid., p. 223.

44. Hansen: "Introduction", p. xxxii.

45. Theory of Film, pp. 261 and 254.

46. Ibid., p. 271.

47. Ibid., p. 46.

48. See, for example, S.M. Eisenstein, W.I. Pudowkin, and G.V. Alexandroff: "The Sound Film: A Statement from U.S.S.R" in: Close Up, 1927-1933: Cinema and Modernism, ed. by James Donald et al., Princeton, New Jersey: Princeton University Press 1998, pp. 83-84.

49. Kracauer, quoting Cavalcanti, in Theory of Film, p. 104.

this emphasis on the spoken word (and the foregrounding of character with which it is associated) results not only in the abandoning of the inanimate world as a subject, but marks a shift in the history of cinema which he describes as "extremely dangerous". What troubles him, in particular, about this foregrounding of dialogue and character is the extent to which it "opens up the region of discursive reasoning, enabling the medium to impart [...] those rational or poetic communications" which – because they "do not depend upon pictorialization to be grasped and appreciated" – are not only "alien to", but fail to engage the capacities of the medium.[50]

In his search for an alternative cinematic practice, Kracauer turns his attention to avant-garde artists of the 1920s (such as Jean Epstein, René Clair, Joris Ivens, and Germaine Dulac) whom he claims were driven by a desire to create a "purified cinema" which was not organised according to the dictates of a theatrical narrative.[51] What particularly interests Kracauer about these filmmakers is not only their disregard for tightly woven narrative structures[52], but the extent to which they employed specifically cinematic techniques and devices (such as "close-up", "slow motion", "quick-cutting" and "unusual camera angles"[53]) in their presentation of "cinematic subjects" such as street scenes and inanimate objects.

For Kracauer, the magnified images revealed by the close-up, in particular, play an important role in disclosing "hidden aspects of the world about us".[54] In a passage reminiscent of Benjamin's analysis of the plant photographs of Karl Blossfeldt, Kracauer claims that "[i]n magnifying the small, the camera exposes to view fantastic shapes too tiny to be normally noticed". These close-ups, he writes, "cast their spell over the spectator, impressing upon him the magic of a leaf or the energies which lie dormant in a piece of cloth".[55]

---

50. Ibid., pp. 104 and 223.

51. Ibid., p. 178.

52. "The avant-garde artists", Kracauer writes, "broke away from the commercialized cinema not only because of the inferior quality of the many adaptations from plays and novels that swamped the screen but, more important, out of the conviction that the story as the main element of feature films is something alien to the medium, an imposition from without". See ibid.

53. Ibid., p. 180.

54. Ibid., p. 49.

55. Ibid., p. 280. See also p. 45, in which Kracauer – quoting Fernand Léger – argues that "only film is equipped to sensitize us, by way of big close-ups, to the

For Kracauer, as for Benjamin, the significance of such images lies not only in the degree to which they disclose – albeit in a larger format – familiar aspects of our environment, but rather the extent to which they fundamentally challenge our previously held conceptions about the material world. Paraphrasing Benjamin, Kracauer claims that the significance of such images (which feature frequently in the work of Hans Richter, René Clair, Jean Epstein and others) lies in the extent to which they "blow up our environment in a double sense: they enlarge it literally; and in doing so, they blast the prison of conventional reality, opening up expanses which we have explored at best in dreams before".[56]

Also reminiscent of Benjamin's analysis of film in the "Work of Art" essay is Kracauer's delineation of the extent to which this opening up of our everyday environment facilitated by the camera revitalises the spectator's senses. "The salient point", Kracauer writes,

> is that these discoveries [...] mean an increased demand on the spectator's physiological make-up. The unknown shapes he encounters involve not so much his power of reasoning as his visceral faculties. Arousing his innate curiosity, they lure him into dimensions where sense impressions are all-important.[57]

---

possibilities that lie dormant in a hat, a chair, a hand, and a foot". Kracauer also quotes Gilbert Cohen-Séat to similar effect: "And I? says the leaf which is falling. – And we? say the orange peel, the gust of wind. [...] Film, whether intentionally or not, is their mouthpiece." Kracauer's analysis of the camera's capacity to reveal aspects of our environment which are ordinarily unseen is not limited to material too small to be noticed, but extends to the revelation of what he describes as "temporal close-ups" of the movement of clouds and waves, "the growth of plants", and "the manes of galloping horses" – all of which are either too transient or too slow to be perceived directly. See pp. 52-53.

56. Ibid., p. 48, and Walter Benjamin: "The Work of Art in the Age of its Technological Reproducibility" (Third Version), in: Benjamin: Selected Writings, Vol. 4, ed. by Howard Eiland/Michael W. Jennings, Cambridge, Mass. and London, England: Harvard University Press 2003, p. 265. Hereafter referred to as "Work of Art".

57. Theory of Film, pp. 158-159. Elaborating on this point, Kracauer states that, although these "images of material moments are meaningful in their own right", their significance lies in the extent to which we "do not confine ourselves to absorbing them but feel stimulated to weave what they are telling us into contexts that bear on the whole of our existence". p. 308. Comparing this tactile,

However, while the commitment to a specifically cinematic language, and the eschewal of narrative that defines the work of directors such as Clair, Epstein, and Richter are characteristics which sit comfortably with Kracauer's analysis of the task of realist cinema, he argues that their conception of film as "an art medium in the established sense" meant that they "rejected the jurisdiction of external reality as an unjustified limitation of the artist's creativity, his formative urges".[58] The results of these "formative urges" can, Kracauer notes, be seen in the rhythmic films and visual symphonies produced by directors such as Oskar Fischinger and Walter Ruttmann, in which images of the environment (of crowds, trains, streetscapes, and inanimate objects) are edited together to produce total works of art which are organised around the creation of rhythmic or symphonic patterns.[59] "All this", Kracauer writes,

> amounts to saying that the real-life shots in the rhythmical *avant-garde* films suffer from emasculation. Instead of suggesting the continuum of physical existence from which they are elicited, they function as elements of compositions which, almost by definition, shut out nature in the raw. True, the devotees of visual music trained their camera on natural objects, but their formative aspirations, manifest in a permanent preoccupation with formal values and sundry movements, blunted their sense of the medium's affinity for the unstaged, the incidental, the not yet shaped.[60]

In addition to his negative assessment of the visual rhythms characteris-

---

creative mode of spectatorship with the mode of spectatorship cultivated by the theatre, Kracauer states that "[w]hile the theatregoer watches a spectacle which affects primarily his mind and only through it his sensibility, the moviegoer finds himself in a situation in which he cannot ask questions and grope for answers unless he is *saturated physiologically*". My emphasis. p. 309.

58. Ibid., p. 81.

59. See, for example, Kracauer's analysis of the formativist impulse apparent in Walter Ruttmann's 1927 Berlin, die Symphonie der Großstadt (a film which Kracauer claims has "the makings of a truly cinematic documentary"). Ibid., p. 207.

60. Ibid., p. 185. As a consequence, Kracauer argues that these films "must be lumped together [with average theatrical films] in spite of all that separates them". This is because "[f]ilms of this kind exploit, not explore, the material phenomena they insert; they insert them not in their own interest but for the purpose of establishing a significant whole; and in pointing up some whole, they refer us from the material dimension back to that of ideology". See ibid., p. 301.

tic of many of the films made by the European avant-garde during this period, Kracauer is also critical of the manner in which music has been employed by both avant-garde and theatrical filmmakers in an attempt to generate a sense of visual and/or dramatic continuity. He claims that any deployment of music which serves to "prop up a theatrical narrative"[61] by aiding or contributing to the creation of drama and/or continuity does a significant disservice to the perceptual and experiential possibilities that he associates with the promise of the medium.

In an attempt to evoke a sense of these possibilities, Kracauer recounts the memory of his own experience of attending a movie theatre where the screening of silent films was habitually accompanied by a drunken pianist, who "under the spell of a pleasant intoxication, [...] improvised freely, as if prompted by a desire to express the vague memories and ever-changing moods which the alcohol stirred in him". Oblivious to the images on screen, Kracauer claims that the pianist was often

> in such a stupor that he played a few popular melodies over and over again, mechanically adorning them with glittering runs and quavers. So it was by no means uncommon that gay tunes would sound when, in a film I watched, the indignant Count turned his adulterous wife out of the house, and that a funeral march would accompany the blue-tinged scene of their ultimate reconciliation.[62]

What delighted Kracauer about this lack of affinity between the musical accompaniment and the image on screen was the extent to which it opened up a space within which he was able to view the film in a manner which differed significantly from the way in which he *would* have viewed it had the narrative and accompaniment been in harmony.[63] What is significant, for Kracauer, about the creation of this sense of discontinuity is the extent to which it shrouds the image on screen with

---

61. Ibid., p. 144.

62. Ibid., p. 137.

63. Kracauer's delineation of the effects produced by this lack of continuity between the musical accompaniment and the images on screen echoes Adorno and Hanns Eisler's analysis of the interesting effects which film music *could* generate if – "instead of limiting itself to conventional reinforcement of the action or mood" – it set "itself in opposition to what is being shown on the screen". See Theodor Adorno and Hanns Eisler: Composing for the Films, London and Atlantic Highlands: The Athlone Press 1994, p. 26.

a veil of "indeterminacy" – a quality which, he argues, is ordinarily stamped out by the formativist aspirations of much narrative oriented cinema.[64]

In contrast to the "utilitarian" structure of the formative/theatrical film, the film practice for which Kracauer argues would be organised around the inclusion of images which have "not yet [been] stripped of their multiple meanings".[65] The director, he states, must "alienate" each shot "from any preconceived meaning" in order that each image may "exert its own independent impact" upon the spectator.[66] Anticipating Alexander Kluge's analysis of the extent to which the indeterminacy of the image fuels the spectator's imagination (the details of which will be discussed in Chapter 6), Kracauer claims that what is significant about the "indeterminacy" of images that have not been pressed into the service of narrative action is the extent to which they prompt the spectator to draw on his/her own imagination in an attempt to engage with the materials on screen.[67] Employing the concept in a manner reminiscent of Charles Baudelaire's delineation of the imagination as a "faculty" which enables one to apprehend "the intimate and secret relations of things, the correspondences and analogies"[68], Kracauer claims that the indeterminacy of the image cultivates "moods, emotions, [and] runs of inarticulate thoughts" in the spectator that no longer revolve around the image on screen.[69]

In keeping, however, with his analysis of the significance of the camera's capacity to extend the spectator's vision beyond the realm of

---

64. See also Kracauer's undated notes on the formative aspirations of Hollywood cinema in "Über die lebensferne Tendenz des Hollywood Films", Kracauer Nachlaß.

65. Theory of Film, p. 69.

66. See "Tentative Outline", p. 87.

67. Upon the advice of Adorno, Kracauer wrote to Alexander Kluge on December 24, 1962, mentioning at the end of his letter that perhaps he had heard about his Theory of Film from Adorno. Kluge wrote back to Kracauer in early 1963 to thank him for the letter and to confirm that Adorno had indeed told him about the book. Unfortunately, however, Kluge does not mention anything in his very short letter about the contents of the book itself. Both letters are contained in the Kracauer Nachlaß.

68. Baudelaire: "Further Notes on Edgar Poe", in: Baudelaire: Selected Writings on Art and Literature, ed. by P.E. Charvet, London: Penguin Books 1992, p. 199.

69. Theory of Film, p. 68.

subjective intention, Kracauer argues that the "correspondences" evoked by the "indeterminacy" of the image are not consciously, but unconsciously generated. Pointing to Proust's analysis of the experiences of the past in the present evoked by involuntary memory, Kracauer claims that the "loosely connected", "indeterminate" images characteristic of realist film are "particularly fit to function as [...] ignition spark[s]" which "touch off" involuntary recollections in the viewer.[70]

4.2 The Child's Capacity for Perception and Imagination

What is interesting to note is the extent to which Kracauer – like Benjamin and Proust before him – foregrounds memories of childhood in his delineation of the significance of the experience of the past in the present evoked by involuntary memory. Although Kracauer does not provide examples of memories pertaining to his own childhood, he does quote extensively from the observations and reminiscences of Hugo von Hofmannsthal and Blaise Cendrars, both of whom argue that film is at its best when it aids the spectator in reviving memories of "childhood days which have sunk into his unconscious"[71]. Relating one such experience, Kracauer – quoting Cendrars – writes:

> The screen showed a crowd, and in this crowd there was a lad with his cap under his arm: suddenly this cap which was like all other caps began, without moving, to assume intense life; you felt it was all set to jump, like a leopard! Why? I don't know.[72]

"Perhaps", Kracauer writes,

> the cap transformed itself into a leopard because the sight of it stirred involuntary memories in the narrator (as did the madeleine in Proust) – memories of the senses resuscitating inarticulate childhood days when the little cap under his arms was the carrier of tremendous emotions, which in a mysterious way involved the spotted beast of prey in his picture book.[73]

---

70. Ibid., p. 165.

71. Kracauer: quoting Hofmannsthal, in ibid., p. 171. See Hugo von Hofmannsthal: "Der Ersatz für Träume", Neue Freie Presse, March 27 (1921).

72. Theory of Film, p. 166. Kracauer is quoting from François and André Berge: "Interview de Blaise Cendrars sur le cinéma" in: Cinéma (Paris, 1939), pp. 138-142.

Hugo von Hofmannsthal takes this argument a step further, claiming not only that film has the capacity to revive childhood memories, but that – in doing so – it provides the spectator with a taste of that "fuller life" which he had dreamed of in his childhood, but which has been denied to him by society.[74] In an interesting connection which implicitly refutes the claims of "naïve realism" that have been directed against *Theory of Film*, Kracauer states that "[i]f Hofmannsthal is right", then "the moviegoer again becomes a child in the sense that he magically rules the world by dint of dreams which overgrow stubborn reality".[75] Although the relationship between cinema and childhood is not pursued explicitly in greater detail in *Theory of Film*, in "Dimanche: Ideen-Entwurf zu einem Kurzfilm" (an unpublished outline for a short film devised, but never made, by Kracauer) the child's capacity to see and experience the world outside of the terms and assumptions which colour and shape the perceptual horizon of adults is described in some detail.[76] Although the film outlined by Kracauer in "Dimanche" does not follow the prescription for realist cinema outlined in *Theory of Film*, its exploration of the child's capacity for perception and imagination is rendered significant when read in the light of Kracauer's delineation of the rejuvenation in the capacity for perception and imagination cultivated by realist cinema.

The film envisaged by Kracauer is divided into two parts, both of which revolve around a Sunday afternoon outing undertaken by "Bébé" (a three or four year old boy) and his parents. In the first part of the film, the family's journey (which begins and ends in their flat, but which includes – amongst other activities – a trip on a bus, and a ride on a merry-go-round, a visit to a café, and a stroll through a park) is shot entirely from the perspective of the child, whose capacity for imagina-

73. Theory of Film, p. 166.

74. Ibid., p. 167.

75. Ibid., p. 171.

76. Kracauer: "Dimanche: Ideen-Entwurf zu einem Kurzfilm" (undated manuscript), Kracauer Nachlaß. A copy of the manuscript in French can also be found in the Kracauer Nachlaß. See "Dimanche: Exposé pour un court sujet". Although the year in which Kracauer wrote this manuscript is not included on the document, the description "Anfang Mai" and "Paris [...] Madison Hotel" appear on the final page, indicating that it was written sometime during his stay at the Madison Hotel in Paris between 1933 and 1936. For an account of this period, see Belke and Renz: Siegfried Kracauer, 1889-1966, pp. 76-84.

tion transforms the outing into a "magnificent adventure".[77] In a series of descriptions reminiscent of Benjamin's analysis of the child's mimetic capabilities, Kracauer describes how – under the gaze of Bébé – the space under the table at the café takes on the appearance of a "primeval forest", while a ride on a merry-go-round is transformed into a marvellous journey through "the landscapes of [Bébé's] coloured children's books".[78]

In contrast to this presentation of events from Bébé's perspective, Kracauer notes that the second half of the film would depict the family's arrival home at their flat, and the recounting of the afternoon's activities from the father's perspective. "The joke", he notes, "lies in the correction of the imaginings of the child". The previous events are shown again from the perspective of the adults, and the occurrences that the child had experienced as wondrous are – through the eyes of the adults – transformed into banal activities and events.[79]

Kracauer's analysis of the child's magical capacity to see and experience the world outside of the terms which govern and shape the perspective of adults is also manifested in a passage in the "Preface" to *Theory of Film*, in which an affinity is drawn between the child's capacity for perception, and the revelatory capacities and possibilities of cinema. Recalling his first trip to see a film at the local moviehouse as a young boy, Kracauer claims that "[t]he impression it made upon [him] must have been intoxicating, for [he] there and then determined to commit [his] experience to writing". "Whether [this project] ever materialized, I have forgotten. But I have not forgotten its long-winded title"[80]: "Film as the Discoverer of the Marvels of Everyday Life" ("*Film als der Entdecker der Schönheiten des alltäglichen Lebens*").[81] "And I remember", he writes, "as if it were today, the marvels themselves":

77. "Dimanche: Ideen-Entwurf zu einem Kurzfilm", p. 1.

78. Ibid., pp. 1-2.

79. Ibid., pp. 2-3.

80. Theory of Film, p. li.

81. See Siegfried Kracauer: Theorie des Films: Die Errettung der äußeren Wirklichkeit, Frankfurt am Main: Suhrkamp 1985, p. 14, and Theory of Film, p. li. As revealed in Kracauer's letter to his former translator Lucienne Astruc (dated March 14, 1962), Kracauer was so unhappy with the German translation of Theory of Film that he re-translated "almost every sentence" from the original English version himself. Kracauer Nachlaß.

What thrilled me so deeply was an ordinary suburban street, filled with lights and shadows which transfigured it. Several trees stood about, and there was in the foreground a puddle reflecting invisible house façades and a piece of the sky. Then a breeze moved the shadows, and the façades with the sky below began to waver. The trembling upper world in the dirty puddle – this image has never left me.[82]

This passage – with its description of the image of an "ordinary suburban street" captured three times: first, by the objective eye of the camera; second, in the reflection of an indifferent puddle; and third, by the imaginative, curious gaze of the child – condenses in a small image much of what is essential to Kracauer's conception of the promise of the alienated mode of perception cultivated by realist cinema. These "marvels" are significant for Kracauer not – as his critics have suggested – because they are faithful reflections of the state of the world "as it is", but because they are the mark of a gaze which is alienated from those preformed ideas and expectations which shape and "delimit our horizon".[83] In a similar vein to his description of the child's capacity for perception and imagination in "Dimanche", the broader significance of Kracauer's analysis of the promise of realist cinema lies in the extent to which it can rejuvenate the way in which we both we perceive, and conceive of the possibilities and limitations of the world around us and, in doing so, fundamentally transform our conception of the possibilities of the future.

82. Theory of Film, p. Ii. Kracauer's description of this image is strongly reminiscent of any number of images which appear in Joris Ivens' 1929 film Regen, which depicts – amongst other things – the reflection of buildings and trees in puddles and other wet surfaces following a rainstorm. Although Kracauer mentions this film in Theory of Film, he does not discuss it in any detail. See pp. 39-40, 181, 203, and 273. It is also interesting to note that the music for the film ("Fourteen Ways to Describe Rain – In honor of Arnold Schönberg's seventieth birthday") was composed by Hanns Eisler. The score is contained in Composing for the Films, pp. 158-165.

83. Theory of Film, p. 296.

Chapter 5:
On the Task of a Realist Historiography in Kracauer's History: The Last Things Before the Last

Siegfried Kracauer's plans for a project on history can be traced back to early 1960, during the busy months in which he was completing the final draft of *Theory of Film: The Redemption of Physical Reality*.[1] In a letter to Leo Löwenthal (dated February 15, 1960) Kracauer states that – upon completion of the book – he plans to have a "creative break", during which time he would like to "read a lot", and write "a couple of essays on history".[2] Upon return from a four month trip to Europe between July and October of the same year, Kracauer notes that, although he has not yet "brought anything to paper", he "meditated a lot about history on the trip". "I am very enthusiastic [*passioniert*]", he writes, "about my attempt to make an incursion in this field. What may come out of it, I don't yet know; perhaps a series of interrelated [*zusammenhaengender*] essays".[3]

By December of 1960, Kracauer's plans for a series of essays on

1. Siegfried Kracauer: Theory of Film: The Redemption of Physical Reality, Princeton, New Jersey: Princeton University Press 1997. Hereafter referred to as Theory of Film.

2. Letter to Löwenthal, Kracauer Nachlaß, Deutsches Literaturarchiv, Marbach am Necker. The source of all references to materials contained in this archive will hereafter be referred to as the Kracauer Nachlaß. The letter has also been published in In Steter Freundschaft, Leo Löwenthal – Siegfried Kracauer: Briefwechsel 1921-1966, ed. by Peter-Erwin Jansen/Christian Schmidt, Springe: zu Klampen 2003, pp. 226-228. Hereafter referred to as In Steter Freundschaft.

3. Letter to Löwenthal, October 29, 1960, Kracauer Nachlaß. See also: In Steter Freundschaft, p. 231.

history had turned into preparations for a book-length project. In a letter to Lucienne Astruc, Kracauer states that he is "deeply steeped in work toward a new book, dealing with problems of history"[4] – the concerns of which are intimately bound with his writings on the significance of the photographic media.[5] Indeed, echoing his analysis – in *Theory of Film* – of the task of the realist photographer, one of the key characteristics which defines his conception of the task of a realist historiographical practice is "the degree to which a historian is able to efface his self in his contacts with the given data".[6] As Kracauer notes to Löwenthal in a letter written during the early stages of the project, the "[h]istorian has traits of the photographer, and historical reality resembles camera-reality".[7]

In Kracauer's "Introduction" to *History: The Last Things Before the Last* (which was completed posthumously in 1969 by Kracauer's friend and associate Paul Oskar Kristeller[8]), the significance of the relationship between Kracauer's final book, and *Theory of Film*, is further confirmed. "[R]ecently", Kracauer writes,

> I suddenly discovered that my interest in history [...] actually grew out of the ideas I tried to implement in my *Theory of Film*. In turning to history, I just continued to think along the lines manifest in that book. And all the time I had not been aware of this but, rather, assumed that I was moving on new ground and thus escaping preoccupations which had kept me under their spell for too long a time. Once I had discovered that I actually became absorbed in history not because it

4. Letter to Astruc, December 12, 1960, Kracauer Nachlaß. See also Kracauer's letters to Löwenthal (March 18, 1961) and Astruc (March 14, 1962) for insights into the research undertaken by Kracauer in the early stages of the project. Kracauer Nachlaß.

5. See Kracauer's letter to Löwenthal, February 10, 1961, Kracauer Nachlaß.

6. Siegfried Kracauer: History: The Last Things Before the Last, Princeton, Markus Wiener Publishers 1995, p. 213. The book will hereafter be referred to as History.

7. Letter to Löwenthal, February 10, 1961, Kracauer Nachlaß.

8. As Kristeller writes in his "Preface" to the book, chapters "one to four, seven, and the first half of chapter five" were pretty much completed by Kracauer prior to his death, while "the second half of chapter five" and "chapters six and eight" were finished by Kristeller, who drew closely on "written drafts or synopses that were quite readable but in need of careful editing". Kristeller also added a foreword and an epilogue to the book. See "Preface" in History, p. vii.

was extraneous to my drawn-out previous concerns but because it enabled me to apply to a much wider field what I had thought before. I realized in a flash the many existing parallels between history and the photographic media, historical reality and camera-reality.[9]

As Kracauer goes on to argue in the book, the similarities between the concerns addressed in *History* and his writings on the photographic media are not, however, limited to comparisons with *Theory of Film*, but can be traced back considerably further to the articles he wrote for the *Frankfurter Zeitung* in the 1920s.[10] "Lately", Kracauer writes, "I came across my piece on 'Photography'[11] and was completely amazed at noticing that I had compared historicism with photography already in this article of the 'twenties". "This discovery", he claims, "made me feel happy for two reasons:"

it unexpectedly confirmed the legitimacy and inner necessity of my historical pursuits; and by the same token it justified, in my own eyes and after the event, the years I had spent on *Theory of Film*. This book of which I had always conceived as an aesthetics of the photographic media, not less and not more, now that I have penetrated the veil that envelops one's most intimate endeavors, appears to me in its true light: as another attempt of mine to bring out the significance of areas whose claim to be acknowledged in their own right has not yet been re-

---

9. History, pp. 3-4.

10. On February 15, 1962, Kracauer wrote to Erika Lorenz (a masters student of Theodor W. Adorno who was writing a thesis on Kracauer's work entitled Siegfried Kracauer als Soziologe) asking her to inform him as to whether any ideas about history could be found in the essays that he wrote for the Frankfurter Zeitung. In her reply to Kracauer's letter (dated February 25, 1962), Lorenz lists 6 articles (all of which were published in the Frankfurter Zeitung between 1923 and 1928): "Die Wissenschaftskrise" ("The Crisis of Science), "Der verbotene Blick", "Die Reise und der Tanz" ("Travel and Dance"), "Das Ornament der Masse" ("The Mass Ornament"), "Die Photographie" ("Photography"), and "Zu den Schriften Walter Benjamins" ("On the Writings of Walter Benjamin"). All of these essays (except for "Der verbotene Blick") have been translated and published in English under the above listed titles in: Siegfried Kracauer: The Mass Ornament: Weimar Essays, ed. by Thomas Y. Levin, Cambridge, Mass. and London, England: Harvard University Press 1995. Both of the letters cited above are contained in the Kracauer Nachlaß.

11. See Kracauer: "Photography", in: The Mass Ornament: Weimar Essays, pp. 47-63.

cognized. [...] So at long last all my main efforts, so incoherent on the surface, fall into line – they all have served, and continue to serve, a single purpose: the rehabilitation of objectives and modes of being which still lack a name and hence are overlooked or misjudged.[12]

However, while Kracauer's delineation of the alienated gaze of the realist historian does (as I will argue in this chapter) bear a number of important similarities to his analysis, in *Theory of Film*, of the rejuvenation in the capacity for perception precipitated by the realist photographer, the relationship between *History* and his 1927 essay on photography is more complicated than is suggested by the theoretically consistent image of his oeuvre outlined in the above passage. Indeed, as Inka Mülder-Bach has argued, although an understanding of the relationship between Kracauer's early and late writings is "crucial for an understanding of *History*", "[i]n order for his 'incoherent efforts' to 'fall into line'", Kracauer's writings would have to be viewed from a perspective that could "transform the discontinuities of his works into a surface expression of an underlying continuity".[13] Taking her lead from Kracauer's own analysis of the shortcomings of historicism (a mode of analysis which irons out the specificities of the past in its charting of a linear narrative driven by progress) Mülder-Bach argues that such a "perspective is not to be trusted". For, she claims, "when one is dealing with totalities, contours become blurred; the overall picture can be obtained only at the price of important specifics".[14]

However, while it is true to say that – in the some thirty-five years separating "Photography" and *History* - the emphasis of Kracauer's analysis of the relationship between photography and history did undergo a change of focus, it is less accurate to claim that this shift of focus "testifies to a fundamental change in [Kracauer's] theoretical position".[15] Indeed, as I will demonstrate in this chapter, Kracauer's analysis, in the final pages of "Photography", of the "confrontation [...] with nature"[16] provoked by photographic images actually serves as a precursor to the positive conception of perceptual alienation that stands at the heart of both *Theory of Film* and *History*.

---

12. History, p. 4.

13. Inka Mülder-Bach: "History as Autobiography: The Last Things Before the Last", New German Critique, No. 54 (Fall, 1991), p. 140.

14. Ibid.

15. Ibid., 142.

16. "Photography", p. 62.

5.1 Photography, History, and Memory

Kracauer's essay on photography revolves around a discussion of two photographs. The first image (which featured on the cover of an illustrated magazine) depicts a twenty-four year old "film diva" in front of the Hotel Excelsior on the Lido. A member of the dance-troupe "The Tiller Girls"[17], the woman (who is sporting a hairstyle with bangs) is depicted holding her head in a seductive pose befitting the caption on the cover that reads "our demonic diva".[18] The second image (which is also "more than sixty years old") was taken in "the studio of a court photographer", and depicts a smiling twenty-four year old woman (who in the proceeding years became a grandmother) wearing a Zouve jacket and a dress with a cinched waist and a crinoline.[19]

The tension around which the essay is structured is borne out of the incongruity between the image of this twenty-four year old woman and the memories of the grandmother retained by her grandchildren. Although the photograph does, to all known accounts, accurately depict the now deceased grandmother as she appeared as a young woman, the image of this twenty-four year old speaks so little to the memories of her grandchildren that she appears to them as a mannequin – a mere sign or representative of her period. "This mannequin", Kracauer writes,

> does not belong to our time; it could be standing with others of its kind in a museum, in a glass case labeled 'Traditional Costumes, 1864'. There the mannequins are displayed solely for the historical costumes, and the grandmother in the photograph, too, is an archaeological mannequin which serves to illustrate the costumes of the period. So that's how women dressed back then: chignons, cinched waists, crinolines, and Zouave jackets. The grandmother dissolves into fashionably old-fashioned details before the very eyes of the grandchildren.[20]

In what appears, in the first part of the essay, to be a reversal of the conception of the promise of photographic alienation elaborated in *Theory of Film*, Kracauer argues that what is troubling about the photograph of this young woman is not only the extent to which the camera's "indifference" to its subject has produced an image that is estranged from the

---

17. For Kracauer's analysis of this troupe, see "The Mass Ornament", in: The Mass Ornament: Weimar Essays, pp. 75-86.

18. "Photography", p. 47.

19. Ibid., p. 48.

20. Ibid.

memories of her grandchildren but, more significantly, the degree to which this indifference reduces the contents of the image to mere spatio-temporal signs or markers of a certain period. In this regard, Kracauer argues, photography could be said to provide the "spatial continuum" which supports the "temporal continuum" established by historicism: "Were it the photograph alone that endowed [the] details [of the photograph] with duration, they would not at all outlast mere time; rather, time would create images for itself out of them".[21] Thus, he argues that

> from the nothingness of the grandmother, the gaze is thrown back onto the chignons. It is the fashion details that hold the gaze tight. Photography is bound to time in precisely the same way as *fashion*. [...] The tightly corseted dress in the photograph protrudes into our time like a mansion from earlier days that is destined for destruction because the city center has been moved to another part of town. [...] Even the landscape and all other concrete objects become costumes in an old photograph.[22]

The significance of this conception of photography for an understanding of Kracauer's criticism of historicism hinges on the sharp distinction he draws between the radically different experiences of the past evoked by photography and memory. In the 1927 essay, Kracauer states that the alienated image of the past preserved by photography is inescapably bound with the time in which it came into existence. Such images, he claims, stand in stark contrast to memory images, which retain only those aspects of the past which have significance for the person who is remembering them. In a similar vein to Proust's delineation of the incongruity between "the calendar of facts" and the impressions evoked by involuntary memory[23], Kracauer argues that "[s]ince what is significant is not reducible to either merely spatial or merely temporal terms, memory images are at odds with photographic representation". "From the latter's perspective", he writes, "memory images appear to be fragments – but only because photography does not encompass the meaning to which they refer and in relation to which they cease to be frag-

21. Ibid., p. 49

22. Ibid., p. 55.

23. Marcel Proust: In Search of Lost Time, London: Vintage 1996, Vol. 4, p. 180.

ments. Similarly, from the perspective of memory, photography appears as a jumble that consists partly of garbage".[24]

Anticipating Benjamin's analysis of the negative effects associated with the rise of "information" as a means of communication[25] (the details of which will be discussed in Chapter 7), Kracauer argues that such "garbage" finds itself at home in the pages of illustrated newspapers. "The aim" of such papers, he claims, "is the complete reproduction of the world accessible to the photographic apparatus. They record the spatial impressions of people, conditions, and events from every possible perspective".[26] For Kracauer, the danger of the proliferation of such images lies not only in the extent to which the alienated gaze of the camera "effaces the contours of its [subject's] history" (sealing such images off from the contexts via which they could be rendered meaningful for the viewer), but also the extent to which they become "eternalized" (that is, *historicised*) as markers or signs of a particular period.[27]

In a passage which clearly influenced Benjamin's analysis of the decline in the capacity for experience precipitated by the proliferation of information[28], Kracauer argues that such images do not aid, but rather "sweep [...] away the dams of memory".[29] "In the hands of the ruling society", he writes, "the invention of illustrated magazines is one of the most powerful means of organizing a strike against understanding". "Never before", he claims, "has a period known so little about itself".[30]

Up to this point, one can see (as Mülder-Bach has argued) that although Kracauer's understanding of photographic alienation – as a mode of vision which bypasses subjective perception and memory – remains largely unchanged across the years which separate his early and late writings, it is true to say that, in "Photography", the effects of this alienated gaze are described as largely negative. In the final pages of the essay, however, Kracauer's delineation of photographic alienation is re-framed within a context in which its effects are rendered significantly more positive – a shift that paves the way for the development, some

24. "Photography", pp. 50-51.

25. Walter Benjamin: "The Storyteller: Reflections on the Works of Nikolai Leskov", in: Benjamin: Illuminations, ed. by Hannah Arendt, London: Fontana Press 1992, pp. 83-107. Hereafter referred to as "The Storyteller".

26. "Photography", pp. 57-58.

27. Ibid., p. 59.

28. "The Storyteller", pp. 88-90.

29. "Photography", p. 58.

30. Ibid.

thirty years later, of the conception of perceptual alienation elaborated in both *Theory of Film* and *History*.

The context within which this change of focus manifests itself is in a discussion of the photographic archive – the significance of which (as elaborated in the introduction) lies in the extent to which images of diverse origin (of "all possible manifestations which present themselves in space"[31]) are "incorporated into [a] central archive in unusual combinations which distance them from human proximity".[32] Employing concepts that also play a central role in both *Theory of Film* and *History*, he argues that this "distance from human proximity" is manifested both at the level of the camera's alienated relationship to its subject, and in the mixed-up jumble of images itself – the meanings of which can no longer be determined by their relationship to the present. "Once the grandmother's costume", Kracauer writes,

> has lost its relationship to the present, it will no longer be funny; it will be peculiar, like an ocean-dwelling octopus. One day the diva will lose her demonic quality and her bangs will go the same way as the chignons. This is how the elements crumble, since they are not held together. The photographic archive assembles in effigy the last elements of a nature alienated from meaning.[33]

If, in the first part of the essay, this alienation from meaning is (via a comparison with the impressions evoked by memory) described as largely negative, in the final pages of the essay, it is injected with a sense of promise. In a passage reminiscent of de Maistre's delineation of the shake-up of the relationship between the past and the present precipitated by the damage sustained by the natural history museum, Kracauer argues that what is significant about the disorganised jumble of materials contained in the photographic archive is the extent to which it prompts a re-thinking of the possibilities of both the past and the future outside of the linear, evolutionary conception of history propagated by historicism. Elaborating on this point in more detail, he claims that, within this schema, it is "incumbent on consciousness to establish the *provisional status* of all given configurations, and perhaps even to awaken an inkling of the right order of the inventory of nature".[34] In a passage in which he draws a connection between his own ideas and those of

---

31. Ibid., p. 60

32. Ibid., p. 62.

33. Ibid.

34. Ibid.

Franz Kafka, Kracauer states, however, that "a liberated consciousness absolves itself of this responsibility by destroying natural reality and scrambling the fragments".[35]

For Kracauer, it is in the space opened up by the "scrambling" of "natural reality" performed by the photographic archive that an emancipatory confrontation with the non-necessary relationship between the past and the present can manifest itself. As he states in "Photography", to create the conditions for such a confrontation is the "go-for-broke game of the historical process"[36] – the political stakes of which he elaborated some thirty-five years later in his analysis of the task of a realist historiography in *History*.

5.2 The Task of a Realist Historiography

In keeping with his analysis, in *Theory of Film*, of the formative/realist split that characterises the history of both film and photography, Kracauer argues in *History* that the history of historiography can also be divided into two groups – one of which is characterised by formative traits, the other by realist tendencies. In a similar vein to his analysis of the "storytelling bias" of the theatrical film (the tightly organised composition of which resembles the form of traditional works of art[37]), Kracauer argues that the historians associated with what he variously describes as the "formativist", "historicist", and/or "narrative" camps are characterised by their attempts to construct an appearance of continuity out of a series of incommensurate and discontinuous events by "synthesizing" a select collection of past occurrences into "a succession of events which lead straight to the present".[38] "The result", Kracauer states, "is a more or less closed success story which, because of its necessary reliance on teleological considerations, not only spawns falsifying hindsight but further tightens the bonds between the elements of the narrative, thereby smoothing away all the existing rifts, losses, abortive starts, inconsistencies"[39].

Citing the work of Benedetto Croce and R. G. Collingwood as

35. Ibid.
36. Ibid.
37. Ibid., p. 181.
38. History, pp. 183, and 170.
39. Ibid., p. 170.

examples[40], Kracauer argues that what underlies the work of the formativist historians is a tendency to construct history according to the concerns and assumptions of the present. Croce's "dictum", he writes, is that "only an interest in the life of the present can move one to investigate past fact", while Collingwood describes the historian as a "'son of his time' who 're-enacts' the past out of his immersion in present-day concerns".[41]

What troubles Kracauer about this "present interest" theory of the task of historiography is the extent to which the present is conceived of as the endpoint and goal of the past, and "historical truth" as a mere "variable of present interest".[42] Underpinning this conception of historiography is an understanding of history which conceives of the relationship between the past and the present as a continuous and linear process, within which each period or event is represented as another step in history's so-called march of progress toward the present. Citing Karl Marx's conception of historical materialism as an example, Kracauer argues that what is troubling about the conception of history as progress which stands at the heart of Marx's project is the extent to which history is imbued with the "kind of necessity" ordinarily associated with the "workings of nature".[43] To reiterate a point made earlier, for Kracauer, what is reactionary about this evolutionary understanding of history is not only the extent to which it is "bound up with the idea of chronological time as the matrix of a meaningful process"[44], but the degree to which it precludes one's capacity to conceive of the possibilities of the future in terms which would challenge the historicist delineation of history as progress.

The alternative conception of the task of historiography outlined by Kracauer in *History* is built upon his analysis of the significance of photographic alienation elaborated in the final pages of "Photography" – the contours of which provided Kracauer with the basis for his delineation of both the realist photographer in *Theory of Film*, and the realist historian

40. See, for example, Benedetto Croce: History: Its Theory and Practice, New York: Russell and Russell 1960, and R.G Collingwood, The Idea of History, New York: Galaxy Books 1956.

41. Kracauer (quoting Croce and Collingwood) in History, p. 63.

42. History, p. 64. For a more detailed account of Kracauer's analysis of the "present interest" theory of the task of historiography, see Chapter 3: "Present Interest" in: History, pp. 62-79.

43. Ibid., p. 36.

44. Ibid., p. 150.

in *History*. According to Kracauer, the task of the latter is to explore the past in the same manner in which the realist photographer explores and penetrates physical reality. In stark contrast to the formative aspirations of the historicists (who seek to shape the past in the image of their own conception and understanding of the period), Kracauer argues that what is crucial to his own conception of the charge of a realist historiography is the extent to which the realist historian is able to alienate himself from his preformed ideas and expectations while engaging with the materials in question. Like the realist filmmaker (whose portrayal of physical reality is not governed by a preoccupation with form) Kracauer argues that it is only by "bracketing" himself off from both the "macro assumptions" of the historicists and the expectations which had previously shaped his understanding of a certain period, that historical data will be able to speak to the realist historian anew on its own terms.

Although Kracauer frequently refers to Proust's novel – and more specifically, to Marcel's alienated encounter with his grandmother – in his analysis of the significant role that this state of "self-transcendence" occupies in his analysis of the task of a realist historiography, it is Kracauer's delineation of the "extraterritorial" state of the exile which serves as the "model" for his analysis of the alienated approach of the realist historian.[45] As Karsten Witte has pointed out[46], Kracauer's employment of the term "extraterritorial" first emerged in the chapter "The Boulevards, Home of the Homeless" in *Orpheus in Paris: Offenbach and the Paris of his Time* (a book which Kracauer wrote between 1934 and 1936 while living under very difficult conditions in exile in France). In a passage in this chapter which anticipates his use of the term in *History* many years later, Kracauer describes the life spent by dandies and exiles in the Parisian boulevards of the 1840s as "extraterritorial" ("*exterritorial*"), owing to the "attitude of aloofness" which they maintained in relation to the existing order.[47]

More than twenty years later, the relationship between exile and "extraterritoriality" emerges again, in *History*, in Kracauer's analysis of

45. Gertrud Koch: "'Not yet accepted anywhere': Exile, Memory, and Image in Kracauer's Conception of History", New German Critique, No. 54 (Fall, 1991), p. 105.

46. Karsten Witte: "Siegfried Kracauer im Exil", Exilforschung: Ein Internationales Jahrbuch, Band 5, München: edition text + kritik 1987, p. 138.

47. Siegfried Kracauer: Orpheus in Paris: Offenbach and the Paris of his Time, New York: Vienna House 1972, p. 68, and Kracauer, Jacques Offenbach und das Paris seiner Zeit, Frankfurt am Main: Suhrkamp 1994, pp. 74-75.

the transformation of one's perceptual and experiential relationship to the world provoked by the experience of exile. Once the exile, Kracauer writes,

settles elsewhere, all those loyalties, expectations, and aspirations that comprise so large a part of his being are automatically cut off from their roots. His life history is disrupted, his 'natural' self relegated to the background of his mind. To be sure, his inevitable efforts to meet the challenges of an alien environment will affect his outlook, his whole mental make-up. But since the self he was continues to smolder beneath the person he is about to become, his identity is bound to be in a state of flux; and the odds are that he will never fully belong to the community to which he now in a way belongs. (Nor will its members readily think of him as one of theirs.) In fact, he has ceased to 'belong'. Where then does he live? In the near-vacuum of extra-territoriality, the very no-man's land which Marcel entered when he first caught sight of his grandmother. The exile's true mode of existence is that of a stranger.[48]

Like Benjamin, Kracauer and his wife Lili experienced firsthand the effects of exile. Within days of the Reichstag fire of February 27, 1933, the Kracauers fled Berlin to France, where they lived in Paris, and later Marseilles, between 1933 and 1941. As revealed in letters written by Kracauer during this period[49], the years spent in France (during which time he was interned for a period of almost two months in camps outside of Paris[50]) were extremely difficult, to say the least. However, in April of 1941 – following a period of nine months spent in "fear and misery" in Marseilles [51] – Siegfried and Lili Kracauer (with the help of

48. History, pp. 83-84.

49. See, for example, Kracauer's letter to Walter Benjamin (dated February 24, 1935) in: Walter Benjamin: Briefe an Siegfried Kracauer (Mit vier Briefen von Siegfried Kracauer an Walter Benjamin), ed. by Rolf Tiedemann/Henri Lonitz, Marbach am Necker: Deutsche Schillergesellschaft 1987, pp. 82-85.

50. Siegfried Kracauer, 1889-1966: Marbacher Magazin, No. 47, ed. by Ingrid Belke/Irina Renz, Marbach am Necker: Deutsche Schillergesellschaft, 1989, p. 95.

51. Letter to Adorno of February 12, 1949, Kracauer Nachlaß. For an account of the atmosphere that characterised Marseilles at the time of Kracauer's (and Benjamin's) stay there, see Klaus Michael: "Vor dem Café. Walter Benjamin and Siegfried Kracauer in Marseille", in: Aber ein Sturm weht vom Paradiese her: Texte zu Walter Benjamin, ed. by Michael Opitz/Erdmut Wizisla, Leipzig: Reclam 1992, pp. 203-204, and 214-215.

Leo Löwenthal and Meyer Schapiro[52]) emigrated to the United States of America, where they settled in New York until their respective deaths in 1966 and 1972.[53]

Despite the many difficulties posed by exile, Kracauer's own experience of "extraterritoriality" clearly had a considerable impact on the development of his conception of an alienated mode of perception through which one's perspective of the world could be fundamentally altered.[54] As Mülder-Bach has pointed out, far from conceiving of this mode of estrangement in negative terms, Kracauer's own experience of extraterritoriality was viewed as a form of liberation: "[A] liberation from the effects of origin and native language, from the ties to a cultural tradition and a social system – and, above all, from the dates of one's own time, the 'labels of chronology'"[55]; the latter of which Kracauer sought to actively maintain by his adamant refusal to reveal his age to his publishers and readers.[56] Indeed, as Kracauer makes clear in a letter to

52. For an account of the difficulties faced by Löwenthal and Schapiro in seeking to secure the Kracauers' emigration to the United States of America, see Leo Lowenthal: "As I Remember Friedel", New German Critique, No. 54 (Fall, 1991), pp. 11-12.

53. For a detailed account of the periods spent in exile in France and the United States, see "Ins Unpolitische abgeglitten? – Pariser Exil: 1933-1940", and "Im Niemandsland der Exterritorialität – Amerika: 1941-1966" in: Momme Brodersen: Siegfried Kracauer, Hamburg: Rowohlt Taschenbuch 2001, pp. 98-119 and 120-137 respectively.

54. Adorno has argued that Kracauer's own conception of himself as an "outsider" did not stem solely from his experience of exile, but was also the product of an unhappy childhood during which he was a victim of anti-Semitism. "Suffice it to say", Adorno writes, "that Kracauer told the story of carrying, in a pitiful parody of the little red book in which the teachers recorded their marks, a similar book in which he graded his fellow students on their behaviour toward him". Theodor W. Adorno: "The Curious Realist: On Siegfried Kracauer", New German Critique, No. 54 (Fall, 1991), p. 161. For an account of some of the difficulties which Kracauer faced as a child, see Martin Jay's comprehensive analysis of Kracauer's "extraterritoriality" in "The Extraterritorial Life of Siegfried Kracauer", in: Jay: Permanent Exiles: Essays on the Intellectual Migration from Germany to America, New York: Columbia University Press 1986, pp. 153-154.

55. Inka Mülder-Bach: "History as Autobiography: The Last Things Before the Last", p. 154.

56. See, for example, Kracauer's letter to Wolfgang Weyrauch (dated June 4, 1962). Kracauer Nachlaß.

Adorno (written on November 8, 1963), this refusal was driven not by a desire "to appear young or younger" to his readers, but by the "fear of being snatched away from chronological anonymity by the fixation of the date, and the unavoidable connotations of such a fixation"[57] – the overcoming of which is a central tenant of his analysis of the "extraterritorial" state of the realist historian.

Like the exile (who, in confronting an "alien environment", finds himself "cut off" from the expectations and assumptions which had previously "comprise[d] so large a part of his being"[58]) Kracauer argues, in *History*, that "[i]t is only in this state of self-effacement, or homelessness that the historian can [effectively] commune with the material of his concern"[59]. "A stranger to the world evoked by [his] sources", he claims that the historian is "faced with the task – the exile's task – of penetrating its outward appearances, so that he may learn to understand that world from within".[60] In contrast to the practices of the formativist camp, he argues that the manner in which this is achieved is not via the "outward projection[s]" of the historian, but rather through a process within which he is transformed into a "divining rod" or "receiving instrument".[61]

In a passage in keeping with Benjamin's criticism of the sovereign, contemplative gaze of the art critic, Kracauer states that the "most promising way of acquiring such knowledge is presumably for [the historian] to heed Schopenhauer's advice to the art student":

> Anybody looking at a picture, Schopenhauer claims, should behave as if he were in the presence of a prince and respectfully wait for what the picture may or may not wish to tell him; for were he to talk first he would only be listening to himself. Waiting in this sense amounts to a sort of active passivity on the historian's part. He must venture on the diverse routes suggested to him by his intercourse with the evidence, let himself drift along, and take in, with all his senses strained, the various messages that happen to reach him.[62]

---

57. Kracauer Nachlaß. See also Kracauer's letters to Adorno (dated October 25, and October 31, 1963) in which he discusses this "idiosyncrasy" in some detail.

58. History, p. 83.

59. Ibid., p. 84.

60. Ibid. See also Kracauer's analysis of those "great historians who owe much of their greatness to the fact that they were expatriates". Ibid.

61. See ibid., pp. 102-103, and 85.

62. Ibid., p. 84.

This state of "active passivity" (which Kracauer argues is "a necessary phase of the historian's work"[63]) bears a number of similarities to his analysis in *Theory of Film* of the alienated, "extraterritorial" state cultivated by realist cinema. Like the viewer of realist film, Kracauer argues that the realist historian's perceptual and cognitive relationship to his material is characterised by a state of "productive absentmindedness".[64] The historian, he writes, "opens himself up to the suggestions of his sources" which "ferment in his mind" and, in doing so, precipitate "a broadening of its scope"[65].

Indeed, in a similar vein to his delineation of the role that realist film can play in triggering involuntary associations and recollections in the viewer, Kracauer argues that the state of self-effacement characteristic of the realist historian's practice prompts him to engage imaginatively with the material of his concern – a mode of engagement which sparks thoughts and associations pertaining to both his specific field of inquiry, as well as connections that are more closely related to his own memories and experiences. Circumscribing this mode of engagement, Kracauer (quoting Isaiah Berlin) argues that the connections experienced by the historian in this context "resemble flashes illumining the night". "This is why", he writes, "their emergence in the historian's mind has been termed a 'historical sensation' and said to 'communicate a shock to the entire system [...] the shock [...] of recognition'".[66] In a similar vein to Benjamin's analysis of the conditions under which a radical historical consciousness could manifest itself, Kracauer argues that this "shock to the [...] system" is borne out of the perception of a moment in which the historicist's linear organisation of the past is burst asunder – laying bare not only the "indeterminacy" of historical events,

63. Ibid., p. 85.

64. Ibid., p. 92.

65. Ibid., pp. 91-92.

66. History, p. 101. See, for example, Benjamin's account of this experience of time in "Convolute N" of The Arcades Project: "In it, truth is charged to the bursting point with time. (This point of explosion, and nothing else, is the death of the intentio, which thus coincides with the birth of authentic historical time, the time of truth.) It is not that what is past casts its light on what is present, or what is present its light on what is past; rather, image is that wherein what has been comes together in a flash with the now to form a constellation." [N3,1], p. 463. See also Kracauer's letter to Rolf Tiedemann (dated February 21, 1966) in which he claims that key aspects of Benjamin's thoughts on history are closely related to his own. Kracauer Nachlaß.

but the extent to which "the idea of a progress of humanity is untenable".[67] "The upshot", Kracauer states, "is that the period [with which the historian is concerned] [...] disintegrates before [his] eyes. From a meaningful spatiotemporal unit it turns into a kind of meeting place for chance encounters"[68] where the possibilities of both the past and the future can be renegotiated and re-explored.

Careful, however, to counteract any criticism of the degree to which the historian's imaginative engagement with his materials could be said to reinstate the highly subjective mode of engagement with the past associated with the formativist historians, Kracauer argues that "subjectivity" in this context "is anything but a limiting factor".[69] As he goes on to explain, this is because the "dynamization" of the historian's character provoked by such an encounter in effect renders his ideas "independent of [their] location in time".[70] In a similar vein to his delineation of the "extraterritorial" state of the exile (whose identity is characterised by a "state of flux"[71]) Kracauer argues that the connections and associations experienced by the historian in this context "invalidate [...] the commonplace assumption that he is the son of his time". "Actually", Kracauer writes, "he is the son of at least two times – his own and the time he is investigating. His mind is in a measure unlocalizable; it perambulates without a fixed abode".[72]

Thus, in contrast to the tightly organised, linear conception of history outlined by the formativist historians (in which history is constructed according to the concerns and assumptions of the present) Kracauer argues that history "is the realm of contingencies, of new beginnings", and that it is the realist historian's task to bring to light "those possibilities which [the formativist historians] did not see fit to explore".[73] If, as Kracauer himself writes, the concerns which he elaborated in *History* actually "grew out of the ideas [he] tried to implement in *Theory of Film*"[74], then it is because his delineation of the promise of the medium rests not, as his critics have suggested, on film's capacity to affirm the state of the world "as it is", but rather on the extent to which realist film

---

67. History, p. 150.
68. Ibid.
69. Ibid., p. 102.
70. Ibid.
71. Ibid., p. 83.
72. Ibid., p. 93.
73. Ibid., pp. 31 and 6 respectively.
74. Ibid., p. 3.

can – in "stir[ring] up the elements of nature"[75] – play a part in re-animating our capacity to conceive of the possibilities of both the past and the future in different terms.

75. "Photography", p. 62.

Part 3: Alexander Kluge

Chapter 6:
From History's Rubble:
Kluge on Film, History, and Politics

The central figure in Alexander Kluge's 1979 film *The Patriot* (*Die Patriotin*) is Gabi Teichert, a high school history teacher from the German state of Hesse, whose dissatisfaction with the shortcomings of her discipline guides us through the eclectic collection of photographs, drawings, poems, stories, maps, posters, and staged and documentary footage out of which the film is constructed. The fictional character of Gabi Teichert (who is played by Hannelore Hoger) does not only feature in *The Patriot*, but actually made her film debut some twelve months earlier in *Germany in Autumn* (*Deutschland im Herbst*) – a collaborative film project undertaken by Kluge and other prominent members of the New German Cinema including Rainer Werner Fassbinder and Volker Schlöndorff.

As Kluge and his co-directors have noted in their brief analysis of the project, the impetus for *Germany in Autumn* sprang from the perceived extent to which the events that took place in Germany during the Autumn months of 1977 – including the kidnapping and murder of Daimler-Benz board member Hanns-Martin Schleyer by the Red Army Faction (RAF), the highjacking of a Lufthansa plane, and the alleged suicides of terrorists Gudrun Ensslin, Andreas Baader, and Jan-Carl Raspe in Stammheim Prison – seemed to pass into the annals of German history without undergoing any rigorous public debate.[1] Constructed out of a series of thematically interrelated episodes (which consist of

1. See Alf Brustellin, Rainer Werner Fassbinder, Alexander Kluge, Volker Schlöndorff, Bernhard Sinkel: "Germany in Autumn: What is the Film's Bias? (1978)", in: West German Filmmakers on Film: Visions and Voices, ed. by Eric Rentschler, New York and London: Holmes and Meier 1988, pp. 132-133. See also Kluge's notes on the film in Alexander Kluge: Die Patriotin: Texte/Bilder 1-6, Frankfurt am Main: Zweitausendeins 1979, pp. 20-37. Hereafter referred to as Die Patriotin.

both fictional and documentary elements), the film seeks to raise a series of questions about the period (and, in particular, its relationship to Germany's Nazi past) without seeking to provide the viewer with any clear-cut answers or firm conclusions. "Autumn 1977", the directors argue, "is the history of confusion", and if the film is to do justice to the complexities of the situation, then it is "[e]xactly this [confusion which] must be held on to".[2]

In *Germany in Autumn*, it is the threat posed by this confusion to the neat conception of German history that Gabi Teichert is expected to teach in the classroom which prompts her to actively go in search of new materials for her lessons. In *The Patriot* too, Teichert is thrown into action, not only by her dissatisfaction with the high school history curriculum, but by the threat to the subject posed by the Hessian Cultural Ministry, which in 1977 decided to amalgamate "history" with "geography" and "social studies".[3] Teichert's reaction to this decision is not only to join the "Hessian School Campaign" in their fight for the preservation of "history" as a subject[4], but – as depicted in both films – to head into the field in search of materials which have been forgotten and/or discarded by the highly reductive, official narratives that appear in the textbooks assigned to her students.

One of Teichert's first ports of call is the Party Convention of the Social Democrats, in which she seeks to encourage a number of real politicians (including Heidi Müller – representative for Niederbayern) to join in her attempts to rejuvenate the high school history curriculum. When questioned by Müller as to whether she has managed to collect anything of value, Teichert states that her first task is – with the cooperation of Müller and another perplexed delegate – to broaden the official version of German history in order to make room for the inclusion of material which has fallen outside of what has been commemorated as historically significant.[5] "I am of the opinion", she states to Müller,

2. "Germany in Autumn: What is the Film's Bias?", p. 133. For a detailed account of the film, see Miriam Hansen: "Cooperative Auteur Cinema and Oppositional Public Sphere: Alexander Kluge's Contribution to Germany in Autumn", New German Critique, No. 24-25 (Fall/Winter, 1981-2), pp. 36-56.

3. See "Gabi Teichert's Geschichtsbegriff", in: Die Patriotin, p. 427. As Anton Kaes has pointed out, this attempt was made despite the fact that "a poll in 1977 had shown enormous deficits in students' historical knowledge". See Anton Kaes: From Hitler to Heimat: The Return of History as Film, Cambridge, Mass. and London, England: Harvard University Press 1989, note 6, p. 239.

4. "Gabi Teichert's Geschichtsbegriff", p. 427.

"that the material for high school history lessons is not positive enough". As revealed, however, throughout the course of the film, Teichert's conception of a more "positive" curriculum is based not on the replacement of a negative chain of events with a narrative which is more salubrious in its focus, but on the opening up of the subject to incorporate materials that could challenge her students to question the extent to which the history of their country could have turned out very differently. "It would be bad", Teichert states, "if that which is known about the history of my country were ultimately the truth. There is always a way out".[6]

This desire to open up the curriculum to include sources and materials which have, in the past, been either ignored and/or disregarded as peripheral and insignificant is – as revealed by Teichert's colleague in a staff meeting about the state of the discipline – driven by the very limited conception of German history she is expected to teach in the classroom. The version, Teichert's colleague states, which draws a line "from Bismarck to Hitler" is the only "consequential extrapolation [*Fortschreibung*]" of the course of German history – a point of view supported by the head of the department who claims that "from now on, we must concentrate on keeping the topic of 'history' limited".

As stated, however, in voiceover in the opening sequence of the film, Gabi Teichert is a "patriot" because "she takes an interest in all the dead of the Reich" – an interest which (as revealed by her activities throughout the course of the film) is more specifically focused on redeeming those voices, memories, and materials that challenge the tightly organised, linear conception of the course of events around which the history curriculum is structured. The disembodied voice of one such member of the Reich is represented by the voiceover narrator of *The Patriot* itself, who is introduced as "a knee" – a character inspired by a Christian Morgenstern poem in which the uninjured knee of a dead soldier abandons its body to travel around the world.[7] As revealed in the opening minutes of the film, the knee in *The Patriot* is the only remaining body-part of Lance Corporal Wieland who was killed during the Battle for Stalingrad on January 23, 1943. The only time we actually get to see Wieland is via black and white, slow motion footage of a young boy with his arm outstretched in the form of a Nazi salute. "This", the knee claims in

---

5. For a transcript of these discussions, see Die Patriotin, pp. 74-85.

6. Ibid., p. 450.

7. This poem is quoted in full in the film and is printed in Die Patriotin, p. 480.

voiceover, "was once my owner Lance Corporal Wieland, eight years before he died in Stalingrad. Wanted to live, found himself in the wrong history".

As revealed by comments made throughout the course of the film, the knee's presence in *The Patriot* is driven by a desire to rectify a series of commonly held misconceptions about the process of learning and writing about history – the interrogation of which forms the basis of Gabi Teichert's activities in the film. Like Teichert (who finds it difficult, if not impossible, to learn about history from "the small print in thick books"[8]) Wieland's knee claims that it is "an error" to think that "the printed letters in libraries have anything to do with history". "We", it claims, "are history, the dead and the dead parts", and it is only the resurrection of the dead which "presupposes a thorough knowledge of history". In a statement in tune with Teichert's faith in the extent to which her students' conception of the possibilities of both the past *and* the future could be rejuvenated by such a resurrection, the knee claims (over footage of the despondent faces of soldiers in the snow-covered battle fields of Stalingrad) that, contrary to those who believe that the "dead are somehow dead", "we dead are full of protest and energy".

In the following scene (part of which also features in *Germany in Autumn*) Gabi Teichert is shown – with a shovel thrown over her shoulder – heading into the field in search of buried, forgotten materials with which she can rejuvenate the high school history curriculum. Armed, at various points throughout the film, with a range of tools (including a hammer, drill, saw, and sickle) *The Patriot* charts her attempts to explore, dig up, discover, crack open, and redeem the traces of the history of her country which have fallen outside of what has been monumentalised as historically significant – a task which is not just confined to the activities of Teichert, but which is the task of *The Patriot* itself.[9]

6.1 Autorenkino and Counter-histories

In his 1979 acceptance speech for the Fontane Prize for Literature, Kluge emphasised the importance of "working on" German history in a fashion reminiscent of the work of Gabi Teichert. "By that", he stated, "I mean something very concrete; one might start by telling stories [*Ge-*

8. See "Gabi Teichert's Geschichtsbegriff", p. 428.

9. Miriam Hansen: "Alexander Kluge, Cinema and the Public Sphere: The Construction Site of Counter-History", Discourse, No. 6 (1983), p. 70.

schichten] in turn about it"[10]. Playing on the double meaning of the German term *Geschichte* (which designates both "history" and "story"), Kluge claims that "[t]elling stories [...] is precisely [his] conception of narrative cinema; and what else is the history of a country but the vastest narrative surface of all? Not one but many stories".[11]

Although Kluge is best known outside of Germany as a prominent member of the New German Cinema, his work spans a broad range of fields, and since the 1960s he has also actively "worked on" German history in his capacity as an author, social theorist, historian and, since 1988, the producer of a number of programs for German television – the highly experimental structure of which is (as we will see in Chapter 7) reminiscent of the structure of his films.

Indeed, despite the associations which Kluge himself has drawn between his own experimental filmmaking practice and "narrative cinema", Kluge's films have – since the release of his first feature film *Yesterday Girl* (*Abschied von gestern*) in 1966 – differed significantly, in both their form and content, from the tightly organised, character driven stories ordinarily associated with narrative cinema. Kluge's distaste for commercial film can be traced back to 1958 to his experience as an assistant on the set of Fritz Lang's film *Journey to the Lost City* (*Das Indische Grabmal*) – a position made possible by a letter of introduction from Kluge's close friend and mentor Theodor W. Adorno.[12] What shocked Kluge about this experience was the extent to which the restrictions imposed upon the director by the film's producer Artur Brauner made it impossible for Lang to realise the project in the form in which he had originally envisioned it.[13] Disappointed by this experience, Kluge spent

---

10. Alexander Kluge: "The Political as Intensity of Everyday Feelings", Cultural Critique, No. 4 (Fall, 1986), p. 127.

11. Alexander Kluge: "On Film and the Public Sphere", New German Critique, No. 24-25 (Fall/Winter, 1981-2), p. 206.

12. See "Die Funktion des Zerrwinkels in zertrümmernder Absicht. Ein Gespräch zwischen Alexander Kluge und Gertrud Koch", in: Kritische Theorie und Kultur, ed. by Rainer Erd et al., Frankfurt am Main: Suhrkamp 1989, pp. 111-112. For a discussion of Kluge's relationship to Adorno in English, see Stuart Liebman: "On New German Cinema, Art, Enlightenment, and the Public Sphere: An Interview with Alexander Kluge", October, No. 46 (Fall, 1988), pp. 23-59.

13. Kluge claims that the producer and his sister-in-law went as far as to give "direct instructions to the chief lighting technician, to the stage architects, to all co-workers who were their employees; every second idea of Fritz Lang was undermined as too expensive, as too erroneous [abwegig]". See "Reibungsverluste.

most of his time in the studio canteen writing the stories which were published in 1962 as *Lebensläufe* (*Case Histories*)[14], travelling in the evenings to the film museum in East Berlin to view a retrospective of German, Soviet, and American films from the silent period.[15] "This was the first time", Kluge notes, "that I encountered noncommercial films from film history"[16] – an experience which not only sparked his interest in early cinema (and the work of Georges Méliès, Louis Lumière, and Alexander Dovzhenko in particular), but had an important impact on the development of his conception of a cinematic practice not bound by the emphasis on continuity and closure characteristic of classical narrative cinema.

It was, however, Jean-Luc Godard's 1959 film *Breathless* (*A bout de souffle*) that inspired Kluge to become a filmmaker.[17] Godard's interest in the writings of Bertolt Brecht – and more specifically, his adaptation of Brecht's conception of theatrical distanciation for a filmmaking practice oriented toward the creation of an active, critical spectator – had an important impact on the development of Kluge's conception of the task of a radical cinema. In more general terms, the production techniques and supportive structure of the French New Wave (of which Godard was a key member) provided Kluge and other German filmmakers with a model for the development of an alternative filmmaking practice – the contours of which were outlined in 1962 in "The Oberhausen Manifes-

Gespräch mit Klaus Eder", in: Alexander Kluge: In Gefahr und größter Not bringt der Mittelweg den Tod. Texte zu Kino, Film, Politik, ed. by Christian Schulte, Hamburg: Vorwerk 1999, pp. 250-251.This book will hereafter be referred to as In Gefahr.

14. Rainer Lewandowski: Alexander Kluge, München: C.H. Beck and edition text + kritik 1980, p. 9. Alexander Kluge, Case Histories, New York: Holmes and Meier 1991. The collection of stories contained in the English edition does, however, vary from the collection of stories published in Lebensläufe.

15. Liebman: "On New German Cinema, Art, Enlightenment, and the Public Sphere: An Interview with Alexander Kluge", p. 50.

16. Ibid.

17. "Reibungsverluste. Gespräch mit Klaus Eder", p. 250. For more detailed analyses of Kluge's relationship to Godard, see Gloria Behrens et al.: "Gespräche mit Alexander Kluge", Filmkritik, Vol. 12 (December, 1976), pp. 569-570, and Christina Scherer: "Alexander Kluge und Jean-Luc Godard. Ein Vergleich anhand einiger filmtheoretischer 'Grundannahmen'", in: Die Schrift an der Wand: Alexander Kluge: Rohstoffe und Materialien, ed. by Christian Schulte, Osnabrück: Universitätsverlag Rasch 2000, pp. 79-102.

to", in which Kluge and twenty-five of his colleagues heralded the birth of the New German Cinema.[18] More specifically, the conception of "*auteur*" cinema advanced by the French New Wave (within which the director – in a similar vein to a literary author – maintains complete control over all aspects of the film's production) provided Kluge with a model of filmmaking which guarded against the kind of directorial interference that he had observed on Fritz Lang's set.

Central to Kluge's conception of *Autorenkino* (*auteur* or author's cinema) is not only the creative independence of the director[19], but the active participation of the spectator, whose task – he claims – is not to "understand" the intentions of the director, but to actively participate in the film's construction.[20] Film, Kluge argues, "is not produced by *auteurs* alone, but by the dialogue between spectators and authors"[21] – a dialogue which is not manifested in the film itself, but rather (in a similar vein to the mode of spectatorship cultivated by the "*separation of*

18. "The Oberhausen Manifesto", in: West German Filmmakers on Film: Visions and Voices, p. 2.

19. "The Autorenfilm", Kluge claims, is "a form of protest against the overhang of the thinking of banks, the thinking of lenders, the thinking of producers in the film". "Reibungsverluste. Gespräch mit Klaus Eder", p. 250.

20. Harmut Bitomsky et al.: "Gespräch mit Alexander Kluge: Über Die Patriotin, Geschichte und Filmarbeit", Filmkritik, No. 275 (November, 1979), p. 510. In a fashion reminiscent of Benjamin's criticism of the sovereign, contemplative gaze of the art critic, Kluge argues that "[u]nderstanding a film completely is conceptual imperialism which colonizes its objects". "If I have understood everything", he claims, "then something has been left out. We must make films that thoroughly oppose such imperialism of consciousness". In an attempt to illustrate this point, Kluge provides an example reminiscent of Kracauer's delineation, in Theory of Film, of the magical image of an ordinary street reflected in a rain puddle: "I cannot understand a puddle on which the rain is falling – I can only see it; to say that I understand the puddle is meaningless. Relaxation means that I myself become alive for a moment, allowing my senses to run wild: for once not to be on guard with the police-like intention of letting nothing escape me". Kluge: "On Film and the Public Sphere", p. 211, and Siegfried Kracauer: Theory of Film: The Redemption of Physical Reality, Princeton, New Jersey: Princeton University Press 1997, p. Ii.

21. Jan Dawson: "But why are the Questions so Abstract: An Interview with Alexander Kluge", in: Dawson: Alexander Kluge and the Occasional Work of a Female Slave, New York: Zoetrope 1977, p. 37.

the elements" characteristic of Epic Theatre[22]) in the associations cultivated in "the spectator's head" by "the gaps [...] between the disparate elements of filmic expression"[23].

In stark contrast to classical narrative cinema (which draws the spectator into the world of the film via an editing system which aligns his or her perspective with that of a lead character), the editing practice favoured by Kluge (and his longtime editor Beate Mainka-Jellinghaus) is characterised by a constant movement between highly eclectic image and sound tracks that consist of both fictional and documentary materials. In *The Patriot*, these materials (the organisation of which is structured around the creation of a series of "montage miniatures" designed to spark thoughts and associations in the spectator's head pertaining to a particular theme, period, or event) include photographs, poems, interviews, maps, sketches, paintings, illustrations from fairytales, movie snippets, clips from the German national anthem, lengthy voiceover statements, newsreel footage, and a frequent use of intertitles that both supplement and challenge the image on screen. (See Figure 1)

Indeed, in stark contrast to Hollywood cinema (which, Kluge argues, limits our capacity to conceive of the past outside of the terms of a tightly woven, character driven story[24]), the form of historiography both represented in – and cultivated by – *The Patriot* (and Kluge's literary work more generally) is more akin to the extracurricular activities of Gabi Teichert, which revolve around "digging up" materials which complicate the highly reductive, official narratives propagated by Hollywood cinema and the commercial media.[25]

---

22. Bertolt Brecht: "The Modern Theatre is the Epic Theatre", in: Brecht on Theatre: The Development of an Aesthetic, ed. by John Willett, New York: Hill and Wang 1998, p. 37.

23. Edgar Reitz, Alexander Kluge, and Wilfried Reinke: "Word and Film", October, No. 46 (Fall, 1988), p. 87. One can hear in this formulation an echo of Theodor W. Adorno, who – in his 1952 analysis of the musical compositions of Arnold Schoenberg – states that "Schoenberg's music demands from the very beginning active and concentrated participation. [...] It requires the listener spontaneously to compose its inner movement and demands of him not mere contemplation but praxis". See "Arnold Schoenberg 1874-1951", in: Adorno: Prisms, Cambridge, Massachusetts: The MIT Press, 1990, pp. 149-150.

24. "There can be no doubt", Kluge states, "that the narrative of an individual fate, unfolded in ninety minutes, can convey historical material only at the price of dramaturgical incest". "On Film and the Public Sphere", p. 206.

25. As stated in Public Sphere and Experience (a book which Kluge co-

Figure 1: Images from The Patriot

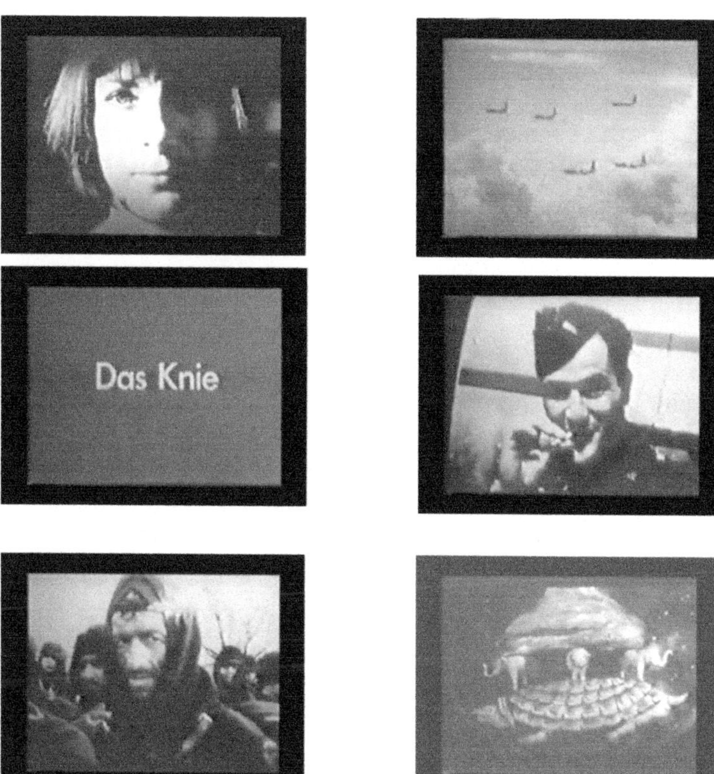

© Alexander Kluge

authored with Oskar Negt in the early 1970s), the simplistic representation of historical events presented by the commercial media has a significant impact on the way in which history is "packaged" for future generations. A media conglomerate, they write, "transfers the propylaeum history of the world onto cassettes; the same selection of images and historical dates is thus programmed into educational cassettes, television programs, educational tools, discussion programs, courses of instruction, and parlor games. It is possible to imagine the uniformity of such a presentation of history by keeping in mind how even today press photos that are distributed by news services overdetermine the polymorphic image world of real political events". Oskar Negt and Alexander Kluge: Public Sphere and Experience: Toward an Analysis of the Bourgeois and Proletarian Public Sphere, London and Minneapolis: University of Minnesota Press 1993, p. 140.

Meaning, Kluge states of the radically heterogeneous imaging practice characteristic of *The Patriot*, is not to be found in any particular image (nor in the film as a whole), but in the thoughts and impressions sparked by the relationship between the materials – connections that encourage the spectator to think about the "place" of the past in different terms.

This idea of a "co-production" between the author and the spectator (which is fundamental to an understanding of the significance of Kluge's film, television, and literary work) stands at the heart of his conception of the role that film can play in prompting the viewer to rethink both the task of historiography, and the futures of the past that have been buried under the highly circumscribed historicist narratives which chart the relationship between the past and the present. For Kluge, what is problematic about these narratives is not only their carefully crafted, linear structure, but the extent to which both the process of exclusion out of which such narratives are fashioned, and the ideology of "historical necessity" through which they are rendered meaningful, prohibit our capacity to conceive of the possibilities of both the past and the future in different terms. Why, Kluge asks, do

> we carry in us such a fixed conception of the probable order of events, which is only the sum of what is impressed upon us by the objective history or the media? Why do we hang on to it so energetically, while the imagination circles elsewhere [...]. and while] the sum of improbabilities is just as great as the sum of all probabilities?[26]

When Kluge announced in a live radio interview conducted at the Frankfurt Book Fair in 2003 that the task of the some five hundred [hi]stories (*Geschichten*) contained in *Die Lücke, die der Teufel läßt*[27] is to "preserve something beyond probability",[28] he reiterated what has, for many years, been the driving force behind his work: A desire to overcome the restrictions imposed upon our conception of the possibilities and limitations of the present by the "probable" order of events around which our conception of history is structured. For Kluge, central to this idea of historical probability is a conception of historical realism that could

26. Claus Philipp: "Vertrauenswürdige Irrtümer: Ein Gespräch", Kolik, No. 13 (2000), p. 10.

27. Alexander Kluge: Die Lücke, die der Teufel läßt. Im Umfeld des neuen Jahrhunderts, Frankfurt am Main: Suhrkamp 2003.

28. "Bücher-Herbst", Deutschland Radio Berlin, October 11 (2003).

more accurately be described as "historical fiction"[29]. He claims that "[w]hat you notice as realistic, [...] is not necessarily or certainly real. The potential and the historical roots, and the detours of possibilities, also belong to reality. The realistic result, the actual result, is only an abstraction that has murdered all other possibilities for the moment".[30]

Both the "highly porous", "chance-bound"[31] nature of events that have been strung together under the guise of "historical necessity", and the degree of "abstraction" that is required in order for that sense of necessity to be rendered meaningful, is revealed by Kluge in a literary montage piece entitled "Der Luftangriff auf Halberstadt am 8. April 1945" ("The Air Raid on Halberstadt on April 8 1945"), the content of which is constructed – in a manner reminiscent of *The Patriot* - out of a diverse collection of fictional and documentary elements (including interviews, stories, quotes, drawings, reports, strategy descriptions, photographs of pilots, and diagrams of weaponry).[32] Remarkable among these elements is a fictional interview (said to have been conducted in London in 1952 at the conference of the *Institute for Strategic Research*) between a German reporter and Brigadier General Frederick L. Anderson of the 8th Division of the US Air Force.[33] The focus of the interview (which is a format employed frequently in Kluge's literary, film, and television work) is the air raid on the German town of Halberstadt in the final weeks of World War II (the late occurrence of which, as An-

29. Kluge: "The sharpest ideology: that reality appeals to its realistic character", On the Beach, No. 3-4 (Summer, 1984), p. 23. Hereafter referred to as "The sharpest ideology".

30. Jan Dawson: "But why are the Questions so Abstract: An Interview with Alexander Kluge", p. 34

31. Claus Phillip: "Vertrauenswürdige Irrtümer: Ein Gespräch", p. 10

32. Kluge: "Der Luftangriff auf Halberstadt am 8. April 1945", in: Kluge: Chronik der Gefühle – Band II: Lebensläufe, Frankfurt am Main: Suhrkamp 2000, pp. 27-82. In keeping with his analysis of the task of the stories contained in Die Lücke, die der Teufel läßt, Kluge has described the collection of stories contained in Chronik der Gefühle as "a carpet of numerous improbable incidents". See Kluge: "Ich liebe das Lakonische", Der Spiegel, No. 45 (2000), p. 338. "Der Luftangriff auf Halberstadt am 8. April 1945" was originally published in 1977 in Kluge: Neue Geschichten, Hefte 1-18: "Unheimlichkeit der Zeit", Frankfurt am Main: Suhrkamp.

33. An abridged version of this fictional interview has been published in English as "The Air Raid on Halberstadt, 8 April 1945", Semiotext(e), No. 11 (1982), pp. 306-315.

drew Bowie has pointed out, "had no strategic significance for the course of the war"[34]).

The questions posed by the reporter (who, like Kluge, was also born in Halberstadt) seek not only to elucidate the purpose of the attack (which levelled 82 per cent of the city, and very nearly killed the then 13 year old Kluge himself[35]) but to challenge General Anderson to explain why the pilots involved in the raid would not have abandoned the attack had they seen the large white surrender flag flying from the tower of the city's church. As revealed in the discussion[36], the reporter's suggestion that the attack *could* have been averted is dismissed by the General as unrealistic. "The goods", he claims, "had to go down onto the city" because it was too dangerous for the pilots to fly back to base with planes fully loaded with explosives. In response to the interviewer's suggestion that the bombs *could* have been dropped on nearby countryside uninhabited by people, the General (whose capacity for imagination has been thwarted by an economic/militaristic logic at odds with the preservation of human life) responds with the claim that the bombs "cost a lot of money" and that it was therefore wrong to "just throw that away, in the mountains or open fields after it was produced at such expense".[37]

Although the text is concerned with a very specific set of circumstances, its method of questioning (which revolves around the creation of a series of gaps within which one is able to conceive of the extent to which an event, or series of events could have turned out very differently) forms the political backbone of much of Kluge's work. "It must", he states, "be possible to present reality as the historical fiction that it is. Its impact on the individual is real [...]. Men die as a result, are pulled apart, are subjected to bombing raids, are dead while alive, are placed in

34. Andrew Bowie: "New Histories: Aspects of the Prose of Alexander Kluge", Journal of European Studies, xii (1982), p. 184.

35. Lewandowski: Alexander Kluge, p. 8. "The form left by the impact of an exploding bomb", Kluge has written of the experience, "is easily remembered. [...] I was there, at a distance of ten metres away, when on April 8 1945 such a thing impacted". Chronik der Gefühle – Band II: Lebensläufe, p. 11. Kluge's comments are also quoted in Lewandowski: Alexander Kluge, p. 8.

36. A similar discussion takes place in Kluge's 1983 film Die Macht der Gefühle (The Power of Feelings) between a German reporter "Frau Pichota" (played by Kluge's sister Alexandra) and "Brigadegeneral Anderson". For a transcript of this discussion, see Kluge: Die Macht der Gefühle, Frankfurt am Main: Zweitausendeins 1984, pp. 94-96.

37. "The Air Raid on Halberstadt, 8 April 1945", p. 313.

asylums as mad etc."[38], but this does not mean that these realities could not have been prevented, that the "deadly outcomes"[39] suffered by these people could not have turned out very differently.

In order to provide a sense of the reality of alternate possibilities, Kluge opposes historical narratives (the outcomes of which are described as "probable" and or "realistic") with his own "counter-histories" – an activity also undertaken by Gabi Teichert who is vehemently opposed to historical narratives that describe a particular outcome as a "necessary consequence"[40]. In response to General Anderson's claim that it is unrealistic to think that the pilots could have dropped their bombs on countryside uninhabited by people, Kluge describes a number of fictional, but nonetheless realistic, "counter-histories" in which human destruction was averted by pilots who – inadvertently or otherwise – dropped their bombs on uninhabited areas in the vicinity of their highly populated, intended targets.

For example, in an interview with Florian Hopf, Kluge recounts Bertolt Brecht's account of a pilot who released his bombs onto an open field as a result of a feeling of indolence. "There was", Kluge narrates,

> a pilot, and in the first world war he had loaded bombs that were supposed to be dropped on a city. He had however the feeling: it is a beautiful morning and I am lazy. Out of indolence, he dropped the bombs in such an unskilful and untimely manner, that they fell on an open field, and the inhabitants of the city were rescued.[41]

Likewise, in his acceptance speech for the 2003 Georg Büchner Prize for Literature, Kluge recounts the story of a "US pilot" who – under the sudden pressure of an attack of colic – "shames himself" in the midst of

---

38. "The sharpest Ideology", p. 23.

39. The phrase is taken from the title of Kluge's 1973 novella Learning Processes with a Deadly Outcome, Durham and London: Duke University Press 1996.

40. Kluge: "Presseheft zum Film", Filmkritik, No. 275 (November, 1979), p. 504. See, for example, the class activity undertaken by Teichert in which she encourages her students to consider the steps that could have been taken to prevent the outcome experienced by Gerda Baethe who, in 1944, found herself under attack in an air raid shelter with her children. Die Patriotin, pp. 146-151.

41. "'Gefühle können Berge versetzen [...]': Interview von Florian Hopf mit Alexander Kluge zu dem Film: Die Macht der Gefühle", in: Die Macht der Gefühle, p. 185.

an air raid against alleged terrorists by "doing it in his combat suit". The result, Kluge claims, is that he drops his "smart bombs" in a swamp adjacent to the building that was his target, inadvertently sparing the lives of the members of a wedding party who had been celebrating there.[42]

As stated by Kluge himself, the politics of such stories lies not in their development along the lines of "a particular political praxis", but in the extent to which they can help "to recuperate [...] what is considered unpolitical as a political matter".[43] For Kluge, it is only by redeeming the non-necessary status of – and relationship between – events (which fall both within and outside of the official narrativization of the relation of the past to the present) that the chain of events out of which our conception of the probable direction of history is structured can be revealed for the "historical fiction" that it actually is. If, he argues, we can free ourselves from conceiving of the past as a linear narrative that leads straight to the present, then it is not only the past – but also the possibilities for the future embedded in the past – which can be renegotiated and re-explored.

6.2 The Construction Site of History

In Kluge's writings on cinema, this attempt to draw attention to the non-necessary relationship between the past and the present also informs

---

42. Alexander Kluge: "Risse", Frankfurter Allgemeine Sonntagszeitung, October 26 (2003), p. 23. See also "Absichtloses Glück: Eine Übersprunghandlung" in which Kluge describes this event in more detail. Die Lücke, die der Teufel läßt, pp. 709-711.

43. "The Political as Intensity of Everyday Feelings", p. 126. In Kluge's films, the gap between "what could have been" and the official account of "realistic outcomes", between the desires and hopes of human beings and the so-called objective realm of facts, is revealed by Kluge most effectively in scenes which show fictional characters such as Gabi Teichert participating in real public events. What is revealed, for example, in the scene in The Patriot in which Teichert is shown at the Convention of the Social Democrats, is the apparent inappropriateness of her questions at a forum for the discussion of so-called "real" political concerns. Indeed, as is rendered clear by the, at times, surprised and impatient responses of the delegates in question, Teichert's desire to open up the history curriculum to make way for the inclusion of different historical imaginaries is not the kind of concern which the delegates can take seriously. See "Reibungsverluste – Gespräch mit Klaus Eder", p. 245.

his analysis of the important role that a return to the "origins" of cinema *could* play in rejuvenating our conception of the possibilities of the medium. In an interview with American filmmaker Richard Linklater in *Primetime Spätausgabe* (one of four of Kluge's weekly programs on German television), Kluge's enthusiasm for early cinema is revealed in a discussion about the silent period:

Linklater: But what pleases me, is the thought that everything that one envisages in the imagination exists, that everything could exist. [cut] I love the early cinema, Griffith is one of my favourite directors, Chaplin, Keaton, the whole silent film actually. [...]
Kluge: You would actually develop the film again anew, if there were more of you. If you were one hundred people, then you would invent the art of film once again [...] *start again from the beginning* [...]
Linklater: [astonished laughter] *From the beginning, to begin again from the beginning.*
Kluge: Yes, yes [...]
Linklater: [with disbelief] Can one do that?
Kluge: Yes, of course, of course, yes.[44]

It is, of course, Kluge's own vision for the rejuvenation of the medium which he is impressing upon Linklater here – a vision driven by a desire for a filmmaking practice which does not seek to reproduce the form and content of films made during the silent period, but which draws inspiration from the alternative conception of the possibilities of the medium embodied in the work of early filmmakers such as Méliès and Lumière[45]. Sidestepping the realist/formative split that Kracauer draws between the two filmmakers, Kluge argues that in "each of these origins,

44. "Durchbruch eines Außenseiters/Der Südstaaten-Regisseur Richard Linklater und sein Erfolgsfilm Before Sunrise", Primetime Spätausgabe, RTL (11 June, 1995). This passage is quoted in Christian Schulte: "Fernsehen und Eigensinn", in: Kluges Fernsehen. Alexander Kluges Kulturmagazine, ed. by Christian Schulte/Winfried Siebers, Frankfurt am Main: Suhrkamp 2002, p. 80. My translation of this segment of the interview (as well as the notes about Linklater's expressions) is based on this extract. The use of italics indicates words spoken in English.

45. "I do not", Kluge claims, "take up the silent film in my films for stylistic reasons but because it is a question of 'radically' keeping open the elementary roots of the film". "The Sharpest Ideology", p. 24.

'cousins' and other relatives of what actually developed can be found, and these can be adapted for the New Media in very interesting ways".[46]

In Kluge's own work, a number of stylistic devices characteristic of early cinema are employed in his own attempts to "reinvent [the] possibilities" of the medium.[47] In films such as *The Patriot* and his 1983 *The Power of Feelings,* these devices include the colour tinting of the image, a frequent use of intertitles, the employment of iris masks to frame the image, and – in a manner reminiscent of Lumière's single-shot films – the extended presentation of natural and urban landscapes which are often divorced from any clear symbolic or narrative function.

The frequent use of these devices, combined with a highly eclectic collection of materials that are edited together in the loose, discontinuous fashion characteristic of much of Kluge's work, results in a film practice that systematically undermines the ordinary channels through which meaning is communicated in classical narrative cinema. As Anton Kaes has argued of *The Patriot,* "[t]he splintering and disintegration of the narrative continuum [...] follow from Kluge's conviction that two thousand years of German history cannot be grasped from the single perspective of a psychological, causal story".[48] "Even an individual historical event like Stalingrad", he claims, "exists only as a multitude of perspectives"[49], the majority of which – like that of Wieland's knee – are excluded from the highly abstract official accounts of the place which Stalingrad occupies in German history.

It is also, as Kaes has pointed out, this "multitude of perspectives" which Kluge has endeavored to represent in his 1964 book *Schlachtbeschreibung*[50] – an experimental historiographical account of the battle of

46. Kluge: "Why Should Film and Television Cooperate?", October, No. 46 (Fall, 1988), p. 99. For a comprehensive analysis of the impact that early cinema has had on the development of Kluge's film and television work, see Miriam Hansen: "Reinventing the Nickelodeon: Notes on Kluge and Early Cinema", October, No. 46 (Fall, 1988), pp. 178-198.

47. Jan Dawson: "But why are the Questions so Abstract: An Interview with Alexander Kluge", p. 37.

48. From Hitler to Heimat: The Return of History as Film, p. 118.

49. Ibid.

50. Ibid., and Alexander Kluge: "Schlachtbeschreibung", in: Chronik der Gefühle – Band I: Basisgeschichten, pp. 509-793. Although originally published in 1964, Kluge has reworked the book a number of times in the proceeding years. The source cited above (to which I will be referring in this chapter) is the most

Stalingrad which (in a manner reminiscent of *The Patriot)* is constructed out of a highly eclectic montage of both fictional and documentary materials (including diary entries, government reports, interviews about strategy, radio messages, responses from the clergy, photographs, drawings, government instructions to the press, medical reports about the dead, the mad, and the wounded, as well as guidelines for German soldiers on how to deal with the treacherous winter conditions without freezing to death).

In a similar vein to Kluge's account of the air raid on Halberstadt, this highly experimental book is also driven by Kluge's longstanding protest against historical narratives which describe events such as those which took place at Stalingrad as "necessary" and/or "inevitable" outcomes of history's so-called march of progress toward the future. Indeed, the highly diverse collection of materials out of which *Schlachtbeschreibung* is constructed could be said to focus primarily on breaking the spell of the aestheticisation of violence and war enacted by Josef Goebbels' likening of Stalingrad to a painting before which one must stand back in order to do it, and presumably the history in which it is embedded, full justice.[51]

Vehemently opposed to the degree of abstraction required to both establish and sustain such a "long-shot" perspective (a term employed by Kracauer in his discussion of the "macro" historical accounts of the formativist historians[52]), Kluge draws his readers in close, encouraging them to generate their own meanings and conclusions from the "micro" materials out of which the book is constructed. Similarly, in "Das Ferne Stalingrad" ("The distant Stalingrad") (a 1989 episode of his television program *10 vor 11*), Kluge presents the viewer with a vast array of "raw materials" (including German radio reports, footage of Russian civilians

recent version. The original version of the book has also been published in English translation as The Battle, New York: Mc Graw-Hill 1967.

51. Goebbels quoted in "Schlachtbeschreibung", p. 562.

52. In his dicussion of the "macro" histories constructed by the formativist historians, Kracauer argues that "[t]he higher the level of generality at which a historian operates, the more historical reality thins out. What he retains of the past when he looks at it from a great distance is wholesale situations, long-term developments, ideological trends, etc. – big chunks of events whose volume wanes or waxes in direct ratio to distance. They are scattered over time; they leave many gaps to be filled. We do not learn enough about the past if we concentrate on the macro units". Kracauer: History: The Last Things Before the Last, Princeton: Markus Wiener Publishers 1995, p. 118.

preparing for the German attack, still images of freezing soldiers, footage from a performance of the "Stalin Cantata", press images of Hitler overlooking a battle plan, clips from a film about Stalingrad made before the attack, and footage taken from German planes of bombs being dropped on the city) all of which (by virtue of the extremely diverse, inherently inconsistent nature of the materials) significantly complicate historical accounts that seek to provide a panoramic overview of events that took place during the period[53].

Indeed, in a similar vein to both *Schlachtbeschreibung* and "The distant Stalingrad", the historical "place" of the events that took place in Germany during the Autumn months of 1977 is, in *Germany in Autumn*, not something which can be easily determined. As in *The Patriot*, the "multitude of perspectives" contained in the highly eclectic montage of materials out of which the film is constructed (including, to cite just a few examples, footage from the State funeral of Schleyer, and the burial of Ensslin, Baader, and Raspe in Dornhalden Cemetery, fictional sequences exploring the security measures put in place by the state, and documentary footage of the Bundeswehr in action, interviews with figures as diverse as Fassbinder's mother, and Horst Mahler – the co-founder of the RAF, and the recurrent presence of the German National anthem) challenge the viewer to both reconsider the events which took place during the Autumn months of 1977, and to actively question the manner in which these events have been packaged by more traditional historical accounts of the period. (See Figure 2).

As Miriam Hansen has claimed of the open, heterogeneous structure of the film, "[i]n the eyes of those who expected a more clear-cut, partisan statement, *Germany in Autumn* certainly lacked in political effectiveness".[54] As she points out, however, the aim of the directors was not to replace the official account of the course of events by simply "pressing one interpretation over another".[55] "As filmmakers", the directors argue, "it is not our concern to provide another statement about terror here and abroad", nor "to add to the hundred thousand theories the first correct one"[56]. Rather, in collating a diverse, inherently inconsistent collection of materials, they have attempted to stimulate the imagination

53. "Das Ferne Stalingrad", 10 vor 11, RTL (February 27, 1989).

54. Hansen: "Cooperative Auteur Cinema and Oppositional Public Sphere: Alexander Kluge's contribution to Germany in Autumn", p. 56.

55. Ibid.

56. "Germany in Autumn: What is the Film's Bias?", p. 132.

of the spectator into reconceiving the possibility of different historical outcomes.

Figure 2: Images from Germany in Autumn

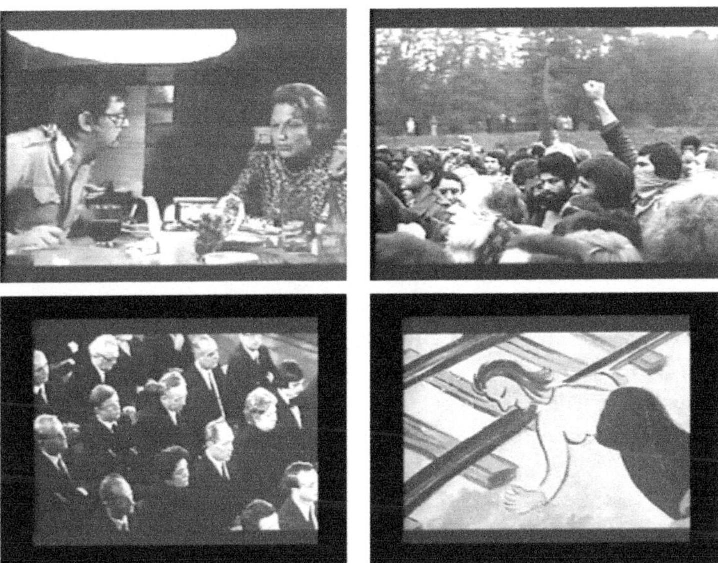

© Alexander Kluge

Kluge is careful, however, to distinguish the active, imaginative conception of spectatorship that he associates with his own films, from the mode of engagement fostered by the style of associative/rhetorical montage employed by filmmakers such as Sergei Eisenstein. Wary of any method of editing which seeks to impose a particular line of thinking upon the spectator, Kluge argues that montage in his films is not used "for explanations (as it is in the rhetorical montage of Eisenstein) but develops an invisible third image directly out of the tension of the incongruousness of the successive images".[57] "We do not", he claims, "fashion [*gestalten*] the associations of the viewers, that is what Hollywood does, we do not channel them once, but we stimulate them, so that

57. "Risse", p. 26. For a more detailed analysis of Kluge's relationship to the films of Eisenstein see Stuart Liebman: "Why Kluge?", October, No. 46 (Fall, 1988), pp. 18-21.

something independent comes into being, something which without these incentives, would not have been actualised".[58]

This independent "third image" (which manifests itself in "the head of the spectator") is not, however, an obvious association established by two images which have been edited together to produce a particular connection or outcome (a practice which he claims "is basically no different from the situation where [...] schoolchildren are forced to memorize [poems]" which have been "conceived in an associative fashion by somebody else").[59] Rather, in a similar vein to Benjamin's delineation of the active, creative mode of spectatorship cultivated by the kind of film practice outlined in the "Work of Art" essay, the active, imaginative mode of spectatorship envisioned by Kluge takes as its model not "the dramaturgy of the school hour, but the school recess; not the moralistic instruction provided by adults, but the imagination of children amongst one another"[60] – the games and activities of whom demonstrate a capacity for the "renewal of existence"[61] which is not hindered by the "imperative [of] practical necessity".[62]

In a passage in "One-Way Street" which clearly influenced the development of Kluge's ideas, Benjamin claims that

> [c]hildren are particularly fond of haunting any site where things are being visibly worked on. They are irresistibly drawn by the detritus generated by buildings, gardening, housework, tailoring, or carpentry. In waste products they recognize the face that the world of things turns directly and solely to them. In using these things, they do not so much imitate the works of adults as bring together, in the

58. "Interview", in Rainer Lewandowski: Die Filme von Alexander Kluge, Hildesheim and New York: Olms Presse 1980, p. 36. See also Florian Rötzer: "Kino und Grabkammer. Gespräch mit Alexander Kluge", in: Die Schrift an der Wand: Alexander Kluge: Rohstoffe und Materialien, p. 35.

59. "On Film and the Public Sphere", p. 220.

60. Alexander Kluge: Gelegenheitsarbeit einer Sklavin. Zur realistischen Methode, Frankfurt am Main: Suhrkamp 1975, p. 196.

61. Walter Benjamin: "Unpacking my Library: A Talk about Book Collecting", in: Benjamin: Illuminations, ed. by Hannah Arendt, London: Fontana Press 1992, p. 63.

62. The phrase is taken from André Breton's analysis of imagination in his "Manifesto of Surrealism", in: Breton: Manifestoes of Surrealism, Ann Arbor: University of Michigan Press 1994, p. 4.

artifact produced in play, materials of widely differering kinds in a new, intuitive relationship.[63]

Drawing on the example of the child at play as the model for his conception of an active, creative spectator, Kluge claims that just as the imagination of children is more readily stimulated by building blocks than by electrical trainsets, so too is the imagination of the spectator more effectively cultivated by films with the unfinished structure of a "construction site" or building in process.[64] "I believe", Kluge states, "that it is [...] easier for the spectator to connect his experiences with a film that has breaks, than with a perfect film. My editor [Beate Mainka-Jellinghaus] always says: Weak films make strong viewers – strong films make weak viewers", to which Kluge adds: "a construction site is more advantageous than complete houses".[65]

In Kluge's writings on film, this metaphor of the construction site is extended to incorporate the spectator as well, as a way of evoking the unfinished, active process of engagement with the past prompted by the eclectic collection of building blocks out of which films such as *The Patriot* and *Germany in Autumn* are constructed.[66] Accordingly, the radical historiographical practice both represented in – and cultivated by – *The Patriot* is not oriented toward a particular endpoint, but channels its energies toward the cleaving open of a series of gaps in the official account of German history within which the possibilities of both the past and the future can be re-imagined and re-explored.

In more general terms, what is significant about the rejuvenation of the capacity for imagination cultivated by Kluge's film and literary work is not only the degree to which it can free us from conceiving of the past and the present as two points bound together by "necessity" but, moreover, the extent to which this capacity for imagination can be brought to bear on the exigencies of the present itself – a present within which the

63. See the section entitled "Construction Site" in "One-Way Street", in: Benjamin: Selected Writings, Vol. 1, ed. by Marcus Bullock/Michael W. Jennings, Cambridge, Mass. and London, England: Harvard University Press 1996, pp. 449-450.

64. "Interview", in: Rainer Lewandowski: Die Filme von Alexander Kluge, p. 42.

65. Bevers, Jürgen et al.: "'Eine Baustelle ist vorteilhafter als ganze Häuser': Ein Gespräch mit Alexander Kluge", Spuren: Zeitschrift für Kunst und Gesellschaft, No. 1 (Februar/März, 1980), p. 17.

66. "The sharpest ideology", p. 24.

destruction of lives and the demolition of cities is too often described as an “unfortunate side-effect” of history’s so-called march of progress toward a better world.

Chapter 7: Raw Materials for the Imagination: Kluge's Work for Television

As Christian Schröder has argued in his review of Alexander Kluge's television programs, tuning in to watch Kluge's work on late night German television is akin to the experience of stumbling upon a literary bookshop in the middle of a red-light district.[1] Wedged between the pornographic movies, crime thrillers, and live competition and shopping programs which constitute the regular evening fare on the commercial stations, Kluge's *10 vor 11 (10 to 11)*, *News and Stories*, *Mitternachtsmagazin* (*Midnight Magazine*), and *Primetime Spätausgabe* (*Prime Time Late Edition*) certainly strike the viewer as strange anomalies. Constructed, in a similar vein to his films, out of a highly diverse collection of raw materials (including photographs, drawings, diagrams, clips from movies, and documentary footage), Kluge's programs are – in both their form and content – certainly unlike anything on German television.

Organised predominantly around interviews with writers, artists, musicians, filmmakers, academics, and directors from both theatre and opera[2], the aim of the programs is to provide what Kluge describes as "cultural windows" for the "old media" within the comparatively "new" medium of television. These interviews (which provide the backbone for

---

1. Christian Schröder: "Das etwas andere Autoren-Fernsehen", Der Tagesspiegel, November 1 (1991).

2. Over the years, these figures have included (to name just a few) Volker Schlöndorff, Christa Wolf, Jean-Luc Godard, Pierre Boulez, Konzaburo Oe, Sophie Rois, Helke Sander, Theo Angelopolous, Jörg Immendorf, Hannelore Hoger, Romuald Karmaker, Wong Kar-Wai, Claude Chabrol, and Werner Herzog, as well as regulars such as Heiner Müller, Oskar Negt, Christoph Schlingensief, Miriam Hansen, Manfred Osten, Joseph Vogl, Joachim Kersten. Ulrike Sprenger, Peter Berling, and Dirk Baeker.

the majority of Kluge's programs) are, however, unlike those conducted on other cultural magazine programs – a format which has become increasingly popular on German television.[3] Although the basic structure of Kluge's work for television resembles the interview format characteristic of these programs, the interviewer (a role regularly performed by Kluge himself) remains predominantly off-screen – his presence marked only by the highly enthusiastic voice guiding and animating the discussions. Although these conversations are organised around the discussion of a particular theme, topic, or event (such as a documentary about techno, Werner Schroeter's staging of an opera by Bellini, the unfinished film projects of Rainer Werner Fassbinder, Siegfried Kracauer's writings on film and mass culture, or the ideas of Deleuze and Foucault[4]) the discussions frequently shoot off in directions that would not appear to be related to the topic in question. Although prompted in large part by Kluge's highly imaginative and, at times, somewhat abstruse mode of questioning, these digressions are also fuelled by the quotes and intertitles which intersperse the shots of the interviewees in conversation – the comments of whom are further complicated, not only by the questions and statements that scroll across the bottom of the screen, but by the manner in which Kluge fragments, duplicates, and rotates the many photographs, diagrams, and other images which flash up throughout the course of the discussion. (See Figure 3).

---

3. For an analysis of Kluge's programs within the broader context of the history of magazine programs in Germany, see Knut Hickethier: "Von anderen Erfahrungen in der Fernsehöffentlichkeit. Alexander Kluges Kulturmagazine und die Fernsehgeschichte", in: Kluges Fernsehen. Alexander Kluges Kulturmagazine, ed. by Christian Schulte/Winfried Siebers, Frankfurt am Main: Suhrkamp 2002, pp. 195-219. This book will hereafter be referred to as Kluges Fernsehen.

4. "196 bpm – Romuald Karmaker filmt Tekknokönig DJ Hell" ("196 beats per minute – Romuald Karmaker films techno king DJ Hell"), Primetime Spätausgabe, RTL (September 14, 2003), "Die Tochter des Miraculix – Vincenzo Bellini's geniale Oper 'Norma'" ("The daughter of Miraculix – Vincenzo Bellini's ingenious opera 'Norma'"), News and Stories, SAT 1 (September 7, 2003), "Fassbinders Gesammelte Hinterlassenschaften" ("Fassbinder's collected legacies"), News and Stories, SAT 1 (September 16, 2001), "Organisiertes Glück" ("Organised Happiness"), News and Stories, SAT 1 (September 19, 1994), "Baustellen der Macht – die französischen Philosophen Foucault und Deleuze über die 'Rhizome der Gewalt'" ("Construction sites of Power – the French philosophers Foucault and Deleuze on the 'rhizome of violence'"), 10 vor 11, RTL (November 10, 2003).

Figure 3: Images from Kluge's television programs.

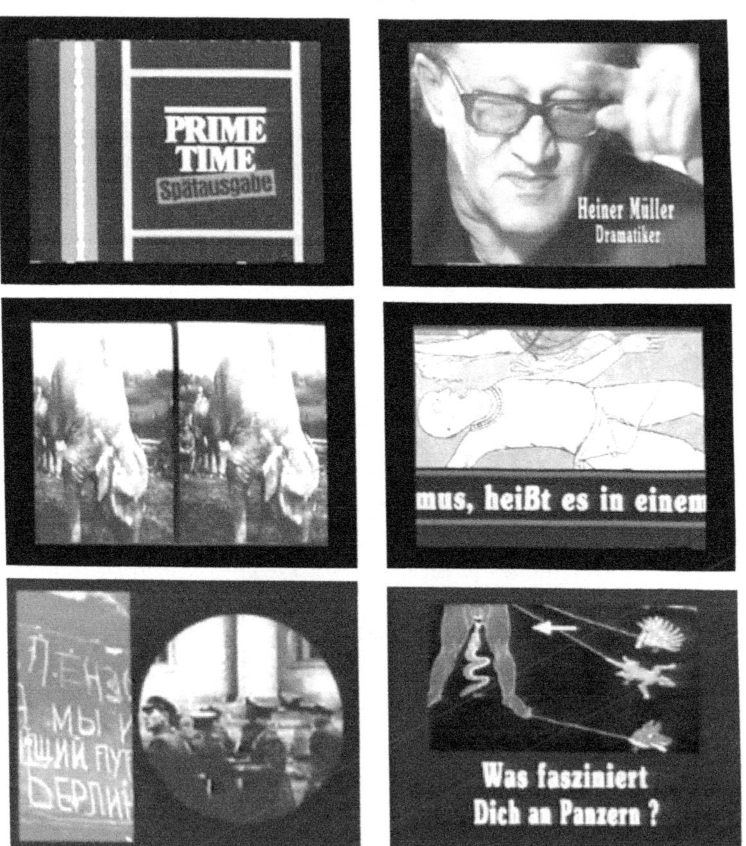

© Alexander Kluge

Even more surprising, however, than the form and content of the programs themselves is the fact that they have, following the establishment of Kluge's DCTP (Development Company for Television Programs) in 1988, been variously broadcast on SAT 1, RTL and VOX – three of the major commercial channels on German television[5]. The roots of this

5. As Matthias Uecker has outlined in his study of Kluge's television programs, DCTP (which is owned jointly by Kluge (50%), *Spiegel-Verlag* (12.5%), and the Japanese advertising agency *Dentsu* (37.5%)) developed out of the *Arbeitsgemeinschaft für Kabel- und Satellitenprogramme*, an organisation established by Kluge (together with book publishers, film directors, and theatre executives) in an

strange alliance can be traced back to 1984 to the establishment of a "dual broadcasting" system in West Germany which saw the introduction of private (commercial) stations alongside ARD and ZDF – the two existing public service channels which had been established in 1953 and 1961 under the aegis of a "commitment to truth, impartiality, and balance and diversity of opinion".[6] In an attempt to preserve (at least, in part) these public service ideals in the face of what it viewed as the onslaught of commercial television, in 1997 the Social Democratic government (SPD) of Nord-Rhein Westfalen instituted a new broadcasting law which stated that commercial stations seeking to gain a broadcasting licence for the state would have to provide programming slots or "window programs" ("*Fensterprogramme*") for independent cultural producers.

Benefitting from this law (and, indeed, from Kluge's profile in Germany as a highly regarded filmmaker and author), in 1988 DCTP was – together with SAT 1 and RTL (then RTL plus) – granted joint broadcasting licences that provided DCTP with weekly program slots within the broader context of the commercial channels; the strict independence of which was, and continues to be, safeguarded by the licensing contract. The result has been that, with the exception of his *Mitternachtsmagazin* (which screens on VOX) Kluge's programs enjoy the extremely rare privilege of occupying regular spaces on the commercial channels which are completely free of commercials.

Needless to say, this carving out of a space within the commercial channels for the creation of what Kluge has described as "*Autoren-Fern-*

attempt to create a "niche" for the so-called "old media" within the sphere of commercial television. The program Die Stunde der Filmemacher (The Hour of the Filmmakers), which first screened on SAT 1 in 1985, developed out of this alliance, and showcased programs produced by German filmmakers which were overseen by Kluge, who served as executive producer). For a detailed account of the events which led to the establishment of these companies, see Chapter 1.3: "Prinzip Gegenproduktion: Alexander Kluge's 'Development Company for Television Programs (DCTP)'", in: Matthias Uecker: Anti-Fernsehen? Alexander Kluges Fernsehproduktionen, Marburg: Schüren 2000, pp. 48-63. Hereafter referred to as Anti-Fernsehen? For an overview in English, see Peter C. Lutze: Alexander Kluge: The Last Modernist, Detroit: Wayne State University Press 1998, pp. 180-184.

6. Peter J. Humphreys: Media and Media Policy in Germany: The Press and Broadcasting since 1945 (Second Edition), Oxford and Providence: Berg 1994, p. 165. For a detailed account of the public service ideals of ARD and ZDF, see pp. 148-152 and 164-168 respectively.

sehen" ("Author's television"), has caused a stir with the directors of the commercial host–stations, including the former head of RTL Helmut Thoma, who has described Kluge as a "ratings killer" who makes "stone--age television"[7]. In critical reviews of Kluge's programs, the so-called "prehistoric" character of his work is often invoked, not only to describe the simple, hand-made quality of the programs (which are produced on a small budget by Kluge and a working team of three or four people) but to question whether the programs are of a suitable calibre to be shown on television at all. Mark Siemons, for example, has argued that Kluge's programs "appear to have absolutely nothing to do with television". "The sound quality", he writes,

> is bad, the questions don't get to the point, things are spoken so quickly that one can hardly follow, and once images appear with which one can draw connections with previously seen material, they are then alienated through doublings, prismatic refractions or incomprehensible blocks of text [*Texttafeln*]. 'That is loveless cobbled-together stuff', say RTL- co-workers.[8]

Anyone, however, who is familiar with the many years of lobbying and negotiations that have enabled Kluge to cleave open a space for his own work (and, indeed, the work of countless others) on German television would know that his programs are not "loveless", "cobbled-together" constructions, but rather the fruit of a longstanding commitment to the creation of alternative forms of communication within the sphere of commercial television.[9] The significance of Kluge's programs (the

---

7. Quoted in Christian Schulte and Winfried Siebers: "Vorwort", in: Kluges Fernsehen, p. 8. Despite Thoma's claim, Kluge argues that his programs often attract over one million viewers. See Astrid Deuber-Mankowsky and Giaco Schiesser: "In der Echtzeit der Gefühle: Gespräch mit Alexander Kluge", in: Die Schrift an der Wand. Alexander Kluge: Rohstoffe und Materialien, ed. by Christian Schulte, Osnabrück: Universitätsverlag Rasch 2000, p. 365. For a detailed breakdown of the ratings figures for Kluge's programs in the first quarter of 1994, see Anti-Fernsehen?, p. 62.

8. Mark Siemons: "Zwölftonmusik im Zirkus: Das Fernsehen Alexander Kluges", in: Fernsehen. Medien, Macht und Märkte, ed. by Helmut Monkenbusch, Reinbeck bei Hamburg: Rowohlt Taschenbuch 1994, p. 108.

9. For an account of Kluge's efforts in this regard, see Gertrud Koch and Heide Schlüpmann: "'Nur Trümmern trau ich [...]': Ein Gespräch mit Alexander Kluge", in: Kanalarbeit: Medienstrategien im Kulturwandel, ed. by Hans Ulrich Reck, Basel and Frankfurt am Main: Stroemfeld/Roter Stern 1998.

form and content of which, far from being arbitrary, is intimately bound with his alternative conception of the possibilities of the medium) can, however, only be fully appreciated when viewed in the light of his long-standing criticism of the monodimensional, information-heavy content of programs which, he argues, have dominated (and continue to dominate) the perceived role and function of the medium.

7.1 Information, Storytelling, and Experience

In *Public Sphere and Experience* (a book which Kluge wrote together with Oskar Negt in the early 1970s[10]) the authors draw implicitly on Benjamin's criticism of the information driven content of modern forms of communication in their criticism of the manner in which television programs such as news broadcasts both address, and communicate with, their audience.[11] Central to Benjamin's analysis of the rise of information as a means of communication is the decline in both the art of storytelling, and the communicability of experience, with which he argues this rise is intimately associated. For both Benjamin and Kluge, what is significant about storytelling as a mode of communication is the extent to which the storyteller is able to recount a tale in such a way that its meaning is not communicated to the listener directly. In a fashion reminiscent of Kluge's delineation of the task of a radical cinema, Benjamin argues that "it is half the art of storytelling to keep a story free from explanation as one reproduces it".[12] "The most extraordinary things, marvellous things", he writes, "are related with the greatest accuracy, but the psychological connection of the events is not forced on the reader".[13] Rather, the tale is recounted in a manner that prompts the listener to draw on his or her own experience and imagination in an attempt to fill out the contours of the story.

10. Oskar Negt and Alexander Kluge: Public Sphere and Experience: Toward an Analysis of the Bourgeois and Proletarian Public Sphere, London and Minneapolis: University of Minnesota Press 1993. Hereafter referred to as Public Sphere and Experience.

11. Walter Benjamin: "The Storyteller: Reflections on the Works of Nikolai Leskov", in: Benjamin: Illuminations, ed. by Hannah Arendt, London: Fontana Press 1992, pp. 83-107. Hereafter referred to as "The Storyteller".

12. "The Storyteller", p. 89.

13. Ibid.

In stark contrast, Benjamin argues that the "prime requirement" of information "is that it appear 'understandable in itself'" – a quality which, in "lay[ing] claim to prompt verifiability", is clearly at odds with "the spirit of storytelling".[14] Taking the form and content of daily newspapers as his prime example, Benjamin argues that the "replacement of the older narration by information [...] reflects the increasing atrophy of experience".[15] "Every morning", he writes,

> brings us the news of the globe, and yet we are poor in noteworthy stories. This is because no event any longer comes to us without already being shot through with explanation. In other words, by now almost nothing that happens benefits storytelling; almost everything benefits information.[16]

In keeping with his analysis, in "Some Motifs in Baudelaire", of the modern decline in the capacity "to assimilate data of the world [...] by way of [one's] experience"[17], Benjamin argues that "[i]f it were the intention of the press to have the reader assimilate the information it supplies as part of his own experience, it would not achieve its purpose"[18]. "But its intention", he claims:

14. Ibid., p. 88. "The value of information", he writes, "does not survive the moment in which it was new. It lives only at that moment; it has to surrender to it completely and explain itself to it without losing any time. A story is different. It does not expend itself. It preserves and concentrates its strength and is capable of releasing it even after a long time". pp. 89-90.

15. Walter Benjamin: "Some Motifs in Baudelaire", in: Benjamin: Charles Baudelaire: A Lyric Poet in the Era of High Capitalism, London and New York: Verso 1997, p. 113.

16. "The Storyteller", p. 89. See also Benjamin's short piece "The Handkerchief" (1932) which anticipates his criticism of newspapers in "The Storyteller" by way of a story about his discussion with a sea captain: "'You can learn nothing from the papers', he said. 'They always want to explain everything to you.' And in fact isn't it half the art of journalism to keep the news free of explanations? And didn't the ancients set an example for us by presenting events, as it were, dry, draining them entirely of psychological explanations and opinions of every sort?" Benjamin: Selected Writings, Vol. 2, ed. by Michael W. Jennings/Howard Eiland/Gary Smith, Cambridge, Mass. and London, England: Harvard University Press 1999, pp. 659-660.

17. "Some Motifs in Baudelaire", p. 112.

18. Ibid.

> is just the opposite, and it is achieved to isolate what happens from the realm in which it could affect the experience of the reader. The principles of journalistic information (freshness of the news, brevity, comprehensibility, and, above all, lack of connection between the individual news items) contribute as much to this as does the make-up of the pages and the paper's style.[19]

In a similar vein to Benjamin, Negt and Kluge argue in *Public Sphere and Experience* that the emphasis on brevity and the cultivation of immediate comprehension characteristic of television news broadcasts impacts negatively, not only on the viewer's capacity to assimilate news items by way of his or her own experience, but on the viewer's ability to conceive of the meaning of a particular situation or event outside of the terms within which it has been framed by the program. "A sensational news item", they argue,

> is broadcast; but it is not accompanied by programs that might meaningfully interpret this news in the light of social contradictions or develop it in relation to the viewer's own experience. It is only on such a broadened basis that grief, sympathy, incorporation into a historical context, or an autonomous reaction by the viewer become possible. [...] Insofar as experiences do manage to penetrate the items on the evening news, they are, in the commentaries, translated into an esoteric language that promotes the rapid consumption of events.[20]

The alternative conception of the possibilities of the medium outlined in *Public Sphere and Experience* takes as its starting point the need to replace

19. Ibid.

20. Public Sphere and Experience, p. 108. Like Benjamin, Negt and Kluge argue that the inability to assimilate information presented by news broadcasts by way of one's experience is further enhanced by the "hodgepodge selection of news items: A train crash, a strike in Italy, the death of a philosopher, the abduction of a young girl, a controversy about the Deutsche mark (appearing in the form of a point-counterpoint between two politicians), a weather report, and so on – all of these items contain, in and of themselves, genuine information, but this information is cut off from its real social roots". p. 119. See also Siegfried Kracauer's 1928 analysis of newsreels and the "hodgepodge" of "shots of ship christenings, destructive fires, sports events, parades, and idyllic scenes of children and animals" out of which they were constructed. Kracauer: "Film 1928", in: Kracauer: The Mass Ornament: Weimar Essays, ed. by Thomas Y. Levin, Cambridge, Mass. and London, England: Harvard University Press 1995, p. 311.

the "monologue"[21] format of information-heavy programs such as news broadcasts with program formats that are genuinely organized around mobilising the participation of the viewer. Drawing on Bertolt Brecht's 1932 analysis of the extent to which radio could be "transformed from an apparatus of distribution into one of communication"[22], Negt and Kluge argue that "the foundation of a possible emancipatory development of television" must be organized around the creation of the "self-determination of [its] viewers".[23] "Radio", Brecht argues,

> would be the greatest conceivable communication apparatus of public life, an enormous system of channels, that is, it would be this if it were to understand how to not only transmit, but also receive, in other words, how to make the listener not only hear but also speak, and how to bring him into the relationship instead of isolating him.[24]

In a similar vein to his delineation of the collaborative nature of the spectatorial relationship cultivated by *Autorenfilm*, Kluge (following Brecht) argues that the greater the degree of reciprocity between the viewer and the program on screen, the more effective the program is in generating a public sphere within which viewers are encouraged to participate in the meaning making process surrounding issues, events and ideas that impact on their own concerns, experiences, and interests.[25]

---

21. Public Sphere and Experience, p. 114.

22. Brecht quoted in Public Sphere and Experience, note 9, p. 103, and Brecht: "The Radio as a Communicative Apparatus", in: Bertolt Brecht on Film and Radio, ed. by Marc Silberman, London: Methuen 2001, pp. 41-46.

23. Public Sphere and Experience, p. 103.

24. Brecht quoted in Public Sphere and Experience, note 9, pp. 103-4, and Brecht: "The Radio as a Communications Apparatus", p. 42. See also Hans Magnus Enzensberger: "Constituents of a theory of the media", New Left Review, No. 64 (Nov/Dec, 1970) in which Brecht's analysis of the possibilities of radio is employed to make a similar argument about the possibilities of television. See also Walter Benjamin's short piece "Reflections on the Radio" which opens with the statement: "The crucial failing of this institution [the radio] has been to perpetuate the fundamental separation between practitioners and the public, a separation which is at odds with its technological basis". Benjamin: Selected Writings, Vol. 2, p. 543.

25. See, for example, "In der Echtzeit der Gefühle: Gespräch mit Alexander Kluge", p. 361.

For Negt and Kluge, one of the greatest obstacles to the cultivation of such a public sphere is what they describe as the "problem of *television realism*".[26] In keeping with Kluge's analysis of the degree to which our capacity to conceive of the possibilities of both the past and the future is foreclosed by historical narratives that describe particular outcomes and occurrences as "necessary" and/or "realistic", Negt and Kluge argue that the tightly organised, unambiguous manner in which news items are packaged on television news broadcasts naturalises the occurrences being represented – providing the viewer with the impression that it is not possible to do anything to change the current situation.[27]

A staunch critic of the manner in which such packaging prohibits us from conceiving of the extent to which things could, in fact, be very different, Kluge argues that an emancipatory television practice would channel its energies toward stimulating the imagination of the audience into reconceiving the possibilities of the present. In the realm of the imagination, he argues,

> [t]he obstacles of reality cease to exist. If the imagination has good reasons to disregard these real obstacles – as a compensation for the reality principle – then the question is how can one, for the sake of whatever cause, encourage the imagination to develop such perspectives on it (ie. perspectives different from those inherent in things as they are). In documentary film this could only be realized via a mixing of forms – the only method which permits radical changes in perspective.[28]

In keeping with Kluge's analysis of the active spectatorial relationship cultivated by the loosely woven, mixed form characteristic of his films, Negt and Kluge argue that "the artisanal production of individual items"[29]

26. Public Sphere and Experience, p. 128.

27. One can detect the influence of Theodor W. Adorno's analysis of magazine stories in Kluge's delineation of "the problem of television realism". Such stories, Adorno writes, "teach their readers that one has to be 'realistic', that one has to give up romantic ideas, that one has to adjust oneself at any price, and that nothing more can be expected of any individual". Adorno: "How to look at television", in: Adorno: The Culture Industry: Selected Essays on Mass Culture, ed. by J.M. Bernstein, London: Routledge 1991, p. 141.

28. Kluge: "On Film and the Public Sphere", New German Critique, No. 24-25 (Fall/Winter, 1981-2), p. 215. Translation modified. See "Die Rolle der Phantasie", in: Klaus Eder and Alexander Kluge: Ulmer Dramaturgien.Reibungsverluste, München and Wien: Carl Hanser 1980, pp. 62-63.

29. Public Sphere and Experience, p. 114.

is more effective in cultivating the imagination and participation of the television audience. For Benjamin, too, it is the simple, handspun quality of the storyteller's tales that is essential to their capacity to engage an audience. "In fact", Benjamin writes, "one can go on and ask oneself whether the relationship of the storyteller to his material, human life, is not in itself a craftsman's relationship, whether it is not his very task to fashion the raw material of experience, his own and that of others, in a solid, useful and unique way".[30]

In the light of these comments, one can begin to get a sense of the extent to which some of the key criticisms that have been levelled at certain characteristics of Kluge's television programs (such as the loose, handcrafted quality of the work, and the perceived inability of the programs to "get to the point") are actually characteristics which are central to Negt and Kluge's alternative conception of the possibilities of television as a medium: a medium which – instead of bombarding the viewer with preprocessed units of information – would actively encourage the audience to draw on their own imagination and experience in an attempt to engage with the materials on screen.

7.2 Raw Materials for the Imagination

In a 1996 episode of the aptly titled *News and Stories* (a forty-five minute program which is broadcast on SAT 1 on Monday evenings) Kluge evokes an image of television that is in keeping with the delineation of the shortcomings of the medium outlined in *Public Sphere and Experience.* The episode in question is entitled "Detonation Deutschland/ Sprengbilder einer Nation von Julian Rosefeldt und Piero Steinle" ("Detonation Germany/Explosive images of a nation by Julian Rosefeldt and Piero Steinle")[31], and revolves around a discussion between Kluge and two German artists – the recent work of whom includes "Detonation Deutschland": an installation of video footage depicting the state-sanctioned demolition of a number of historically and/or architecturally significant buildings in Germany. (See Figure 4).

Towards the end of the program (and over an intertitle announcing "Detonation Deutschland" as the third project of Rosefeldt and Steinle) Kluge asks the latter (who subsequently appears in medium close-up) whether the remains of a demolition typically consist of "raw material"

30. "The Storyteller", p. 107.

31. News and Stories, SAT 1 (July 8, 1996).

Figure 4: Images from "Detonation Deutschland/Sprengbilder einer Nation von Julian Rosefeldt und Piero Steinle"

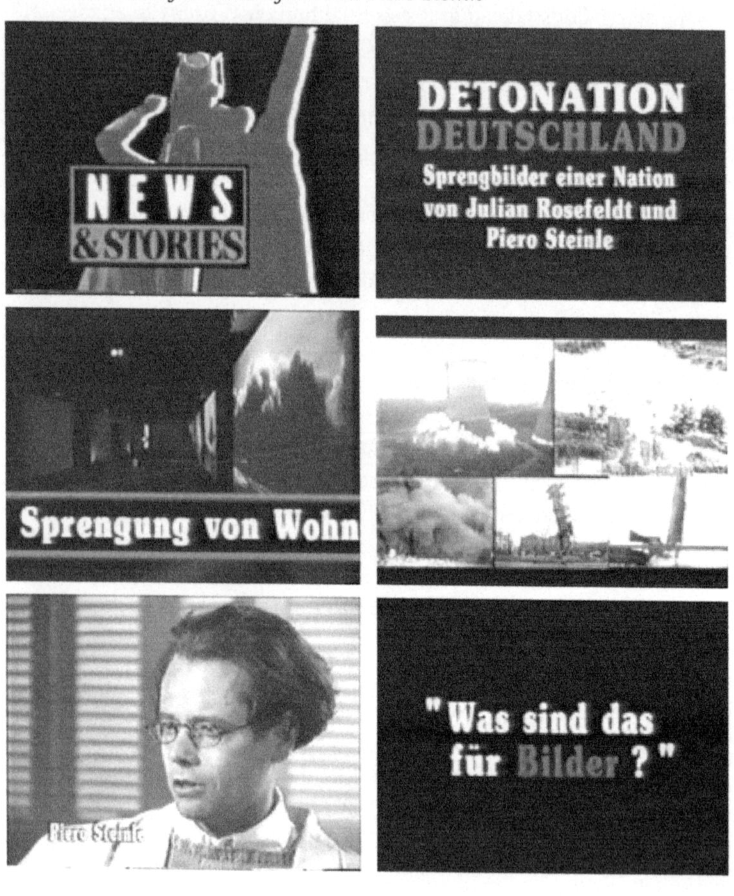

© Alexander Kluge

("*Rohstoff*"), or whether it is "scrap metal and rubbish" ("*Schrott und Schutt*") that remain after such an explosion. After listening to Steinle (who confirms that, "as a matter of principle", it is scrap metal and rubbish which constitute the remains of a demolition) Kluge enthusiastically suggests that television, too, could be likened to such an explosion.[32] Although located off-screen, Kluge's highly enthusiastic presence is reflected in the somewhat bewildered, politely smiling face of Steinle, who

32. See also Uecker's analysis of this discussion in Anti-Fernsehen?, p. 100.

pauses uncomfortably before seeking to respond to Kluge's observation. Although cryptic within the immediate context of the program, viewers familiar with Kluge's conception of the task of a radical cinema would have already drawn a connection between his observations about the installation, and his frequent likening of his own films to "construction sites" or buildings in process[33] – the unfinished, open structure of which encourages the spectator to engage creatively with the raw materials out of which films such as *The Patriot* and *The Power of Feelings* are constructed.

In the context of the program, Kluge's likening of television to an explosion that produces scrap metal and rubbish (rather than the raw materials favoured by Kluge) could be said to echo his and Negt's negative delineation of the closed-off, monodimensional content of information-heavy programs elaborated in *Public Sphere and Experience*. Indeed, in stark contrast to these programs, Kluge's work for television does not provide the audience with preprocessed units of information which – like the scrap metal and rubbish left behind after a demolition – cannot easily be incorporated into new constructions (nor the structures of meaning generated in the spectator's head which are frequently discussed by Kluge[34]). Rather, in keeping with both Kluge's delineation of the task of a radical cinema, and the call – in *Public Sphere and Experience* – for program formats that are genuinely organised around mobilising the participation of the audience, Kluge's television programs are constructed out of a diverse collection of raw materials – the unfinished, open structure of which encourages the spectator to draw upon his/her own experience and imagination in an attempt to fill out the contours of the program.

The central device employed by Kluge for generating these raw materials is the interview format around which the majority of his programs are constructed.[35] What is unique about these interviews (which

---

33. See, for example, Jürgen Bevers et al.: "'Eine Baustelle ist vorteilhafter als ganze Häuser': Ein Gespräch mit Alexander Kluge", Spuren: Zeitschrift für Kunst und Gesellschaft, No. 1 (Februar/März, 1980), p. 17.

34. See, for example, Alexander Kluge: "Pact with a Dead Man", in: West German Filmmakers on Film: Visions and Voices, ed. by Eric Rentschler, New York and London: Holmes and Meier, 1988, p. 236, and Edgar Reitz, Alexander Kluge, and Wilfried Reinke: "Word and Film", October, No. 46 (Fall, 1988), p. 87.

35. Although the interview serves as an anchor for the majority of Kluge's programs, a significant number of the programs do not feature interviews, but are constructed out of a diverse montage of materials (such as photographs, dia-

typically take place in busy public spaces such as bars, cafes, theatres, museums or, alternatively, in the storeroom of Kluge's Munich office) is the dynamic way in which Kluge as interviewer seeks to engage the interviewee in a conversation which ricochets imaginatively between a broad range of topics while seeking to address the complexity of the issue in question. In the majority of these interviews, it is Kluge's highly enthusiastic mode of questioning which sets the tone of the conversation, and which ensures that the topic is addressed from multiple perspectives. Although this is sometimes achieved through the presentation of interviews with a range of different subjects[36], these multiple perspectives are more regularly generated by Kluge himself who demonstrates, what Christian Schulte has described as, the "extraordinary capacity, through unexpected changes in perspective, to [both] stimulate [...] the imagination of his dialogue partner", and to "set his capacity for memory into action".[37]

The example provided by Schulte (which is taken from one of the many dynamic interviews that Kluge conducted with Heiner Müller[38]) is an interesting example of the way in which Kluge's curious mode of questioning animates the conversation by seeking to ignite the associative and imaginative capacities of his interview partner. In this particular

---

grams, clips from films, quotes, and electronically generated images) which address a particular theme or topic. See, for example, "Das Xmas Project" ("The Xmas Project"), 10 vor 11, RTL (December 12, 1993), "Darwins Waltzer", Primetime Spätausgabe, RTL (August 26, 1990), and "Jahresüberblick" ("Overview of the year"), News and Stories, SAT 1 (January 3, 1994).

36. See, for example, "Ein Straßenbahnfahrt durch eine Stadt in den neuen Bundesländen" ("A tram ride through a city in the new federal states"), 10 vor 11, RTL (March 9, 1992). In this program (which provides a portrait of the history of tram travel in Halberstadt) these multiple perspectives are generated through discussions with a range of interviewees, including a tram driver, transport superintendent, mechanic, passenger, and town chronicler.

37. Christian Schulte: "Fernsehen und Eigensinn", in: Kluges Fernsehen, p. 78.

38. "Im Zeichnen des Mars" ("In the Sign of Mars"), Primetime Spätausgabe, RTL (January 23 1994). This interview, and several others with Müller, have been published in two volumes. See Alexander Kluge and Heiner Müller: "Ich schulde der Welt einen Toten": Gespräche, Hamburg: Rotbuch 1996, and Alexander Kluge and Heiner Müller: "Ich bin ein Landvermesser": Gespräche mit Heiner Müller, Hamburg: Rotbuch 1996. The interview in question appears as "Charakterpanzer und Bewegungskrieg" in: Ich Schulde der Welt einen Toten: Gespräche, pp. 85-91.

example, the process begins with Kluge enthusiasically encouraging Müller to describe "the moon" to the television audience:

Müller: The first thing would be that the moon is something that one shouldn't walk on. All other planets first, then the moon. The moon is something that one shouldn't colonise, shouldn't touch, one should simply let it stand, the way it is, or let it continue, the way it is. I'm saying this now in a very associative fashion [...]
Kluge: But how would you begin to narrate the moon, would you begin with the sun, would you begin with the planets, would you begin with the stars? You have begun: It should not be walked on. I find that very consequential, but attempt to describe, to describe to a stranger, what it is.
Müller: With the moon, one has something that one needs to sleep. It is something that one needs to know what time it is, where one can sleep.[39]

As is revealed in the discussion that follows, the moon also plays an important role in an unpublished poem written by Müller, the recollection of which leads him (via a childhood memory) to recall his first experience of politics:

Müller: And I remember, 1934, it was nearly evening, the bells rang in this village [...] because Hindenburg had died. And that was very strange, that was actually my first experience of politics or history. I noticed that it was something like a decisive point [*Einschnitt*] for the adults. Something had come to an end, some kind of protection or[...].
Kluge: A sense of security [...]
Müller: [...] a sense of security was gone, and a sense of agitation, a sense of fear were there, and everyone stood completely dumb at the fence and heard the bells.
Kluge: And what does that have to do with the moon?
Müller: For me, that has something to do with the moon. I don't know why, I can't give reasons for that now. The moon was a source of agitation, but also a source of security.[40]

---

39. "Charakterpanzer und Bewegungskrieg" in: Ich Schulde der Welt einen Toten: Gespräche, pp. 88-89.

40. Ibid., pp. 90-91. Sections of this interview are also quoted in "Fernsehen und Eigensinn", p. 76-78. See also Kluge's interview with Jeff Mills – "Jeff Mills/Godfather des Techno"), News and Stories, SAT 1 (September 7, 1998) – which is also partly animated by a mutual fascination with the solar system. A transcript of this interview has been published in Alexander Kluge: Verdeckte

Although the mode of questioning demonstrated by Kluge in this passage is typical of the highly associative, imaginative manner in which interviews are conducted on his programs, not all of Kluge's interviewees demonstrate Müller's willingness to partake in a conversation that is continually shifting in its parameters and focus. Jean-Luc Godard, for example (whom Kluge interviewed in 1990 at a press conference for the release of Godard's *Nouvelle Vague*[41]), responded in an impatient and somewhat indifferent fashion to Kluge's curious line of questioning, resulting in a one-way conversation that was stilted and uninspiring in its awkwardness.[42]

In more general terms, it is also true to say that a number of figures who appear on Kluge's programs exhibit signs of frustration when their answers and/or explanations are re-diverted by Kluge, preventing them from being able to communicate their ideas in a manner which is systematic and linear in orientation. Indeed, such frustration appears to be particularly pronounced when it becomes clear that the direction in which Kluge is diverting the conversation leads directly to his own area of interest and/or expertise – a tendency that could, at times, be said to stunt (rather than stimulate) the imaginative and associative capacities of his interview partner.[43]

Kluge does not, however, conceive of the interview format as a fo-

---

Ermittlung: Ein Gespräch mit Christian Schulte und Rainer Stollmann, Berlin: Merve 2001, pp. 127-139.

41. "Wie in der Liebe: 'Keine Erklärungen'/Magazin zu Godards 60. Geburtstag" ("Just like in love: 'No explanations'/Magazine for Godard's sixtieth birthday"), 10 vor 11, RTL (March 12, 1990).

42. The questions posed by Kluge in the interview revolve around what Godard's parents did for a living, and whether he could describe the wallpaper and the position of the bed in his childhood bedroom. Surprised and unimpressed by Kluge's line of questioning, Godard simply responds by stating that it would take too long – and require too much effort – to answer such questions.

43. Uecker goes a step further, arguing that Kluge's "way of steering the conversation in the direction of his own interests can at times appear aggressive, even violent, rather than just persistent; for example, when he loses patience with an opera singer and starts to explain the character of Wozzeck in Alban Berg's opera to him rather than giving him a chance to make any more statements". Matthias Uecker: "'Für Kultur ist es nie zu spät!'- Alexander Kluge's Television Productions", in: "Whose Story?": Continuities in contemporary German-language literature, ed. by Arthur Williams et al., Bern: Peter Lang 1998, p. 345. See also Uecker's discussion of this topic in Anti-Fernsehen?, p. 109.

rum within which the interviewee is simply required to rehearse his or her fully formed ideas about a particular topic for the benefit of an attentive television audience.[44] Indeed, the interviews conducted on Kluge's programs do not (save those moments in which Kluge himself dominates the conversation) seek to close down meaning by instructing or persuading the audience of the benefits of a certain interpretation of events, or a particular line of thinking. Rather, in keeping with the call for interactivity outlined in *Public Sphere and Experience*, the interviews conducted by Kluge are both dynamic and porous in their structure – prompting both the interviewee *and* the audience to establish their own connections with the raw materials generated by the discussions.

This emphasis on interactivity (which is absolutely crucial for an understanding of the significance of Kluge's television, film, and literary work) is also evident in the highly eclectic "mixed form" of the programs themselves, which (in a manner reminiscent of Kluge's films) are constructed out of a diverse collection of raw materials. Also reminiscent of films such as *The Patriot* and *The Power of Feelings* is the manner in which Kluge employs devices and techniques redolent of early cinema in his attempt to create program formats that are organised around cultivating the active participation of the television audience.[45] In Kluge's programs, these devices (which include a frequent use of intertitles, iris masks to frame the image, the shooting of landscapes from moving vehicles[46], and a liberal use of colour tinting) are supplemented by a plethora of possibilities opened up by digital video (including the layering of image and text through superimposition, the production of complex collage effects created by montage within the frame, the generation and animation of digital images, the employment of scrolling text mes-

44. See, for example, Rainer Lewandowski's interview with Kluge, and Kluge's annoyance at Lewandowski's frequent attempts to draw the conversation back into the direction that he had anticipated when forming his questions. In response to Lewandowski's claim that Kluge's response did not address the point which he had wanted to make, Kluge states that he should focus on participating in the discussion, rather than seeking to "pedagogically" draw out a certain opinion. Die Filme von Alexander Kluge, p. 47.

45. For Kluge's comments on his attempts to "reclaim film history for television", see "In der Echtzeit der Gefühle: Gespräch mit Alexander Kluge", p. 363, and "Nur Trümmern trau ich [...]': Ein Gespräch mit Alexander Kluge", p. 21.

46. See, for example, "Ein Straßenbahnfahrt durch eine Stadt in den neuen Bundesländen", 10 vor 11, RTL (March 9, 1992).

sages to pose questions and display quotes, and the fragmentation, duplication, magnification, and rotation of the image).[47] (See Figure 5).

Figure 5: Images from Kluge's television programs

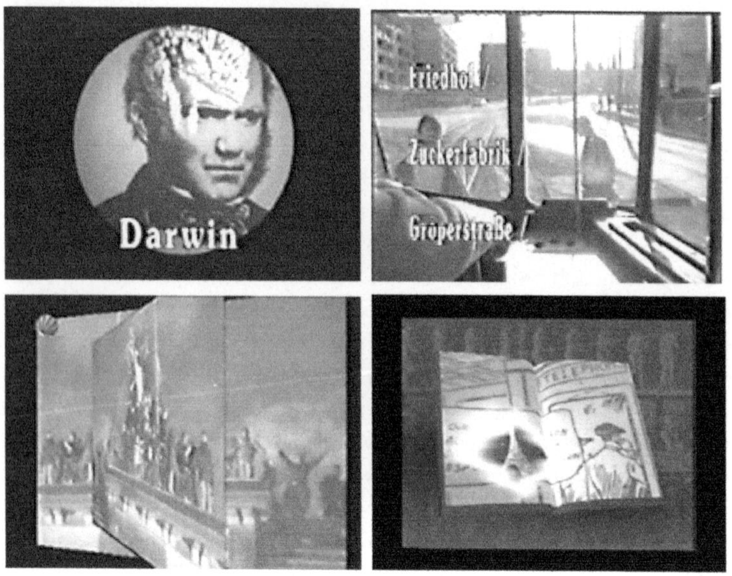

In the opening sequence of "Geisterstunde mit Bildern" ("Ghost-hour with Images")[48], for example, a black and white intertitle announcing the themes of the program (which include "What is real?", "Plato's Cave Parable in *The Republic*", "The 100th Anniversary of the death of Karl Marx", and "The Philosopher in front of the electrical monitor") is followed by an elaborately crafted collage of both still and moving images. The screen is divided into two parts: The right hand section features a monitor which is stacked with yellow tinted books, and which displays a

47. As Uecker has pointed out, it is this manipulation of the image that enables Kluge to incorporate a broad range of materials into his programs without having to seek copyright permission. See Uecker: "'Für Kultur ist es nie zu spät!'- Alexander Kluge's Television Productions", p. 347. See also Arno Makowsky's comments in this regard, to which Uecker also refers: "Der Pate als Quotenkiller", Süddeutsche Zeitung, No. 240, 16-17 October (1993), p. 10.

48. 10 vor 11, RTL (August 27, 1990).

montage of black and white footage of crowd scenes and the public display of Lenin's body, while the left hand section consists of a full-screen montage of black and white footage of planes in bomber formation which is overlaid with iris-framed, red and blue colour-tinted footage of what appears to be army personnel. In the sequence which follows (which is briefly preceded by a montage of still images of iris-framed maps, and a photograph of a bust of Socrates) Oskar Negt is shown seated in a dark room in front of two monitors – both of which display black and white documentary footage of war scenes, including images of burning buildings, and bomber pilots in action. (See Figure 6).

Figure 6: Images from "Geisterstunde mit Bildern"

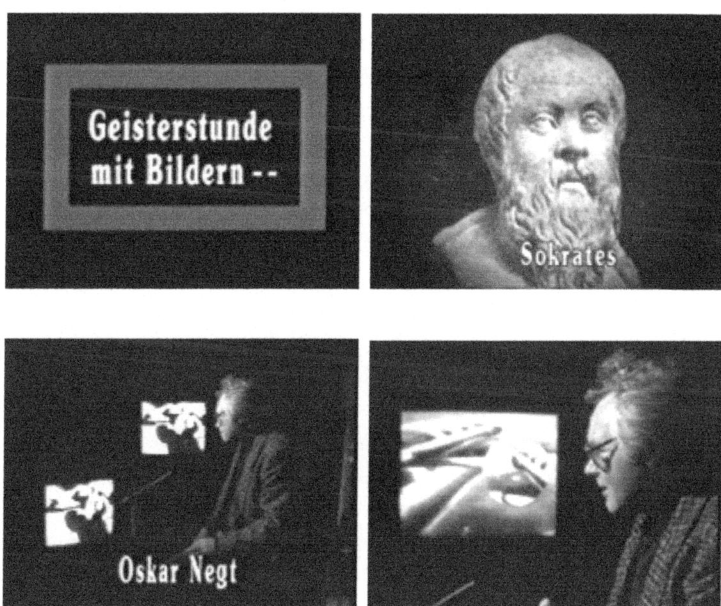

© Alexander Kluge

In a similar vein to the active television viewer envisioned by Negt and Kluge in *Public Sphere and Experience*, Negt uses the raw materials that appear before him on the monitors as springboards for the formation of his own associations, connections, and ideas. These associations (which provide a form of voiceover narration reminiscent of Kluge's films) prompt him to question both the goal of warfare, and the image of reality projected by such images – a train of thought that leads him to a consideration of Plato's cave allegory (in which prisoners mistake the shadows projected on the wall of the cave in which they are imprisoned for reality itself).[49] Pointing to the images of warfare on the monitors, Negt states in a critical tone that, according to Plato, such images are shadows of ideas, and that it is ideas (and not the source of the shadows) which constitute reality – a point which Negt then correlates with Hegel's analysis of the spirit of progress driving world history, stating critically (as he gestures toward the monitors) that it is not the progress of history, nor the progress of consciousness, which is unfolding before us in this footage.

Apart from providing the audience with a model of a highly imaginative, dynamic mode of spectatorship, what is interesting about this sequence is the extent to which Negt's observations and associations speak (albeit in an opaque, condensed fashion) to Kluge's analysis of the extent to which the highly circumscribed image of events presented by the mainstream media actively shapes our understanding of what is appropriate and/or acceptable behaviour, and impacts negatively upon our capacity to conceive of the extent to which an event, or series of events, could in fact have turned out very differently.

In keeping with his criticism of both films and television programs which seek to pedagogically impress their ideas upon the viewing audience, Kluge's work for television does not provide alternative "readings" of topical issues or events, nor do his programs endeavour to channel the observations and associations of viewers into conceiving of the benefits of a particular idea or outcome. Rather, in cleaving open a series of "cultural windows" within the commercial channels for the so-called "old media", Kluge has endeavoured not only to rejuvenate our conception of the possibilities of television as a medium, but to actively encourage the viewing audience to draw on their own imagination and experience in the aid of the creation of different cultural and historical imaginaries.

---

49. See "The Simile of the Cave" in: Plato: The Republic (Part Seven, Book 6), London: Penguin Books 1987, pp. 316-325.

Conclusion

The current amazement that the things we are experiencing are 'still' possible in the twentieth century is not philosophical. This amazement is not the beginning of knowledge – unless it is the knowledge that the view of history which gives rise to it is untenable.
Walter Benjamin[1]

There is a line in our time, and in every time, between those who believe all men are created equal, and those who believe that some men and women and children are expendable in the pursuit of power. There is a line in our time, and in every time, between the defenders of human liberty and those who seek to master the minds and souls of others. Our generation has now heard history's call, and we will answer it.
George W. Bush, The 43rd President of the United States of America[2]

Among the some five hundred (hi)stories contained in Kluge's 2003 book, *Die Lücke, die der Teufel läßt*, is a short, but nonetheless, significant account of a series of events that transpired at the 39th international conference on security policy which took place in Munich in February, 2003. As is the case with most of Kluge's work, the story – which is entitled "*Wenn es hart auf hart kommt, braucht Politik das Unmögliche*" ("When it comes to the crunch, politics needs the impossible") – is constructed out of a diverse collection of fragments, among which is included a short piece which recounts a heated exchange about the then im-

1. "On the Concept of History", in: Benjamin: Selected Writings, Vol. 4, ed. by Howard Eiland/Michael W. Jennings, Cambridge, Mass. and London, England 2003, p. 392.

2. "President's Remarks to the Nation" (Ellis Island, New York: September 11, 2002). Speech available online at the Office of the Press Secretary at the White House: http://www.whitehouse.gov/news/releases/2002/09/20020911-3.html (Last accessed May 21, 2007).

pending war against Iraq between US defence secretary Donald Rumsfeld, and German foreign minister Joschka Fischer.

As described by Kluge (who attended the conference to gather material for his television programs), this heated exchange sprang from Rumsfeld's refusal (upon the invitation of Fischer) to join him on stage while he delivered his report. The German foreign minister, Kluge writes, was so irritated by this refusal "that he could not control the pitch of his voice".[3] Abandoning his prepared speech, Fischer (in an attempt to gain the attention of Rumsfeld) broke into English – stating of the defence secretary's case for war against Iraq: "I am not convinced. That is my problem. I cannot go to the public and say these are the reasons because I don't believe them".[4] According to an observer named Becker (whose thoughts and observations are quoted by Kluge), Fischer's response was delivered in a "'pleading', 'imperious', 'incredulous' tone, all of which [...] is appropriate for a discussion in the personal sphere", adding, however, that it is "totally inappropriate when PERSONAL PRONOUNCEMENTS of this type are rejected by the opposition".[5]

What is significant about Becker's analysis of the inappropriateness of Fischer's comments (which received broad coverage in the international media) is the extent to which they corroborate Kluge's delineation of the degree to which "politics" has come to be understood as a "specialized area" that is divorced from the everyday beliefs, concerns, feelings, and experiences of individuals. Elaborating on this point in 1979 in a speech entitled "The Political as Intensity of Everyday Feelings", Kluge argues that the delayed emotional reaction experienced by Germans in relation to events which took place in Auschwitz is a symptom of this perceived split between the political and personal spheres:

You see, it is thoroughly unpractical if the emotional shock of German families, which would have meant something important for the victims of Auschwitz in 1942, is made up for in 1979; for today it is an essentially useless, that is, timeless form of shock. The fact that we in our country are always shocked at the wrong moments and are not shocked at the right ones – and I am now talking about

---

3. Alexander Kluge: Die Lücke, die der Teufel läßt. Im Umfeld des neuen Jahrhunderts, Frankfurt am Main: Suhrkamp 2003, p. 616.

4. Fischer quoted in Anonymous: "Germany, France work on plan to avert Iraq war", ABC News Online: http://www.abc.net.au/news/newsitems/200302/s779900.htm (Last accessed May 21, 2007).

5. Die Lücke, die der Teufel läßt, p. 616. This emphasis is contained within the text.

something very bad – is a consequence of our considering politics as a specialized area which others look after for us and not as a degree of intensity of our own feelings.[6]

For Kluge, it is the highly abstract manner in which political decisions and events are packaged for public consumption that is largely responsible for the maintenance of this perceived split between political and personal spheres. In a similar vein to the "*aestheticizing of political life*"[7] undertaken by the fascists (whose heinous crimes were, "in the name of progress", viewed as "a historical norm"[8]) George W. Bush's justification of violence and war on the basis that he is answering "history's call" not only naturalises the war against Iraq, but provides the public with the impression that it is not possible to do anything to prevent or change the situation. For within the paradigm outlined by Bush and his cohorts, the US government and its allies are merely the torchbearers of a war that is but a stepping-stone in history's so-called march of progress toward the future.[9]

For Kluge, what is problematic about the historicisation of political events (which regularly takes place in the mainstream media) is not only the extent to which it naturalises their occurrence, but the degree to which it subsumes their specificities under abstract categories (such as "civilization", "freedom", and "progress") about which "our direct senses tell us very little".[10] In an attempt to illustrate this point, Kluge com-

6. Alexander Kluge: "The Political as Intensity of Everyday Feelings", Critical Inquiry, No. 4 (Fall, 1986), p. 126.

7. Walter Benjamin: "The Work of Art in the Age of its Technological Reproducibility", in: Benjamin, Selected Writings, Vol. 4, p. 269.

8. "On the Concept of History", p. 392.

9. See also the speech delivered by Bush at a national prayer service in Washington three days after the events of September 11, 2001: "Just three days removed from these events, Americans do not yet have the distance of history, but our responsibility to history is already clear: to answer these attacks and rid the world of evil". Available online: http:www.whitehouse.gov/nsc/nss3.html (Last accessed May 21, 2007). In his 2002 "State of the Union Address", Bush also states something very similar: "History has called America and our allies to action, and it is both our responsibility and our privilege to fight freedom's fight". See http://www.whitehouse.gov/news/releases/2002/01/2002012911.html (Last accessed May 21, 2007).

10. "The Political as Intensity of Everyday Feelings", p. 121. In his "Paralipomena to 'On the Concept of History'", Benjamin states something similar: "In

pares Friedrich Hölderlin's highly evocative description of a piece of earth in his poem "The Autumn" ("*Der Herbst*") with the account of a section of forest ground contained in a biology textbook; the latter of which (with its description of "16 x 10 to the 57th lice", "10 to the minus 7 foxes and twice 10 to the minus 6 deer"[11]) serves to illustrate what Benjamin describes as the highly abstract, "'scientific' character"[12] of historicist accounts of history.

As Kluge makes clear, what you notice very quickly is that we are dealing here with two very different kinds of languages:

> One is the language of statistics: we deal with our surroundings in an *unsensuous* way, exactly as we do with the real relations in history. And we deal with lyric poetry in a *sensuous* way with our direct sense for what is near. The two fall apart. The big decisions in history are not made in the realm of what we can experience close at hand.[13]

In each of the chapters in this book, what I have endeavoured to demonstrate (via an analysis of topics as diverse as literature, film, photography, historiography, and television) is the extent to which the work of Benjamin, Kracauer, and Kluge is driven by a desire to "fan [...] the spark of hope"[14] in the role that a political film/literary/historiographical/television practice could play in reigniting the link between the world of politics and that which "we can experience close at hand".[15] In contrast to the aestheticisation of politics undertaken by the Nazis (a practice

order for all the moments in the history of humanity to be incorporated in the chain of history, they must be reduced to a common denominator – 'culture', 'enlightenment', 'the objective spirit,' or whatever one wishes to call it". p. 403.

11. "The Political as Intensity of Everyday Feelings", p. 122.

12. "Paralipomena to 'On the Concept of History'", p. 401.

13. "The Political as Intensity of Everyday Feelings", p. 122.

14. "On the Concept of History", p. 391.

15. As Christopher Pavsek has argued, Benjamin's capacity to ignite this link between the political and personal spheres is partly responsible for the appeal of his work. "Benjamin", Pavsek writes, "attracts so many reverent readers because he can, with such poignancy, make politics [...] seem to be a matter of such great personal, emotional concern. And vice-versa, by telescoping the universal into the particular, he manages to evoke the political imbedded in small, personal, everyday matters". See "The Storyteller in the Age of Mechanical Reproduction: Alexander Kluge's Reworking of Walter Benjamin", Found Object, Vol. 1, Issue 2 (1992), p. 90.

which is alive and well in the contemporary media) the role of the filmmaker/writer/historian/television producer is, within this context, not only to put us *back in touch* with the political sphere but, in doing so, to encourage us to draw on our own capacity for imagination and experience in an attempt to rethink the possibilities of both the past and the future outside of the evolutionary conception of history propagated by both historicists, and those in positions of power who seek to naturalise their choices and decisions.

As I hope to have made clear in these concluding remarks, although the concerns and ideas of Benjamin, Kracauer, and Kluge were (and, in Kluge's case, continue to be) profoundly shaped by their experiences of Nazi Germany, their ideas are no less relevant for a world in which – at the start of the twenty-first century – wars are waged, and lives destroyed, in the name of the progress of humanity.

Bibliography

Adorno, Theodor W.: "Transparencies on Film", New German Critique, No. 24-25 (Fall/Winter, 1981-2), pp. 199-205.

Adorno, Theodor W.: "Arnold Schoenberg, 1874-1951", in: Adorno: Prisms, Cambridge, Mass.: The MIT Press 1990.

Adorno, Theodor W.: "On Proust", in: Adorno: Notes to Literature: Volume 1, New York: Columbia University Press 1991.

Adorno, Theodor W.: "The Curious Realist: On Siegfried Kracauer", New German Critique, No. 54 (Fall, 1991), pp. 159-157.

Adorno, Theodor W.: "How to Look at Television", in: The Culture Industry: Selected Essays on Mass Culture, ed. by J.M. Bernstein, London: Routledge 1991.

Adorno, Theodor W./Eisler, Hans: Composing for the Films, London and Atlantic Highlands: The Athlone Press 1994.

Adorno, Theodor W./Benjamin, Walter: The Complete Correspondence: 1928-1940, ed. by Henri Lonitz, Cambridge, Mass.: Harvard University Press 1999.

Adorno, Theodor W.: Kindheit in Amorbach, ed. by Reinhard Pabst, Frankfurt am Main, Leipzig: Insel 2003.

Andrew, Dudley: The Major Film Theories: An Introduction, London, Oxford, New York: Oxford University Press 1976.

Andrew, Dudley: Concepts in Film Theory, Oxford and New York: Oxford University Press 1984.

Anonymous: "Germany, France work on plan to avert Iraq war", ABC News Online: http://www.abc.net.au/news/newsitems/200302/s779900.htm (Last accessed May 21, 2007).

Aragon, Louis: Paris Peasant, London: Pan Books 1987.

Arnheim, Rudolf: "Melancholy Unshaped", The Journal of Aesthetics and Art Criticism (Spring, 1993), pp. 291-297.

Barg, Werner: "Ein Dokumentarist des Protestes. Alexander Kluges Theorie des Dokumentarfilms. Beobachtungen zu seinen Essay-Filmen und Fernsehmagazinen", in: Perspektiven des Dokumentarfilms, ed. by Manfred Hattendorf, München: Diskurs Film 1995.

Barnouw, Dagmar: Critical Realism: History, Photography, and the Work of Siegfried Kracauer, Baltimore and London: The Johns Hopkins University Press 1994.

Baudelaire, Charles: The Painter of Modern Life and Other Essays, London: Phaidon Press 1964.

Baudelaire, Charles: Artificial Paradise, New York: Herder and Herder 1971.

Baudelaire, Charles: Art in Paris: 1845-1862, Salons and other Exhibitions, Oxford: Phaidon Press 1981.

Baudelaire, Charles: Baudelaire in English, ed. by Carol Clarke/Robert Sykes, London: Penguin Books 1997.

Baudelaire, Charles: The Flowers of Evil, Oxford and New York: Oxford University Press 1998.

Behrens, Gloria et al.: "Gespräche mit Alexander Kluge", Filmkritik, 12 (December, 1976), pp. 562-600.

Belke, Ingrid/Renz, Irina (Ed.): Siegfried Kracauer, 1889-1966: Marbacher Magazin, No. 47, Marbach am Necker: Deutsche Schillergesellschaft 1989.

Benjamin, Andrew/Osborne, Peter (Ed.): Walter Benjamin's Philosophy: Destruction and Experience, London and New York: Routledge 1994.

Benjamin, Walter: Über Haschisch, ed. by Tillman Rexroth, Frankfurt am Main: Suhrkamp 1972.

Benjamin, Walter: Reflections: Essays, Aphorisms, Autobiographical Writings, ed. by Peter Demetz, New York: Schocken Books 1986.

Benjamin, Walter: Moscow Diary, ed. by Gary Smith, Cambridge, Mass. and London, England: Harvard University Press 1986.

Benjamin, Walter: Briefe an Siegfried Kracauer (Mit vier Briefen von Siegfried Kracauer an Walter Benjamin), ed. by Rolf Tiedemann/Henri Lonitz, Marbach am Necker: Deutsche Schillergesellschaft, 1987.

Benjamin, Walter: Gesammelte Schriften (7 Volumes), ed. by Rolf Tiedemann/Hermann Schweppenhäuser, Frankfurt am Main: Suhrkamp 1991.

Benjamin, Walter: Illuminations, ed. by Hannah Arendt, London: Fontana Press 1992.

Benjamin, Walter: The Correspondence of Walter Benjamin: 1910-1940, ed. by Gershom Scholem/Theodor W. Adorno, Chicago and London: University of Chicago Press 1994.

Benjamin, Walter: Selected Writings, Volume 1, ed. by Marcus Bullock/Michael W. Jennings, Cambridge, Mass. and London, England: Harvard University Press 1996.

Benjamin, Walter: One-Way Street and Other Writings, London and New York: Verso, 1997.

Benjamin, Walter: Charles Baudelaire: A Lyric Poet in the Era of High Capitalism, London and New York: Verso 1997.

Benjamin, Walter: Understanding Brecht, London and New York: Verso 1998.

Benjamin, Walter: Selected Writings, Volume 2, ed. by Michael W. Jennings, Howard Eiland, and Gary Smith, Cambridge, Mass. and London, England: Harvard University Press 1999.

Benjamin, Walter: The Arcades Project, Cambridge, Mass. and London, England: Harvard University Press 1999.

Benjamin, Walter: Selected Writings, Volume 3, ed. by Howard Eiland/ Michael W. Jennings, Cambridge, Mass. and London, England: Harvard University Press 2002.

Benjamin, Walter: Selected Writings, Volume 4, ed. by Howard Eiland/ Michael W. Jennings, Cambridge, Mass. and London, England: Harvard University Press 2003.

Bevers, Jürgen et al.: "'Eine Baustelle ist vorteilhafter als ganze Häuser': Ein Gespräch mit Alexander Kluge", Spuren: Zeitschrift für Kunst und Gesellschaft, 1 (Februar/März, 1980), pp. 16-19.

Bitomsky, Harmut et al.: "Gespräch mit Alexander Kluge: Über Die Patriotin, Geschichte und Filmarbeit", Filmkritik, 275 (November, 1979), pp. 505-520.

Bowie, Andrew: "New Histories: Aspects of the Prose of Alexander Kluge", Journal of European Studies, xii (1982), pp. 180-208.

Brandon, Ruth: Surreal Lives: The Surrealists, 1917-1945, London: Macmillan 2000.

Brecht, Bertolt: Journals: 1934-1955, ed. by John Willett, New York: Routledge 1996.

Brecht, Bertolt: Brecht on Theatre: The Development of an Aesthetic, ed. by John Willett, London: Methuen 1990.

Brecht, Bertolt: Bertolt Brecht on Film and Radio, ed. by Marc Silberman, London: Methuen 2001.

Breton, André: Nadja, New York: Grove Press 1960.

Breton, André: Manifestoes of Surrealism, Ann Arbor: University of Michigan Press 1972.

Breton, André: Mad Love, Lincoln and London: University of Nebraska Press 1987.

Breton, André: Communicating Vessels, Lincoln and London: University of Nebraska Press 1997.

Broderson, Momme: Walter Benjamin: A Biography, ed. by Martina Dervis, London and New York: Verso 1997.

Broderson, Momme: Siegfried Kracauer, Reinbeck bei Hamburg: Rowohlt Taschenbuch 2001.

Bruck, Jan: "Brecht's and Kluge's Aesthetics of Realism", Poetics, No. 17 (1988), pp. 57-68.

Brustellin, Alf et al.: "Germany in Autumn: What is the Film's Bias?", in: West German Filmmakers on Film: Visions and Voices, ed. by Eric Rentschler, New York and London: Holmes and Meier 1988.

Buck-Morss, Susan: The Origin of Negative Dialectics: Theodor W. Adorno, Walter Benjamin, and the Frankfurt Institute, New York: The Free Press 1979.

Buck-Morss, Susan: "Aesthetics and Anaesthetics: Walter Benjamin's Artwork Essay Reconsidered", New Formations, No. 20 (Summer, 1993), pp. 123-143.

Buck-Morss, Susan: The Dialectics of Seeing: Walter Benjamin and the Arcades Project, Cambridge, Mass. and London, England: The MIT Press 1995.

Bullock, Marcus: "The Rose of Babylon: Walter Benjamin, Film Theory, and the Technology of Memory", MLN, 105 (1988), pp. 1098-1120.

Bullock, Marcus: Romanticism and Marxism: The Philosophical Development of Literary Theory and Literary History in Walter Benjamin and Friedrich Schlegel, New York: Peter Lang 1989.

Bush, George W.: "National Prayer Service Speech, September 14, 2001": http:www.whitehouse.gov/nsc/nss3.html (Last accessed May 21, 2007).

Bush, George W.: "2002 State of the Union Address": http://www.whitehouse.gov/news/releases/2002/01/20020129-11.html (Last accessed May 21, 2007).

Bush, George W.: "President's Remarks to the Nation": http://www.whitehouse.gov/news/releases/2002/09/20020911-3.html (Last accessed May 21, 2007).

Caygill, Howard: Walter Benjamin: The Colour of Experience, London and New York: Routledge 1998.

Cohen, Margaret: Profane Illumination: Walter Benjamin and the Paris of Surrealist Revolution, Berkeley, Los Angeles, London: University of California Press 1993.

Collingwood, R.G.: The Idea of History, New York: Galaxy Books 1956.

Cook, Roger.F.: "Film Images and Reality: Alexander Kluge's Aesthetics of Cinema", Colloquia Germanica, 18, No. 4 (1985), pp. 281-299.

Corliss, Richard: "The Limitations of Kracauer's Reality", Cinema Journal, Vol. 10.1 (Fall, 1970), pp. 15-22.

Corrigan, Timothy: New German Film: The Displaced Image, Bloomington and Indianapolis: Indiana University Press 1994.

Croce, Benedetto: History: Its Theory and Practice, New York: Russell and Russell 1960.

Dawson, Jan: Alexander Kluge and the Occasional Work of a Female Slave, New York: Zoetrope 1977.

Dawson, Jan: "'But Why are the Questions so Abstract?': An Interview with Alexander Kluge", in: Dawson: Alexander Kluge and the Occasional Work of a Female Slave, New York: Zoetrope 1977.

Deuber-Mankowsky, Astrid/Schiesser, Giaco: "In der Echtzeit der Gefühle: Gespräch mit Alexander Kluge", in: Die Schrift an der Wand. Alexander Kluge: Rohstoffe und Materialien, ed. by Christian Schulte, Osnabrück: Universitätsverlag Rasch 2000.

Doderer, Klaus: "Walter Benjamin and Children's Literature", in: With the Sharpened Axe of Reason: Approaches to Walter Benjamin, ed. by Gerhard Fischer, Oxford and Herndon: Berg 1996.

Eagleton, Terry: The Ideology of the Aesthetic, Oxford: Blackwell 1990.

Eder, Klaus/Kluge, Alexander: Ulmer Dramaturgien, München and Wien: Carl Hanser 1980.

Eder, Klaus/Kluge, Alexander: "Reibungsverluste. Gespräch mit Klaus Eder", in: In Gefahr und größter Not bringt der Mittelweg den Tod. Texte zu Kino, Film, Politik, ed. by Christian Schulte, Hamburg: Vorwerk 1999.

Elsaesser, Thomas: "Cinema – The Irresponsible Signifier or 'The Gamble with History': Film Theory or Cinema Theory", New German Critique, No. 40 (Winter, 1987), pp. 65-89.

Elsaesser, Thomas: "New German Cinema and History: The Case of Alexander Kluge", in: The German Cinema Book, ed. by Tim Bergfelder et al., London: British Film Institute 2002.

Eisenstein, S.M. et al.: "The Sound Film: A Statement from the USSR", in: Close Up, 1927-1933: Cinema and Modernism, ed. by James Donald et al., Princeton, New Jersey: Princeton University Press 1998.

Enzensberger, Hans-Magnus: "Constituents of a Theory of the Media", New Left Review, 64 (Nov/Dec, 1970), pp. 13-36.

Fischer, Gerhard: "Benjamin's Utopia of Education as Theatrum Mundi et Vitae: On the Programme of a Proletarian Children's Theatre, in: With the Sharpened Axe of Reason: Approaches to Walter Benjamin, ed. by Gerhard Fischer, Oxford and Herndon: Berg 1996.

Fränkel, Fritz/Joël, Ernst: "Der Haschisch-Rausch: Beiträge zu einer experimentellen Psychopathologie", Klinische Wochenschrift, 5, Nr. 37 (September, 1926), pp. 1707-1709.

Freud, Sigmund: "Creative Writers and Day-dreaming", in: Art and Literature – Vol. 14: The Penguin Freud Library, ed. by Albert Dickson, London: Penguin 1990.

Freud, Sigmund: "Beyond the Pleasure Principle", in: On Metapsychology: The Theory of Psychoanalysis, ed. by Angela Richards, London: Penguin 1991.

Frisby, David: Fragments of Modernity: Theories of Modernity in the Work of Simmel, Kracauer, and Benjamin, Cambridge, Mass.: The MIT Press 1988.

Gilloch, Graeme: Myth and Metropolis: Walter Benjamin and the City, Cambridge: Polity Press 1997.

Gilloch, Graeme: Walter Benjamin: Critical Constellations, Cambridge: Polity Press 2002.

Gregor, Ulrich: "Interview", in: Herzog/Kluge/Straub, ed. by Peter W. Jansen/Wolfram Schütte, München and Wien: Carl Hanser 1976.

Habermas, Jürgen: "Consciousness-Raising or Redemptive Critique", New German Critique, No. 17 (Spring, 1979), pp. 30-59.

Hansen, Miriam: "Cooperative Auteur Cinema and Oppositional Public Sphere: Alexander Kluge's contribution to Germany in Autumn", New German Critique, No. 24-25 (Fall/Winter, 1981-2), pp. 36-56.

Hansen, Miriam: "Introduction" to Adorno: "Transparencies on Film", New German Critique, No. 24-25 (Fall/Winter, 1981-2), pp. 186-198.

Hansen, Miriam: "Alexander Kluge, Cinema, and the Public Sphere: The Construction Site of Counter-History", Discourse, No. 6 (1983), pp. 53-74.

Hansen, Miriam: "Alexander Kluge: Crossings between Film, Literature, Critical Theory", in: Film und Literatur: Literarische Texte und der neue deutsche Film, ed. by Susan Bauschinger et al., Bern: Francke 1984.

Hansen, Miriam: "Benjamin, Cinema, and Experience: 'The Blue Flower in the Land of Technology'", New German Critique, No. 40 (Winter, 1987), pp. 179-224.

Hansen, Miriam: "Reinventing the Nickolodeon: Notes on Kluge and Early Cinema", October, No. 46 (Fall, 1988), pp. 179-198.

Hansen, Miriam: "Decentric Perspectives: Kracauer's Early Writings on Film and Mass Culture", New German Critique, No. 54 (Fall, 1991), pp. 47-76.

Hansen, Miriam: "With Skin and Hair: Kracauer's Theory of Film, Marseilles 1940", Critical Inquiry, 19 (Spring, 1993), pp. 437-469.

Hansen, Miriam: "Introduction", in: Siegfried Kracauer: Theory of Film: The Redemption of Physical Reality, Princeton, New Jersey: Princeton University Press 1997.

Hansen, Miriam: "The Stubborn Discourse: History and Story-Telling in the Films of Alexander Kluge", in: Die Schrift an der Wand. Alexander Kluge: Rohstoffe und Materialien, ed. by Christian Schulte, Osnabrück: Universitätsverlag Rasch 2000.

Hansen, Miriam: "Benjamin and Cinema: Not a One-Way Street", in: Benjamin's Ghosts: Interventions in Contemporary Literary and Cultural Theory, ed. by Gerhard Richter, Stanford, California: Stanford University Press 2002.

Hansen, Miriam: "Room-for-Play: Benjamin's Gamble with Cinema", October, No. 35 (Summer, 2004), pp. 3-45.

Hickethier, Knut: "Von anderen Erfahrungen in der Fernsehöffentlichkeit. Alexander Kluges Kulturmagazine und die Fernsehgeschichte", in: Kluges Fernsehen: Alexander Kluges Kulturmagazine, ed. by Christian Schulte/Winfried Siebers, Frankfurt am Main: Suhrkamp 2002.

Hopf, Florian: "'Gefühle können Berge versetzen [...]': Interview von Florian Hopf mit Alexander Kluge zu dem Film: Die Macht der Gefühle", in: Alexander Kluge: Die Macht der Gefühle, Frankfurt am Main: Zweitausendeins 1984.

Humphreys, Peter J.: Media and Media Policy in Germany: The Press and Broadcasting Since 1945 (Second edition), Oxford and Providence: Berg 1994.

Ingram, Susan: "The Writing of Asja Lacis", New German Critique, No. 86 (Spring/Summer, 2002), pp. 159-177.

Jay, Martin: The Dialectical Imagination: A History of the Frankfurt School and the Institute of Social Research, 1923-1950, Boston, Toronto, London: Little, Brown, and Company 1973.

Jay, Martin: Permanent Exiles: Essays on the Intellectual Migration from Germany to America, New York: Columbia University Press 1986.

Jay, Martin: "The Extraterritorial Life of Siegfried Kracauer", in: Jay: Permanent Exile: Essays on the Intellectual Migration from Germany to America, New York: Columbia University Press 1986.

Jay, Martin: "Adorno and Kracauer: Notes on a Troubled Friendship", in: Jay, Permanent Exiles: Essays on the Intellectual Migration from Germany to America, New York: Columbia University Press 1986.

Kael, Pauline: "Is There a Cure for Film Criticism? Or: Some Unhappy Thoughts on Siegfried Kracauer's Nature of Film: The Redemption of Physical Reality", Sight and Sound, 31.2 (Spring, 1962), pp. 56-64.

Kaes, Anton: From Hitler to Heimat: The Return of History as Film, Cambridge, Mass. and London, England: Harvard University Press 1992.

Kessler, Michael/Levin, Thomas Y. (Ed.): Siegfried Kracauer: Neue Interpretationen, Tübingen: Stauffenburg 1990.

Kluge, Alexander: Letter to Siegfried Kracauer, circa 1963, Kracauer Nachlaß, Deutsches Literaturarchiv, Marbach am Necker.

Kluge, Alexander: The Battle, New York: McGraw-Hill 1967.

Kluge, Alexander: "Presseheft zum Film", Filmkritik, 275 (November, 1970), pp. 503-504.

Kluge, Alexander: Gelegenheitsarbeit einer Sklavin: Zur realistischen Methode, Frankfurt am Main: Suhrkamp 1975.

Kluge, Alexander: Neue Geschichten. Hefte 1-18: "Unheimlichkeit der Zeit", Frankfurt am Main: Suhrkamp 1977.

Kluge, Alexander: Die Patriotin: Texte/Bilder 1-6, Frankfurt am Main: Zweitausendeins 1979.

Kluge, Alexander: "On Film and the Public Sphere", New German Critique, No. 24-25 (Fall/Winter, 1981-2), pp. 206-220.

Kluge, Alexander: "The Air Raid on Halberstadt, 8 April 1945", Semiotext(e), No. 11 (1982), pp. 306-315.

Kluge, Alexander: "The sharpest ideology: that reality appeals to its realistic character", On the Beach, No. 3-4 (Summer, 1984), pp. 23-24.

Kluge, Alexander: Die Macht der Gefühle, Frankfurt am Main: Zweitausendeins, 1984.

Kluge, Alexander: Der Angriff der Gegenwart auf die übrige Zeit. Das Drehbuch zum Film, Frankfurt am Main: Syndikat 1985.

Kluge, Alexander: "The Political as Intensity of Everyday Feelings", Cultural Critique, No. 4 (Fall, 1986), pp. 119-128.

Kluge, Alexander: Case Histories, New York and London: Holmes and Meier 1988.

Kluge, Alexander: "Why Should Film and Television Cooperate?", October, No. 46 (Fall, 1988), pp. 96-102.

Kluge, Alexander: "Pact with a Dead Man", in: West German Filmmakers on Film: Visions and Voices, ed. by Eric Rentschler, New York and London: Holmes and Meier 1988, pp. 234-241.

Kluge, Alexander/Müller, Heiner: "Ich schulde der Welt einen Toten": Gespräche, Hamburg: Rotbuch 1996.

Kluge, Alexander/Müller, Heiner: "Ich bin ein Landvermesser": Gespräche, Hamburg: Rotbuch 1996.

Kluge, Alexander: Learning Processes with a Deadly Outcome, Durham and London: Duke University Press 1996.

Kluge, Alexander: In Gefahr und größter Not bringt der Mittelweg den Tod: Texte zu Kino, Film, Politik, ed. by Christian Schulte, Berlin: Vorwerk 8 1999.

Kluge, Alexander: "Ich liebe das Lakonische", Der Spiegel, 45 (2000), pp. 336-340.

Kluge, Alexander: Chronik der Gefühle (2 Volumes), Frankfurt am Main: Suhrkamp 2000.

Kluge, Alexander: "Der Luftangriff auf Halberstadt am 8. April 1945", in: Kluge: Chronik der Gefühle. Band II: Lebensläufe, Frankfurt am Main: Suhrkamp 2000.

Kluge, Alexander: "Schlachtbeschreibung", in: Kluge: Chronik der Gefühle. Band I: Basisgeschichten, Frankfurt am Main: Suhrkamp 2000.

Kluge, Alexander: Facts & Fakes 1: Verbrechen, ed. by Christian Schulte/Reinald Gußmann, Berlin: Vorwerk 8 2000.

Kluge, Alexander: Verdeckte Ermittlung: Ein Gespräch mit Christian Schulte und Rainer Stollmann, Berlin: Merve 2001.

Kluge, Alexander: Facts & Fakes 2-3: Herzblut trifft Kunstblut – Erster imaginärer Opernführer, ed. by Christian Schulte/Reinald Gußmann, Berlin: Vorwerk 8 2001.

Kluge, Alexander: Facts & Fakes 4: Der Eiffelturm, King Kong und die weiße Frau, ed. by Christian Schulte/Reinald Gußmann, Berlin: Vorwerk 8 2002.

Kluge, Alexander: Facts & Fakes 5: Einar Schleef-der Feuerkopf spricht, ed. by Christian Schulte/Reinald Gußmann, Berlin: Vorwerk 8 2003.

Kluge, Alexander: Die Lücke, die der Teufel läßt. Im Umfeld des neuen Jahrhunderts, Frankfurt am Main: Suhrkamp 2003.

Kluge, Alexander: "Risse", Frankfurter Allgemeine Sonntagszeitung, No. 43, October 26 (2003), pp. 23 and 26.

Koch, Gertrud: "Die Funktion des Zerrwinkels in zertrümmernder Absicht. Ein Gespräch zwischen Alexander Kluge und Gertrud Koch", in: Kritische Theorie und Kultur, ed. by Rainer Erd et al., Frankfurt am Main: Suhrkamp 1989.

Koch, Gertrud: "'Not yet accepted anywhere': Exile, Memory, and Image in Kracauer's Conception of History", New German Critique, No. 54 (Fall, 1991), pp. 95-109.

Koch, Gertrud: "Cosmos in Film: On the Concept of Space in Walter Benjamin's 'Work of Art' Essay", in: Walter Benjamin's Philosophy: Destruction and Experience, ed. by Andrew Benjamin/Peter Osborne, London and New York: Routledge 1994.

Koch, Gertrud/Schlüpmann, Heide: "'Nur Trümmern trau ich[...]': Ein Gespräch mit Alexander Kluge", in: Kanalarbeit: Medienstrategien im Kulturwandel, ed. by Hans-Ulrich Reck, Basel and Frankfurt am Main: Stroemfeld and Roter Stern 1998.

Koch, Gertrud: Siegfried Kracauer: An Introduction, Princeton, New Jersey: Princeton University Press 2000.

Kracauer, Siegfried: "Dimanche: Ideen-Entwurf zu einem Kurzfilm" (undated manuscript), Kracauer Nachlaß, Deutsches Literaturarchiv, Marbach am Necker.

Kracauer, Siegfried: "Entwurf über das Verhältnis direktor visueller Erfahrung und der durch Photographie vermittelten" (undated manuscript), Kracauer Nachlaß, Deutsches Literaturarchiv, Marbach am Necker.

Kracauer, Siegfried: "Über die lebensferne Tendenz des Hollywood Films" (undated manuscript), Kracauer Nachlaß, Deutsches Literaturarchiv, Marbach am Necker.

Kracauer, Siegfried: Letter to Theodor W. Adorno, February 12, 1949, Kracauer Nachlaß, Deutsches Literaturarchiv, Marbach am Necker.

Kracauer, Siegfried: Letter to Rudolf Arnheim, September 14, 1951. Kracauer Nachlaß, Deutsches Literaturarchiv, Marbach am Necker.

Kracauer, Siegfried: Letter to Lucienne Astruc, September 10, 1959, Kracauer Nachlaß, Deutsches Literaturarchiv, Marbach am Necker.

Kracauer, Siegfried: Letter to Leo Löwenthal, February 15, 1960, Kracauer Nachlaß, Deutsches Literaturarchiv, Marbach am Necker.

Kracauer, Siegfried: Letter to Rudolf Arnheim, October 16, 1960, Kracauer Nachlaß, Deutsches Literaturarchiv, Marbach am Necker.

Kracauer, Siegfried: Letter to Leo Löwenthal, October 29, 1960, Kracauer Nachlaß, Deutsches Literaturarchiv, Marbach am Necker.

Kracauer, Siegfried: Letter to Lucienne Astruc, December 12, 1960, Kracauer Nachlaß, Deutsches Literaturarchiv, Marbach am Necker.

Kracauer, Siegfried: Letter to Leo Löwenthal, February 10, 1961, Kracauer Nachlaß, Deutsches Literaturarchiv, Marbach am Necker.

Kracauer, Siegfried: Letter to Leo Löwenthal, March 18, 1961, Kracauer Nachlaß, Deutsches Literaturarchiv, Marbach am Necker.

Kracauer, Siegfried: Letter to Erika Lorenz, February 15, 1962, Kracauer Nachlaß, Deutsches Literaturarchiv, Marbach am Necker.

Kracauer, Siegfried: Letter to Lucienne Astruc, March 14, 1962, Kracauer Nachlaß, Deutsches Literaturarchiv, Marbach am Necker.

Kracauer, Siegfried: Letter to Wolfgang Weyrauch, June 4, 1962, Kracauer Nachlaß, Deutsches Literaturarchiv, Marbach am Necker.

Kracauer, Siegfried: Letter to Alexander Kluge, December 24, 1962, Kracauer Nachlaß, Deutsches Literaturarchiv, Marbach am Necker.

Kracauer, Siegfried: Letter to Theodor W. Adorno, October 25, 1963, Kracauer Nachlaß, Deutsches Literaturarchiv, Marbach am Necker.

Kracauer, Siegfried: Letter to Theodor W. Adorno, October 31, 1963, Kracauer Nachlaß, Deutsches Literaturarchiv, Marbach am Necker.

Kracauer, Siegfried: Orpheus in Paris: Offenbach and the Paris of his Time, New York: Vienna House 1972.

Kracauer, Siegfried: From Caligari to Hitler: A Psychological History of the German Film, Princeton, New Jersey: Princeton University Press 1974.

Kracauer, Siegfried: Das Ornament der Masse: Essays, Frankfurt am Main: Suhrkamp 1977.

Kracauer, Siegfried: Theorie des Films: Die Errettung der äußeren Wirklichkeit, Frankfurt am Main: Suhrkamp 1985.

Kracauer, Siegfried: Jacques Offenbach und das Paris seiner Zeit, Frankfurt am Main: Suhrkamp 1994.

Kracauer, Siegfried: The Mass Ornament: Weimar Essays, ed. by Thomas Y. Levin, Cambridge, Mass. and London, England: Harvard University Press 1995.

Kracauer, Siegfried: History: The Last Things Before the Last, Princeton: Markus Wiener Publishers 1995.

Kracauer, Siegfried/Panofsky, Erwin: Siegfried Kracauer – Erwin Panofsky Briefwechsel: 1941-1966, ed. by Volker Breidecker, Berlin: Akademie 1996.

Kracauer, Siegfried: "Tentative Outline of a Book on Film Aesthetics [1949]", in: Kracauer/Panofsky: Siegfried Kracauer – Erwin Panofsky Briefwechsel: 1941-1966, ed. by Volker Breidecker, Berlin: Akademie 1996.

Kracauer, Siegfried: Theory of Film: The Redemption of Physical Reality, Princeton, New Jersey: Princeton University Press 1997.

Kracauer, Siegfried: The Salaried Masses: Duty and Distraction in Weimar Germany, London and New York: Verso 1998.

Lacis, Asja: Revolutionär im Beruf: Berichte über proletarisches Theater, über Meyerhold, Brecht, Benjamin, und Piscator, ed. by Hildegard Brenner, München: Rogner and Bernhard 1971.

Lehmann, Hans-Thies: "An Interrupted Performance: On Walter Benjamin's Idea of Children's Theatre", in: With the Sharpened Axe of Reason: Approaches to Walter Benjamin, ed. by Gerhard Fischer, Oxford and Herndon: Berg 1996.

Levin, Thomas Y.: Siegfried Kracauer: Eine Bibliographie seiner Schriften, Marbach am Necker: Deutsche Schillergesellschaft 1989.

Lewandowski, Rainer: Alexander Kluge, München: C. H. Beck and edition text + kritik 1980.

Lewandowski, Rainer: Die Filme von Alexander Kluge, Hildesheim and New York: Olms Press 1980.

Liebman, Stuart: "On New German Cinema, Art, Enlightenment, and the Public Sphere: An Interview with Alexander Kluge", October, No. 46 (Fall, 1988), pp. 23-59.

Liebman, Stuart: "Why Kluge?", October, No. 46 (Fall, 1988), pp. 5-22.

Lindroos, Kia: Now-Time/Image-Space: Temporalization of Politics in Walter Benjamin's Philosophy of History and Art, Jyväskylä: Jyväskylä University Print House 1998.

Lorenz, Erika: Letter to Siegfried Kracauer, February 25, 1962, Kracauer Nachlaß, Deutsches Literaturarchiv, Marbach am Necker.

Lowenthal, Leo: "As I remember Friedel", New German Critique, No. 54 (Fall, 1991), pp. 5-17.

Löwenthal, Leo/Kracauer, Siegfried: In steter Freundschaft, Leo Löwenthal – Siegfried Kracauer: Briefwechsel 1921-1966, ed. by Peter-Erwin Jansen/Christian Schmidt, Springe: zu Klampen 2003.

Lutze, Peter: Alexander Kluge: The Last Modernist, Detroit: Wayne State University Press 1998.

Mankowsky, Arno: "Der Pate als Quotenkiller", Süddeutsche Zeitung, No. 240, 16-17 October (1993).

Marder, Elissa: Dead Time: Temporal Disorders in the Wake of Modernity (Baudelaire and Flaubert), Stanford, California: Stanford University Press 2001.

Marx, Karl: Selected Writings, ed. by David McLellan, Oxford: Oxford University Press 1978.

McCole, John: Walter Benjamin and the Antinomies of Tradition, Ithaca and London: Cornell University Press 1993.

Mehlman, Jeffrey: Walter Benjamin for Children: An Essay on his Radio Years, Chicago and London: The University of Chicago Press 1993.

Michael, Klaus: "Vor dem Café. Walter Benjamin und Siegfried Kracauer in Marseille", in: Aber ein Sturm weht vom Paradiese her: Texte zu Walter Benjamin, ed. by Michael Opitz/Erdmut Wizisla, Leipzig: Reclam 1992.

Mülder-Bach, Inka: "'Mancherlei Fremde': Paris, Berlin und die Exterritorialität Siegfried Kracauers", Juni, 3, 1 (1989), pp. 61-72.

Mülder-Bach, Inka: "History as Autobiography: The Last Things Before the Last", New German Critique, No. 54 (Fall, 1991), pp. 139-157.

Nadeau, Maurice: The History of Surrealism, Middlesex: Pelican Books 1978.

Negt, Oskar/Kluge, Alexander: Public Sphere and Experience: Toward an Analysis of the Bourgeois and Proletarian Public Sphere, Minneapolis and London: University of Minnesota Press 1993.

Pavsek, Christopher: "The Storyteller in the Age of Mechanical Reproduction: Alexander Kluge's Reworking of Walter Benjamin", Found Object, Vol. 1, 2 (1992), pp. 83-92.

Pensky, Max: "Tactics of Remembrance: Proust, Surrealism, and the Origins of the Passagenwerk", in: Walter Benjamin and the Demands of History, ed. by Michael P. Steinberg, New York: Cornell University Press 1996.

Pensky, Max: Melancholy Dialectics: Walter Benjamin and the Play of Mourning, Amherst: University of Massachusetts Press 2001.

Petro, Patrice: "Kracauer's Epistemological Shift", New German Critique, No. 54 (Fall, 1991), pp. 127-138.

Phillip, Claus: "Vertrauenswürdige Irrtümer: Ein Gespräch", Kolik, 13 (2000), pp. 5-15.

Plant, Sadie: Writing on Drugs, London: Faber and Faber 1999.

Plato: The Republic, London: Penguin Books 1987.

Proust, Marcel: The Letters of Marcel Proust, ed. by Nina Curtiss, New York: Random House 1949.

Proust, Marcel: Marcel Proust on Art and Literature: 1896-1919, New York: Carroll and Graf Publishers 1984.

Proust, Marcel: In Search of Lost Time (6 Volumes), London: Vintage 1996.

Proust, Marcel: The Complete Short Stories of Marcel Proust, New York: Cooper Square Press 2001.

Reitz, Edgar/Kluge, Alexander/Reinke, Wilfried: "Word and Film", October, No. 46 (Fall, 1988), pp. 83-95.

Rodowick, D. N: "The Last Things Before the Last: Kracauer and History", New German Critique, No. 41 (Spring-Summer, 1987), pp. 109-139.

Rötzer, Florian: "Kino and Grabkammer. Gespräch mit Alexander Kluge", in: Die Schrift an der Wand. Alexander Kluge: Rohstoffe und Materialien, ed. by Christian Schulte, Osnabrück: Universitätsverlag Rasch 2000.

Scherer, Christina: "Alexander Kluge und Jean-Luc Godard. Ein Vergleich anhand einiger filmtheoretischer 'Grundannahmen'", in: Die Schrift an der Wand. Alexander Kluge: Rohstoffe und Materialien, ed. by Christian Schulte, Osnabrück: Universitätsverlag Rasch 2000.

Scherpe, Klaus R.: "Alexander Kluge: Germany – An Experience of Words and Images", in: European Memories of the Second World War, ed. by Helmut Peitsch et al., New York and Oxford: Berghahn Books 1999.

Schlüpmann, Heide: "Phenomenology of Film: On Siegfried Kracauer's Writings of the 1920's", New German Critique, No. 40 (Winter, 1987), pp. 97-114.

Schlüpmann, Heide: "The Subject of Survival: On Kracauer's Theory of Film", New German Critique, No. 54 (Fall, 1991), pp. 111-126.

Schlüpmann, Heide: Ein Detektiv des Kinos: Studien zu Siegfried Kracauers Filmtheorie, Basel and Frankfurt am Main: Stroemfeld 1998.

Scholem, Gershom: "Walter Benjamin", in: Scholem: Jews and Judaism in Crisis, ed. by Werner J. Dannhauser, New York: Schocken Books 1976.

Scholem, Gershom: Walter Benjamin: The Story of a Friendship, Philadelphia: The Jewish Publication Society of America 1981.

Scholem, Gershom (Ed.): The Correspondence of Walter Benjamin and Gershom Scholem: 1932-1940, New York: Schocken Books 1989.

Schröder, Christian: "Das Etwas Andere Autoren-Fernsehen", Der Tagesspiegel, November 1 (1991).

Schulte, Christian (Ed.): Die Schrift an der Wand. Alexander Kluge: Rohstoffe und Materialien, Osnabrück: Universitätsverlag Rasch 2000.

Schulte, Christian/Siebers, Winfried (Ed.): Kluges Fernsehen: Alexander Kluges Kulturmagazine, Frankfurt am Main: Suhrkamp 2002.

Schulte, Christian/Siebers, Winfried: "Vorwort", in: Kluges Fernsehen: Alexander Kluges Kulturmagazine, ed. by Schulte/Siebers, Frankfurt am Main: Suhrkamp 2002.

Schulte, Christian: "Fernsehen und Eigensinn", in: Kluges Fernsehen: Alexander Kluges Kulturmagazine, ed. by Schulte/Siebers, Frankfurt am Main: Suhrkamp 2002.

Schweppenhäuser, Hermann: "Propaedeutics of Profane Illumination", in: On Walter Benjamin: Critical Essays and Recollections, ed. by Gary Smith, Cambridge, Mass. London, England: The MIT Press 1995.

Shattuck, Roger: Proust's Binoculars: A Study of Memory, Time, and Recognition in A la recherche du temps perdu, New York: Random House 1963.

Siemons, Mark: "Zwölftonmusik im Zirkus: Das Fernsehen Alexander Kluges", in: Fernsehen. Medien, Macht und Märkte, ed. by Helmut Monkenbusch, Reinbeck bei Hamburg: Rowohlt Taschenbuch 1994.

Simmel, Georg: "The Metropolis and Mental Life", in: Simmel on Culture – Selected Writings, ed. by David Frisby/Mike Featherstone, London, Thousand Oaks, New Delhi: Sage Publications 1997.

Smith, Gary (Ed.): Benjamin: Philosophy, History, Aesthetics, Chicago and London: University of Chicago Press 1989.

Smith, Gary (Ed.): On Walter Benjamin: Critical Essays and Recollections, Cambridge, Mass. and London, England: The MIT Press 1995.

Steinberg, Michael P. (Ed.): Walter Benjamin and the Demands of History, Ithaca and London: Cornell University Press 1996.

Stollmann, Rainer: Alexander Kluge zur Einführung, Hamburg: Junius 1998.

Stüssi, Anna: Erinnerung an die Zukunft: Walter Benjamins "Berliner Kindheit um Neunzehnhundert", Göttingen: Vandenhoeck and Ruprecht 1977.

Szondi, Peter: "Hope in the Past: On Walter Benjamin", Critical Inquiry, Vol. 4, No. 3 (Spring, 1978), pp. 491-506.

Taussig, Michael: The Nervous System, New York and London: Routledge 1992.

Taussig, Michael: Mimesis and Alterity: A Particular History of the Senses, New York and London: Routledge, 1993.

Tiedemann, Rolf et al. (Ed.): Walter Benjamin, 1892-1940: Marbacher Magazin, No. 55, Marbach am Necker: Deutsche Schillergesellschaft 1990.

Uecker, Matthias: "'Für Kultur ist es nie zu spät': Alexander Kluges Television Productions", in: "Whose Story?" – Continuities in Contemporary German – language literature, ed. by Stuart Parkes et al., Bern: Peter Lang 1998.

Uecker, Matthias: Anti-Fernsehen? Alexander Kluges Fernsehproduktionen, Marburg: Schüren 2000.

Weber Nicholsen, Shierry: Exact Imagination, Late Work – On Adorno's Aesthetics, Cambridge, Mass. and London, England: The MIT Press 1999.

Wiggerhaus, Rolf: The Frankfurt School: Its History, Theories, and Political Significance, Cambridge, Mass.: The MIT Press 1995.

Willett, John (Ed.): Brecht on Theatre: The Development of an Aesthetic, New York: Hill and Wang 1998.

Willett, John: Brecht in Context, London: Methuen 1998.

Wilte, Bernd: Walter Benjamin: An Intellectual Biography, Detroit. Wayne State University Press 1991.

Witte, Karsten: "Siegfried Kracauer im Exil", Exilforschung: Ein Internationales Jahrbuch, Band 5, München: edition text + kritik, 1987), pp. 135-149.

Wohlfarth, Irving: "Et Cetera? The Historian as Chiffonnier", New German Critique, No. 39 (Fall, 1986), pp. 142-168.

Wolin, Richard: Walter Benjamin: An Aesthetic of Redemption, Berkeley and Los Angeles: University of California Press 1994.

Other Works Cited

Ivens, Joris: Regen (Rain), 1929.

Kluge, Alexander: Abschied von Gestern (Yesterday Girl), 1966.

Kluge, Alexander et al: Deutschland im Herbst (Germany in Autumn), 1978.

Kluge, Alexander: Die Patriotin (The Patriot), 1979.

Kluge, Alexander: Die Macht der Gefühle (The Power of Feelings), 1983.

Kluge, Alexander: "Das Ferne Stalingrad", 10 vor 11, RTL, February 27, 1989.

Kluge, Alexander: "Wie in der Liebe: 'Keine Erklärungen'/Magazin zu Godards 60. Geburtstag", 10 vor 11, RTL, March 12, 1990.

Kluge, Alexander: "Darwins Waltzer", Primetime Spätausgabe, RTL, August 26, 1990.

Kluge, Alexander: "Geisterstunde mit Bildern", 10 vor 11, RTL, August 27, 1990.

Kluge, Alexander: "Ein Straßenbahnfahrt durch eine Stadt in den neuen Bundesländen", 10 vor 11, RTL, March 9, 1992.

Kluge, Alexander: "Das Xmas Project", 10 vor 11, RTL, December 12, 1993.

Kluge, Alexander: "Jahresüberblick", News and Stories, SAT 1, January 3, 1994.

Kluge, Alexander: "Im Zeichnen des Mars", Primetime Spätausgabe, RTL, January 23, 1994.

Kluge, Alexander: "Organisiertes Glück", News and Stories, SAT 1, September 19, 1994.

Kluge, Alexander: "Durchbruch eines Außenseiters/Der Südstaaten-Regisseur Richard Linklater und sein Erfolgsfilm Before Sunrise", Primetime Spätausgabe, RTL, June 11, 1995.

Kluge, Alexander: "Detonation Deutschland/Sprengbilder einer Nation von Julian Rosefeldt und Piero Steinle", News and Stories, SAT 1, July 8, 1996.

Kluge, Alexander: "Jeff Mills/Godfather des Techno", News and Stories, SAT 1, September 7, 1998.

Kluge, Alexander: "Fassbinders Gesammelte Hinterlassenschaften", News and Stories, SAT 1, September 16, 2001.

Kluge, Alexander: "Die Tochter des Miraculix – Vincenzo Bellini's geniale Oper 'Norma'", News and Stories, SAT 1, September 7, 2003.

Kluge, Alexander: "196 bpm – Romuald Karmaker filmt Tekknokönig DJ Hell", Primetime Spätausgabe, RTL, September 14, 2003.

Kluge, Alexander: "Bücher-Herbst", Deutschland Radio Berlin, October 11, 2003.

Kluge, Alexander: "Baustellen der Macht – die französischen Philosophen Foucault und Deleuze über die 'Rhizome der Gewalt'", 10 vor 11, RTL, November 10, 2003.

Riefenstahl, Leni: Der Triumph des Willens (The Triumph of the Will), 1935.

Acknowledgements

This book began as a doctoral thesis undertaken at the University of New South Wales. I am grateful to UNSW for providing me with a scholarship that sustained my research throughout the course of the project. I would also like to thank the Deutscher Akademischer Austausch Dienst (DAAD) for a grant that enabled me to undertake research at the J.W. Goethe Universität, Frankfurt am Main. The Goethe Institute, Sydney, the Faculty of Arts and Social Sciences, UNSW, and the Faculty of Humanities, University of Technology, Sydney also generously supported my work at various stages of the project.

I owe a debt of gratitude to my doctoral supervisors Dr. Jodi Brooks and Assoc. Prof. Gerhard Fischer for their advice, support, and detailed, thorough engagements with my work. I am also very grateful to Demetrios Douramanis who has read every chapter and provided me with much critical insight, inspiration, and support. I would also like to thank a number of people who have supported my work in various ways: Thank you to Prof. Dr. Heide Schlüpmann, Prof. Patrice Petro, Prof. Dr. Klaus Scherpe, Prof. David Roberts, Prof. Andrew Benjamin, Prof. Marcus Bullock, Assoc. Prof. Olaf Reinhardt, Prof. Martyn Lyons, Prof. Lesley Stern, Assoc. Prof. George Kouvaros, Dr. Dag Petersson, Dr. Gerald Hartung, Prof. Alun Munslow, Dr. Katrina Schlunke, Dr. Roland Goll, Claudia Kühn, and the staff at the Deutsches Literaturarchiv, Marbach am Necker, the Deutsches Filmmuseum, and the Mediathek at the J.W. Goethe Universität.

I am also grateful to Dr. Alexander Kluge for providing me with access to materials from the DCTP archive, and for generously allowing me to reproduce images from his work in the book. Thank you also to Beata Wiggen at DCTP for answering my inquiries, and for providing me with copies of hard-to-find materials. Finally, I would like to thank the Deutsches Literaturarchiv, Marbach am Necker, and Suhrkamp Verlag for granting me permission to quote from unpublished materials contained in the Siegfried Kracauer Nachlaß.

Previous versions of sections of the book have appeared in: *Literature and Aesthetics*, No. 12 (2002); *Rethinking History: The Journal of Theory and Practice*, Vol. 9, No. 4 (2005); *The International Journal of Media and Cultural Politics*, Vol. 1, No. 1 (2005); Dag Petersson and Erik Steinskog (Ed.), *Actualities of Aura: Twelve Studies of Walter Benjamin*, Svanesund, NSU Press 2005; and Gerald Hartung and Kay Schiller (Ed.), *Weltoffener Humanismus. Philosophie, Philologie und Geschichte in der deutsch-jüdischen Emigration*, Bielefeld, transcript 2006.